HOW THE
CELTS
CAME TO
BRITAIN

DRUIDS, ANCIENT SKULLS AND THE
BIRTH OF ARCHAEOLOGY

HOW THE
CELTS
CAME TO
BRITAIN

DRUIDS, ANCIENT SKULLS AND THE
BIRTH OF ARCHAEOLOGY

MICHAEL A. MORSE

TEMPUS

Front cover illustration: An imaginative view of a Druidical ceremony at Stonehenge. Samuel Rush Meyrick and Charles Hamilton Smith, *The Costume of the Original Inhabitants of the British Islands*, 1815. © *Society of Antiquaries*

Back cover illustration: A 'typical' Briton. Joseph Barnard Davis and John Thurnam, *Crania Britannica*, 1856-65

First published 2005
Tempus Publishing Limited
The Mill, Brimscombe Port,
Stroud, Gloucestershire, GL5 2QG
www.tempus-publishing.com

Typesetting and origination by Tempus Publishing Limited
Printed in Great Britain

CONTENTS

For Dimitra

So Jove usurping reigned. These, first in Crete
And Ida known, thence on snowy top
Of cold Olympus ruled the middle air
Their highest heaven; or on the Delphian cliff,
Or in Dodona, and through all the bounds
Of Doric land; or who with Saturn old
Fled over Adria to the Hesperian fields
And o'er the Celtic roamed the utmost isles

John Milton, *Paradise Lost*, 1667 (I: 514-521)

ACKNOWLEDGEMENTS

During the past decade of wrestling with the issue of the Celts, I have received generous support on both sides of the Atlantic. In particular, this book represents a blend of influences from the Universities of Chicago and Cambridge, and I am grateful to my friends and colleagues at these two institutions. I am also thankful for the supportive environment at the British Museum and for the assistance of the library and archive staff at the Royal Society.

An earlier version of this book was written as a doctoral dissertation under the guidance of George W. Stocking, Jr., at the Morris Fishbein Center for the History of Science, University of Chicago. I am especially indebted to Professor Stocking as well as to Robert Richards, Michael Dietler and to colleagues in Chicago from a wide variety of disciplines within the History of Human Sciences workshop.

On the other side of the ocean, I was fortunate to discover that John Collis was trying to solve the same puzzle, for which we had each assembled different pieces. He will recognise much in here that arose from our discussions. I am grateful to Christopher Chippindale who read through many versions of the manuscript over the years. I am also grateful to Jonathan Williams, who read a late draft and helped me to focus my thinking on the epilogue. Simon James, Lloyd Laing and an anonymous reviewer saved me from some embarrassing errors. The challenging students at Madingley Hall reminded me that the interested amateur can sometimes be more efficient than the professional scholar at spotting weak arguments.

While these individuals have been generous in helping me with this project, they did not necessarily agree with my interpretations. Responsibility for these, as well as for any errors, is mine alone.

I am grateful for the generous support of the University of Chicago and the Andrew W. Mellon Foundation. An earlier version of Chapter VI appeared in the *Proceedings of the Prehistoric Society* in 1999. Finally and most importantly, I am grateful for the support of my family – on both sides of the Atlantic.

CHAPTER I

INTRODUCTION

Britain's Celtic Origins

Everyone knows that Great Britain and Ireland were populated by the Celts before the Romans arrived. But the Romans did not call them by that name. When Julius Caesar led the first Roman incursion into Britain, he referred to the natives simply as Britons. There is no record of what these Britons called themselves. Classical descriptions of northwestern European peoples, called 'Keltoi' in Greek sources and 'Galli' in Latin, were vague, contradictory and never mentioned the British Isles.

Only in the early eighteenth century did scholars begin to write of ancient Celtic migrations to these islands. Since then, ideas about the Celts evolved and changed in unexpected ways. Each generation employed its own definition of the Celts and favoured a particular method of studying them. Not until the beginning of the twentieth century did a conception of the Celts emerge that we would find familiar. During these formative 200 years, 'the Celts' was the name given to a series of quite different imagined ancient peoples. They were described as speakers of an ancestral pan-European tongue, speakers of a language unique to the western shores of the Continent, practisers of one of the world's oldest and purest religions, possessors of a certain head shape and authors of a unique type of art and literature. Each of these definitions carried with it an implicit notion of how peoples can be categorised. The history of British ideas about Celtic ancestors is a window into the development of the social science disciplines that address the problem of human diversity.

Today, the very notion of Celtic heritage is embroiled in controversy. Within the United Kingdom, regions often described as Celtic are obtaining an increasing amount of self-governance through the process of devolution. For many European integrationists, the Celts symbolise an ancient continent-wide unity that is the modern aspiration of the European Union. Fringe pan-Celticists draw upon a vision of a unified Celtic past as they work toward a political partnership for Brittany, Ireland, Scotland, Wales and even Cornwall. Popularly, the Celts have come to represent a spiritual counter-culture or ancient wisdom. A growing number of scholars, meanwhile, dismiss the very idea of 'Celtic' Britain as a modern and fallacious invention.

In the midst of these competing ideas, a confusing number of books promise to explain who the Celts either were or were not. But the label is so fluid that no single definition has enjoyed a long shelf life. All that has really persisted since the early eighteenth century is the notion that Britain was once Celtic, albeit with a host of differing interpretations about what this might mean. Before we draw our own conclusions about the place of the Celts in ancient Britain, we must first look at how they got there – not how the Celts *themselves* arrived, however we might define them, but how the Celtic *label* became attached to a cultural phenomenon in pre-Roman Britain.

The history of Celtic scholarship in Britain can be broadly divided into two periods, each associated with its own dominant approach to the problem of peopling. From the early eighteenth century, when the term was first applied to the British Isles, to the mid nineteenth century, the Celts were mainly defined as a linguistic group. Part One covers this time, when most new ideas about the ancient Celts developed through the study of language. From the 1840s to the end of the nineteenth century, the study of material remains eclipsed linguistics as the main source of new definitions of the Celts. This is the subject of Part Two, which begins back in the early eighteenth century, when Celtic material remains were simply described in reference to the linguistic group of that name, and concludes with the formation of archaeology, the discipline in which the modern, popular understanding of the Celts emerged.

During the eighteenth and nineteenth centuries, *Celtic* referred to a variety of human groupings such as tribe, race, culture and civilisation. Today, many researchers discuss a Celtic ethnicity. As theories about the peopling of Britain changed, *Celtic* developed into a widely recognised term, readily adapted to new approaches and ideas. By tracing this common thread of research into the origins of Britain, we can understand how writers who described themselves variously as a historian, chorographer, antiquary, ethnologist, anthropologist and even Celticist, conceived of boundaries that separate one group from the rest of humanity. This process of redefining the Celts culminated at the end of the nineteenth century with the emergence of archaeology. Since that moment, new ideas about the Celts were no longer associated with the development of new disciplines. For more than a century now, archaeology has provided a forum for researchers to debate what constitutes an ancient people. Ironically, having developed in tandem with the modern understanding of the Celts, British archaeology is now moving toward a rejection of the term in relation to the nation's prehistory. Today, many archaeologists understand human cultural diversity to be too complex to accommodate any single definition of the ancient Celts.

Partly through these new ideas in archaeology, the question of the place of the Celts in Britain's past has grown in prominence. But this interest has not hitherto involved a thorough examination of how ideas about the ancient Celts developed and changed. Instead, a number of misconceptions and caricatures have arisen in relation to British intellectual history and key figures in the story have been forgotten. The main reason for this is that up to now, the history of British scholarship on the Celts has never been the focus of research, but has been co-opted as a (usually) small aspect of a wider argument.

In 1992, the anthropologist Malcolm Chapman critiqued traditional treatments of the Celts and denied any special connection between the ancient Celts and the modern 'Celtic fringe'. He concluded that the terms *Celt* and *Celtic*, both in antiquity and modern times, arose from a particular kind of culture-meeting, characterised by the presence of a strong economic and cultural centre (Rome and London respectively) and a peripheral region in the process of incorporation into the political rule of the centre. In both cases, he argued that the concept of the Celts originated in the centre as a term for the periphery. In this interpretation, the Celts were not a self-defined ethnic group in antiquity, but an externally defined collection of peoples who may or may not have had a group identity. Chapman's theory also means that modern peoples who consider themselves Celts, having derived their Celtic identity in the context of a different culture-meeting in a different place from that in antiquity, share little or no unique and continuous traditions with ancient Celts. While this book offers a fascinating insight into the inner workings of cultural boundary formation, it is mainly focused on the literary sphere and adds little to the story of how the term *Celtic* actually arose in the eighteenth and nineteenth centuries. Chapman dedicated just eight pages to the history of Celtic scholarship.[1]

Chapman's work precipitated a wider enthusiasm for examining the historical roots and socio-political contexts of modern images of the Celts. Starting in the mid 1990s, a number of articles and conference papers were published on these issues, but added little to the history of Celtic scholarship. The archaeologist Simon James attempted to give the intensifying academic debate a wider audience when he wrote *The Atlantic Celts: Ancient People or Modern Invention?* This ambitious volume traces the whole ethnic history of the British Isles and, echoing Chapman, concludes that the ancient Celts represent a modern invention in an example of what he calls ethnogenesis. Yet the section on the history of Celtic scholarship merely repeats what had been said before by Chapman and others.[2]

As in the books by Chapman and James, overviews of British ideas about the ancient Celts typically appear in an abbreviated form, leading to misconceptions about the evolution of the Celtic label and the history of the social sciences more generally. On the one hand, general interest books on the Celts tend to portray the history of Celtic scholarship through a series of heroic figures who, in a gradual march toward the truth, replaced supposed rampant speculation about the past with serious scientific endeavour. This selective version of history is normally designed to provide a pedigree for a certain view of the Celts and omits alternative ideas that may have been dominant in the past. The converse narrative, offered by the deconstructionists, is that popular understandings of the term are the product of a succession of biased and eccentric scholars. This version of history, often part of an argument that disputes the depiction of ancient Britain as Celtic, can lead to a similarly one-sided view of intellectual history.

In the debate between the Celticists and the sceptics, the history of Celtic scholarship has rarely been explored in detail, but has been used to support a particular viewpoint. One consequence of this situation is that there is a widespread belief that, as the archaeologist Stuart Piggott wrote in 1966, 'the words "Celt" and "Celtic" had taken on more or less their present popular usage' by the beginning of the eighteenth century.[3] In fact, these words did not acquire their present meanings until the beginning of the twentieth century, following a dynamic 200 years in which practitioners in a host of different disciplines used the terms for their own ends. To compound the spread of simple misreadings like this, many significant historical figures have been forgotten. Researchers such as Thomas Brown, Evan Evans, James Cowles Prichard, William Wilde, Samuel Birch, Joseph Anderson, Robert Munro and John Romilly Allen ought to be household names for any student of the Celts, but they hardly appear in any discussion of how the term *Celtic* evolved.

An exception to these trends is the archaeologist John Collis' recent book, *The Celts: Origins, Myths and Inventions.* Firmly in the deconstructionist camp,

Collis explores the introduction and evolution of the idea of the ancient Celts, not just in relation to Britain but more generally and in much greater detail than had Piggott, Chapman or James.[4] His research, which focuses more on the history of French scholarship, is in many ways complementary to the story that appears here. Collis' motives, however, are principally to demonstrate how the modern idea of the ancient Celts that appears in general interest books is based on a series of fallacies. The story he presents is, in fact, similar (albeit more robust) to the heroic tale of discoveries often recounted by the 'pan-Celticists', except that he is interested in where these past researchers went wrong. Collis' history, while key to his argument about modern interpretations of the European Iron Age, is not intended to put earlier Celtic scholarship in historical context and does not explore the relationship between past researchers of the Celts and the emergence of social science disciplines like archaeology.

With the contributions of scholars like James and Collis, the Celtic debate today has turned bitter and at times extreme, with accusations that the sceptics are somehow involved in 'ethnic cleansing' countered by claims that the Celtic label reflects the kind of 'false and dangerous' methodology used by Nazi ideologues.[5] While this rhetoric has clearly lost any sense of proportion, it is indicative of a wider trend that reduces interpretations to the social context and political leanings of past scholars. For the Celtic deconstructionists in particular, the history of Celtic scholarship is often attributed to nationalism, romanticism or the religious and social background of researchers. As ideas about the ancient Celts evolved in the eighteenth and nineteenth centuries, however, the socio-political motives of scholars were tremendously varied. In a sense, the term developed a life of its own, outlasting the theories of those who used it and adapting itself to most new approaches that arose.

Of course the backgrounds of researchers were a contributing factor at each step in the intellectual development of the idea of the Celts. These backgrounds, however, were as varied as the many definitions of the Celts put forward. For example, some scholars were Breton, Welsh, Scottish or Irish patriots, looking to the Celts to provide their home nation with a glorious past. Others, often with opposing motives, were English patriots, who nevertheless tried to define the place of the Celts in their own ancestry. Yet others had no discernable political leanings. Some were romantics who saw the Celts as the parent-peoples of all Europeans. Other romantics saw the Celts as fundamentally different from other European peoples. Socio-political factors no doubt played a part in the formulation of ideas about the Celts, but the wider phenomenon, of how the Celts entered and remained a part of so many different models of the peopling of Britain, overwhelmed all such motives. While each generation defined the Celts differently, these definitions were not necessarily a simple reflection of the political biases of researchers. Only by examining the scholarly contexts in which the term has been used, can we appreciate how it supported a variety of different approaches to the question of the peopling of Britain and, ultimately, why the term has endured.

What follows is the history of a concept, articulated through the use of a particularly resonant word. This word is as familiar as it is elusive. Along the way there are many surprises. We cannot assume, as others have, that older uses of the word *Celtic* have anything like the meaning we give it today. Only by looking at the history of scholarship addressing how the Celts came to Britain, can we begin to understand what it means to talk about the Celtic heritage of these islands.

Before the Celts 'Arrived'

The sudden introduction of the Celts into debates over the peopling of the British Isles at the start of the eighteenth century is best understood in the context of earlier origins scholarship. In the eighteenth century, the Celts appeared within a linguistic argument in a departure from previous work which was based almost entirely on historical sources. With new ideas came new terminology, and *Celtic*, as the name of an ancestor language, filled a void left by the discrediting of earlier accounts of British origins.

For many centuries before anyone conceived of Celts in ancient Britain, the investigation of the early peopling of the British Isles was dominated by the *Historia Regum Britanniae* written by the Welshman Geoffrey of Monmouth around 1135, in a tradition of scholarship that linked the origins of a people to king lists. Before Geoffrey, the Saxons, who had long dominated political life in Britain, understood that they came from the Continent relatively recently and had little interest in the island's ancient past. Geoffrey avoided the time's political controversy over Norman versus Saxon rights to power by claiming the earliest peoples and rulers of Britain to have been 'Britons', or Welsh, by then found only in the far west of the island. In Geoffrey's history, the Britons were originally descended from Brutus (considered to be a refugee of the Trojan War) and underwent a golden age under King Arthur before the arrival of the Saxons.

With the exception of a handful of writers, there was little opposition to the Brutus story before the sixteenth century. In the sixteenth and seventeenth centuries, however, Geoffrey's history became the object of controversy. A sustained attack began with John Major in 1521 in *Historia Majoris Britanniae* and with the Italian Polydore Vergil, who had come to Britain in 1502 and who wrote *Anglica Historia* in 1535.

For some, these critiques of the Brutus story were unpatriotic. The foremost defender of Geoffrey's history to emerge in the mid sixteenth century was John Leland, whose loyalty to the Tudors led Henry VIII to appoint him King's Antiquary in 1533, with the task of travelling Britain in search of sources on ancient times. The result of this endeavour, *Commentarii de Scriptoribus Britannicis,* supported Geoffrey's history.

By the mid sixteenth century, a curious new source on ancient times began to influence British debates over peopling. In 1498, the major domo of Pope Alexander VI, Annius of Viterbo, claimed to have discovered lost books written by Berosus, a Babylonian chronicler from Alexandrian times. Though an ambitious forgery, Annius' supposed translation of Berosus had an enormous impact on contemporary models of peopling because the text provided the detail lacking from the biblical account of the post-Flood re-peopling of the world. Annius' account, published as *Commentaria Super Opera Diversorum Auctorum de Antiquitatibus*, provided a list of kings descended from Japhet, the son of Noah generally thought to have gone westward from the resting place of the ark. In addition to inventing kings outright, Annius integrated information emerging from translated classical sources into the biblical framework. He introduced Samothes, a descendant of Japhet, as king of the Celts in Gaul, and forefather both to Druys, the founder of the Druids, and to a king named Celtes (*pl. 1*).

Knowledge of Berosus reached England in the context of a running debate over the relative antiquity of Oxford and Cambridge. In 1548, John Bale, Bishop of Ossory, turned to Berosus to provide the ancient universities of Britain with a past older than the Trojan Brutus story when he wrote *Illustrium Majoris Britanniae Scriptorum*. John Caius built on this argument when, in 1568, he wrote in *De Antiquitate Cantebrigiensis Academiae* that the first Britons came from Celtica under Samothes. These works became widely known in the 1570s when Richard White used both the Samothes and Brutus stories in his *Historiarum (Britanniae)*, written in religious exile on the Continent.[6]

Due to the declining prestige of Geoffrey's history and the growing controversy over Annius' forgery, however, this tenuous version of a colonisation of Britain from Celtic areas did not hold for long. In 1582, the Celts played a role in an alternative version of migrations to Britain in George Buchanan's *Rerum Scotarium Historia*. Buchanan, a Scottish scholar and tutor of Mary Stuart and James VI, wrote most of his history of Scotland by the mid 1560s, partly as a political tract promoting the rights to the throne of Moray, the brother of Queen Mary. In the *Historia*, Buchanan drew on classical descriptions of the Celts, whom he defined as 'a numerous People Inhabiting principally about *Lyons*, from whom one part of *France* was called *Gallia Celtica*'.[7] Defining the Celtae and Belgae as speakers of separate dialects, he expanded on classical accounts by writing that the Celts came to Ireland and Scotland through Spain, while the Belgic tribes came straight to Britain, bringing the language that became Welsh:

> I say, when I ponder within my self, such an agreement in Speech, which as yet preserves its ancient Affinity of Words, and no obscure markes of its Original; I am easily induc'd to believe; that, before the coming in of the Saxons, all the Britains used a Language, not much different from each other; and it is probable, that the Nations, adjoyning to the Gallick shore, used the Belgick Tongue, from whose limits a good part of the Britans, bordering on France, had made a Transmigration, as Caesar informs us. But the Irish, and the Colonies sent from them, being derived from the Celtae, Inhabitants of Spain, 'tis probable, they spake the Celtick Tongue. I suppose, that these Nations returning, as it were, from a long Pilgrimage, and possessing themselves of the neighbour-Seats, and almost coalescing into one People, did confound the Idioms of their several Tongues respectively; so that, it was neither wholly Belgick, nor wholly Celtic, nor yet wholly unlike either of them.[8]

Though Buchanan's *Historia* went through many editions in the century after its publication, his association of the ancient Celtae with a Celtic language was not adopted by other authors. By the early eighteenth century, his reputation was so tarnished, especially by Thomas Innes, that the new idea of Celtic languages emerging in that period seems to be unrelated to Buchanan. Despite Buchanan's lack of influence in spreading the idea of a Celtic language, he did play a role in the growing scepticism over the Brutus story.

In the 1580s, two other developments further diminished the reputation of Geoffrey's history: the creation of a Society of Antiquaries which treated historical sources with newfound scepticism, and, more significantly, the

1586 publication of William Camden's *Britannia*, which followed Polydore Vergil's critique. *Britannia* was a comprehensive topographical and chorographical description of the entirety of the British Isles and was noteworthy for connecting different parts of Britain with particular tribes of Roman times. The book went through several editions and was continually expanded for 200 years, retaining a predominant position in British antiquarianism. In *Britannia*, as in the Brutus story, the peopling of Britain was linked to the etymology of the very word, 'Britain'. For Geoffrey, the Britons, who encompassed only the Welsh and Cornish, derived their name directly from Brutus himself. For Camden to use *Britannia* as the title of his topography of the entire island, he needed not just a new derivation of the word, but a new meaning, whereby it referred to the whole island. For his derivation, he looked to ancient languages, 'in which lieth the maine strength of this disputation and the surest proofe of peoples originall', giving momentum to the study of languages as an alternative to the strict biblical-historical framework.[9] In Camden's model, the 'Britons' took their name from an old word, 'brith', meaning painted, recalling the blue-painted men that Caesar found on these islands.[10]

At the beginning of the seventeenth century, with the Brutus story in decline, a set of alternative methods emerged to answer the related questions of the peopling of British Isles and the source of insular civilisations. The most significant development was the exploration of America, providing 'savages' as an alternative to civilised Trojans as possible first inhabitants. Some of the first comparisons between native Americans and the original Britons were in the form of illustrations, as early drawings of American 'savages' were used as analogues for the first 'Picts' and 'Britons' (*pl.2*). This novel framework for interpreting Britain's past is known as ethnographic analogy – where the ancient past is explained through comparison with observed modern behaviour – and is one of the central means of interpreting ancient monuments in archaeology.

Ethnographic analogy decoupled the questions of peopling and the origins of civilisation. With the first Britons now considered to be an unnamed 'savage' people, the Saxons emerged in the seventeenth century to replace Brutus and King Samothes as a favoured source of Britain's distinctiveness.

In the seventeenth century, as Saxonism and ethnographic analogy gradually replaced the Brutus story, the only new alternative to emerge was the idea that the first Britons were Phoenicians. The main proponents of this position were Samuel Bochart, who published *Geographica Sacra* in 1646, and Aylett Sammes, whose *Britannia Antiqua Illustrata* of 1676 joined

Phoenicians to the Druids, who had appeared sporadically in peopling debates since the mid sixteenth-century contributions of Bale and Caius (*pl.3*). Sammes included a list of 'Celtick Kings', beginning with Samothes, but, because he had seen them mentioned by a number of 'learned Antiquaries', seems to have included the list 'only to inform the World of the cheat and forgery of *Annius* in his pretended *Berosus*'.[11] Neither Sammes nor Bochart gained much support for the Phoenician theory, probably because the fall of the Brutus story led to a general expectation that the first Britons would not be a known civilised people.

By the end of the seventeenth century, the question of the peopling of the British Isles was in disarray. With the fall of the Brutus story, the exposure of Annius' forgery, and the expectation that the first Britons were 'savages' probably not chronicled in the Bible, no named people or source point was agreed. Then, at the turn of the century the study of language – in conjunction with biblical and classical scholarship, and, later, the study of ancient remains – emerged with the promise of new answers. The key catalyst for this new synthesis came when a French writer named Paul-Yves Pezron proposed a general history of Europe centred on the ancient Celts. This novel origins model was quickly imported to Britain, where it filled the void left by the departure of the Trojan Brutus from the historical landscape.

PART ONE

LANGUAGES

In 1701, the Welsh scholar Edward Lhuyd returned to Oxford after a series of journeys through the lesser-known regions of Ireland, Great Britain and Brittany, to consider the question of the first inhabitants of the British Isles. Subscribers to his 1707 *Archaeologia Britannica* were surprised that his conclusions focused on the languages people spoke, rather than their customs, ancient monuments or oral traditions. He wrote that the search for the 'Original Language' spoken in these areas in ancient times could 'contribute not a little towards a Clearer Notion of the First Planters'.[1] Echoing previous claims that there are great similarities between Welsh and Breton, Lhuyd was the first to demonstrate that Irish Gaelic was part of the same language family. In contemplating how these languages came to be spoken on the western edge of Europe, Lhuyd looked for roots in Spain and France. He did not name this family of languages, however, and mentioned the Celts only in reference to possible ancient migrations from Gaul, where Caesar observed that one-third of the population went by that tribal name.

More than 120 years later, the Bristol physician James Cowles Prichard explored how the languages of Cornish, Welsh, Manx, Irish Gaelic, Scottish Gaelic and Breton were closely related in a family. By this time, however, Prichard felt that he could not avoid 'the term *Celtic languages*' as 'the most proper epithet for the class of idioms.' Despite his own firm objections to the term, Prichard, 'in compliance with custom' designated this family of languages as Celtic and, by extension, the speakers of these languages as Celts.[2]

How, between 1707 and 1831, did it become customary to call Britain's original inhabitants by the name of 'Celts', although leading scholars

thought that the word was mis-applied and although the term had not previously been used in that manner, either in ancient times by Greek and
Roman authors or in medieval and early modern scholarship? Because linguists were among the first to use the term *Celtic* in reference to ancient
Britain, our story begins with the history of this discipline, which set the
pattern for other strands of research into Britain's origins. Linguistics in this
period was not an isolated discipline, but was used in harmony with other
modes of inquiry, particularly history and literary studies in a broader intellectual pursuit. We must also look to these disciplines to understand how
linguists came to put the Celtic label on a family of languages whose ties to
the ancient Celts of classical texts is not at all straightforward.

    The next three chapters examine this period, from the introduction of
the Celts into the story of the peopling of Britain until the study of 'Celtic'
languages became a dominant form of evidence for scholars in the 1840s.
Though this period is characterised by the growth of linguistics, the definition of 'Celtic' languages emerged slowly and unevenly through three broad
stages. Chapter II examines the first of these stages in the early eighteenth
century, when the idea of ancient Celts in Britain was born, though with
competing and contradictory definitions. Chapter III looks at the subsequent distinction that emerged in the mid eighteenth century between Celts
and Goths, and how this came about through a linking of Celtic language-
speakers with the Druids described by Caesar and Tacitus. Finally Chapter
IV explores the ironic situation in the early nineteenth century, when an
emerging discipline with globalist research goals reluctantly employed the
Celtic label, thanks to the influence of romantic writers who had little interest
beyond their local region.

    From Lhuyd to Prichard, the idea that Britain was Celtic first emerged
and passed through a series of changes in just over a century of linguistic
research. In all of these novel linguistic applications of *Celtic*, the name
enabled scholars to articulate new theories of peopling and origins. Only
Prichard's definition of the word has endured, but as even he acknowledged, this does not mean that it was correct. To say that a usage was correct
or incorrect implies that there is – somewhere – a privileged meaning to
Celtic. The very flexibility of the term proved to be a strength as it played a
crucial role in the development of modern linguistics.

CHAPTER II

FROM NOAH'S ARK TO EUROPE

Pezron, Lhuyd and the Celtic Languages

At the very moment when the term *Celtic* was first associated with ancient Britain, it already had at least two contradictory meanings and supported rival theories of the peopling of the British Isles. A great deal of misunderstanding has surrounded readings of early eighteenth-century scholarship of the Celts on account of the frequent assumption that thinkers at that time used *Celtic* more or less in the same way we do today, blurring the distinction between these two theories. Edward Lhuyd, by virtue of having used the term, is widely regarded as being co-originator of the modern idea of the Celtic language family. Yet his definition of the Celts referred to just a fraction of the peoples who spoke languages that we call Celtic. And Paul-Yves Pezron, the other supposed co-originator of the idea, neither recognised all these languages as being part of the same family nor described them as being uniquely Celtic. What Lhuyd and Pezron had in common was that they both wrote books that were among the first to mention Celts in connection with ancient Britain and that their books were both published in English at about the same time. Not only did they employ different definitions of the Celts than we do, but they disagreed with each other on fundamental points.

Lhuyd's friend Henry Rowlands, in his own contribution to the peopling of Britain, noted what distinguished their conclusions:

> These two now mention'd Gentlemen, having by different Methods open'd a Way of resolving diverse Tongues in Europe, to one Mother-Language, which Language indeed Mr Lhwyd leaves modestly undecided, but by Monsieur Pezron is determin'd to be the Celtick.[1]

In other words, both scholars looked to language to trace origins and both employed a concept of an original language from which closely related modern languages descended. Lhuyd, however, did not give a name to this 'Mother-Language'. Instead, he simply argued that the historically documented tribe called the Celts was involved in bringing a proportion of modern languages to the British Isles. Pezron, meanwhile, named as 'Celtic' the original language which was the ancestor, not just of Welsh and Breton, but of all European languages. Most writers on the topic in the early eighteenth century followed Pezron, who argued that the Celts were the ancestors of all Europeans with no particularly close connection to the regions that we call the 'Celtic fringe'.

Pezron

The first published account that the Celts were the original inhabitants of the British Isles appeared in Pezron's 1703 *L'Antiquité de la Nation et la Langue des Celtes* and became widely known in Britain in the form of a 1706 English translation titled *The Antiquities of Nations*.[2] Pezron, a Breton monk, argued that the Celts were the first inhabitants of Europe and that their speech could be traced in many of the major European languages, of which he considered Breton and its close relative, Welsh, to be the purest modern examples. This idea caught the attention of Welsh scholars, one of whom, David Jones, provided the 1706 translation. This English edition contained a notice for the imminent publication of the first volume of Lhuyd's *Archaeologia Britannica*.

In *L'Antiquité de la Nation*, Pezron reintroduced a fifteenth-century idea that the Celts, integrated into the biblical-historical framework in which they appeared in Berosus, were the true ancestors of the French. In the Middle Ages, the prevailing view of French origins looked back no further than the arrival of post-Roman Frankish tribes. In 1485, however, the Italian scholar Paolo Emilio, reading the newly available Roman texts such as Caesar's *Gallic Wars*, proposed that the Gauls, also known as Celts in ancient Rome, were France's true ancestors.[3] The appearance of Annius' forged translation of Berosus in the following decade strengthened the Gallic/Celtic argument. With the exposure of Berosus, however, the Franks resumed their position as the accepted source of the French bloodline until Pezron's challenge.

Pezron's argument involved a revival, not just of the debate over France's Frankish versus Gallic origins, but of Genesis-based national histories. He gave this already outdated idea new-found currency through a linguistic argument linking the languages of Breton, Welsh, Greek, Latin and Teutonic (or German). Such linguistic connections, especially between Breton and Welsh, had been noted as early as the twelfth century. The introduction of the term *Celtic*, however, signifying the ancestor of these and other languages, was Pezron's innovation and his lasting legacy, for he is the ultimate source of all subsequent uses of the term in relation to ancient Britain.

By the time Pezron's book was published in 1703, his argument had been circulating for several years, explaining why a handful of seventeenth-century linguistic works employed the term before that date. In 1693, in one of a series of letters between John Aubrey, who first proposed the theory of the Druidical origins of Stonehenge, and Professor James Garden of King's College, Aberdeen, discussing possible Druidical monuments in Scotland, Garden proposed alternative derivations of the word 'Druid' in Greek and in 'the Celtick tongue'.[4] Garden cited Gerhard Johann Voss in arguing that 'Druid is a word of Celtick extract, and that the origine thereof is to be sought for in the celtick tongue such as both the old Gallick and British tongues were'. But Voss' own derivation of the word Druid did not mention the Celtae, and Voss' use of the term in other contexts is not specific to Gaul and Britain.[5] It is likely, therefore, that Garden's source for this idea comes from Pezron. Like Pezron, Garden was interested in the relationship between the biblical chronology and other ancient sources and he probably came across Pezron's work in the context of that endeavour, adopting Pezron's linguistic terminology. Later uses of the term can be traced directly to Pezron. One of Pezron's many correspondents, the great mathematician Gottfried Wilhelm Leibniz, had published his own interpretation of the Celtic languages and helped spread Pezron's definition shortly before the publication of *L'Antiquité de la Nation*. And news of Pezron's theory that 'Celtick' was 'the Original language, even that Spoken in Paradise itself' reached the Royal Society in 1700.[6]

In *L'Antiquité de la Nation* Pezron took as his starting point the problematic absence of the Celts from the biblical account of the peopling of the world and the unhelpful attempt of Annius to fill this gap through forgery. In order to fill the gap himself, he made the then-conventional argument that a people speaking a single language could be known under different, yet often similar-sounding names. Using this principle, he traced the origin of the Celts through the following sequence of name changes: Gomer, the grandson of Noah and son of Japhet, ruled a tribe called the Gomerites or Gomarians, described by Josephus; this group was later known as the Sacae or Saques; then it was known as the Titans, linking the story with Greek

mythology; a group of Titans travelled northward from Greece and became
known as Cimbri or Cimbrians, in fact a northern tribe from Roman
times; 'after which these Warlike People took the name of Celtae, when
they settled in the Provinces of Europe'.[7]

Aside from naming the Celts as the tribe that was first to reach western
Europe and crediting them with great advances in philosophy, the novelty
of Pezron's work was his use of linguistics to describe certain modern peoples as preserving, with few corruptions, the original language of the first
inhabitants:

> I shall conclude with one Thing, that Men ought not to be ignorant of, and
> that is, That the Language of the Titans, which was that of the Ancient Gauls,
> is after a Revolution of above Four Thousand Years, preserved even to our
> Time: A strange Thing, that so ancient a Language should now be spoken by
> the Amorican Britons in France, and by the Ancien [sic] Britains in Wales.[8]

Pezron went on to support this argument with a series of language tables
meant to demonstrate that Celtic words can still be found in Greek, Latin
and Teutonic.

Lhuyd

In 1691, Edward Lhuyd* became interested in contacting Pezron after hear-
ing about his work on the origins of the Gauls, but failed to reach him,
despite repeated efforts, until late in the decade.[9] Lhuyd's scholarly context
contrasted sharply with the monastic setting of Pezron's work. Lhuyd came
to Jesus College, Oxford, in 1682 and started a career in natural history at
the Ashmolean Museum at a time when it was among the country's foremost institutions in antiquarianism. The keeper of the museum then was
Robert Plot, who was producing the kind of county surveys that were pro-
liferating in conjunction with the natural history movement in the Royal
Society. Lhuyd soon became involved in similar surveys, examining botani-
cal, geological, genealogical, linguistic and antiquarian materials as a part of
the investigation of human and world history. On Plot's retirement in 1691,
Lhuyd took over the post of keeper and soon embarked on a series of

---

*Edward Lhuyd spelled his name 'Lhwyd' in his letters, but chose to spell it
'Lhuyd' on the basis of a revised Welsh orthography proposed in 'A Translation of
the Welsh Preface to the Glossography', *Archaeologia Britannica, 2*. This revised
spelling reflects Lhuyd's preference after his extensive studies of linguistics.

collecting trips that would establish him as a major figure in the study of Britain's fossils and earliest inhabitants.

In 1693, Lhuyd toured Wales for seven weeks, collecting materials for Edmund Gibson's enlarged edition of Camden's *Britannia*. Two years later, he tried to make this trip the basis for a larger endeavour when he solicited subscribers for multi-volume surveys titled *The Natural History and Antiquities of Wales* and *Archaeologia Britannica*. Soon, he distributed queries and then, in 1696, set out on a five-month tour of Wales. The next year, he hired three assistants and began a series of comprehensive collecting tours of Britain, Ireland and Brittany, lasting until 1701.

One of Lhuyd's earliest mentions of the Celts occurred during the years of these tours, around the time he made contact with Pezron. In 1697, in a report sent to the Royal Society, he described an inscription he found on a step of a tower at Kaerphily castle as possibly being in 'the old *Celtic* character, which *Caesar* says was like the *Greek*', adding that 'our Ancestors (if ever they had any Writing) have left us none upon Stones'.[10] In the following year, a mutual acquaintance told Lhuyd that Pezron was working on a 'Celtic Dictionary' and 'labours to prove all Europe and the Greek language originally Celtic'.[11] By this point, Lhuyd seems to have understood that by 'Celtic' Pezron was referring to Breton and Welsh as the purest living examples. He wanted to check Pezron's theory about Celtic by comparing 'British' (i.e. Welsh and Cornish) with Greek.[12] Lhuyd was intrigued by Pezron's ideas which confirmed his own observation of similarities among the languages he came across in the course of his journeys. After receiving further details of Pezron's work during the summer of 1698, however, Lhuyd became aware of differences with his own research and hoped to hear more from Pezron in order to settle their disagreements about how these languages were connected:

> His notion of the Greek, Roman and Celtic Languages being of one common origin, agrees exactly with my observations. But I have not advanced so far as to discover the Celtic to be the Mother-tongue, tho' perhaps he may not want good grounds, at least plausible arguments, for such an assertion. The Irish comes in with us, and is a dialect of the Old Latin, as the British is of the Greek, but the Gothick or Teutonick, tho' it has also much affinity with us, must needs make a Band apart.[13]

Probably because Lhuyd disagreed with Pezron's interpretation of Celtic as the parent language of Europe, Lhuyd started to shy away from using the term *Celtic*. When describing his conclusion that Welsh and Cornish 'are but so many dialects of one and the same language,' he did not mention the Celts.[14]

Lhuyd's further attempts to contact Pezron proved fruitless before the 1703 publication of *L'Antiquité de la Nation*.[15] Upon seeing the book in that year, Lhuyd thought Pezron went too far in using linguistics as a basis for connecting Breton-speakers to Celts who migrated directly from Mount Ararat. Lhuyd seems to have been criticising Pezron's argument when he wrote that Pezron 'has infinitely outdone all our Countrymen as to national zeal.'[16]

Lhuyd shared Pezron's basic method of using comparative tables in order to find the origins of languages, but, despite offering a much more comprehensive collection of data, was less ambitious in his conclusions. Lhuyd did not address the question of European origins and confined his study to tracing the source of the non-English languages of the British Isles. Like Pezron, he concluded that these languages descended from ancient Celtic. But Lhuyd's definition of the Celts was not the same as the biblical-historical Celts of Pezron's elaborate genealogy. For Lhuyd, the Celts were merely a tribe that Caesar described as living in Gaul in ancient times:

> as the Gauls were a People that consisted of three several Nations, of so many
> different Languages, some of those Words attributed to them in general, might
> have been Celtic properly so called, some Aquitanian and others Belgic.[17]

And unlike Pezron, who traced Celtic speech in all European languages, Lhuyd argued that aside from a few Latin words which derived from 'the old *Gaulish* or *Celtic*', Celtic has left its mark only in Brittany, Wales, Cornwall and the Gaelic parts of Ireland and Scotland.[18] Despite their differences, Lhuyd was clearly influenced by Pezron's argument that the close relationship between Breton and Welsh pointed to a lineage that included the ancient Celts: the search for the 'Original Language' could 'contribute not a little towards a Clearer Notion of the First Planters'.[19] Lhuyd diverged from Pezron's approach to tracing the language of the ancient Celts, however, in two crucial respects. First, Lhuyd downplayed the potential contributions of Breton, 'because we cannot distinguish what they may have borrow'd from the *French*', while for Pezron, Breton had been the purest descendant of ancient Celtic.[20] And secondly, Lhuyd introduced the Irish language as being not just a member of the same language family as Breton and Welsh, but as being closely linked, 'rather more than ours [i.e. Welsh], with the *Gaulish*'.[21]

Before Lhuyd demonstrated the relationships among the Irish language, Breton and Welsh, the origins of the Irish had generally been traced to Spain and were considered to have been separate. Lhuyd's innovation was to put Ireland at the heart of British origins: 'We see then how necessary the *Irish* language is to those who would understand or write of the Antiquity of the Isle of *Britain*.'[22] In Lhuyd's model of early migrations, however, the peopling of Ireland derived equally from immigrants from Gaul and Spain:

> Having now related what none have hitherto made mention of; viz. First, that the old Inhabitants of *Ireland* consisted of two Nations *Gwydhelians* & *Scots*. Secondly, that the *Gwydhelians* descended from the most ancient *Britains*, & the *Scots* from *Spain*. Thirdly, that the *Gwydhelians* lived in the most ancient times, not only in *North-Britain* (where they still continue intermix'd with *Scots, Saxons, & Danes*) but also in *England* & *Wales*. And fourthly, that the say'd *Gwydhelians* of *England* & *Wales* were the Inhabitants of *Gaul* before they came into this Island. [...]
>
> The next thing to be prov'd is that those ancient Gwydhelians were a Colony of those Nations whom the Romans call'd Galli or Celtae. And this will also appear evident from a Comparison of both their Languages.[23]

Lhuyd supported these statements with language lists connecting the Irish language to Spanish and to ancient Celtic words drawn from Latin sources. He also found a relationship between Irish Gaelic and Teutonic, but explained this as the product of language mixing between the ancient Celtae and Belgae, who, he thought, spoke a Germanic language.

The culmination of Lhuyd's language lists was one based on a Latin-Irish dictionary but expanded 'to a sort of *Latin-Celtic Dictionary*' by comparing Latin words with their Irish and Welsh equivalents.[24] This dictionary represented the product of Lhuyd's endeavours to reconstruct the ancient Celtic language using modern sources. While Pezron saw Breton and Welsh as the purest living descendants of ancient Celtic, Lhuyd argued that Welsh and Irish Gaelic were the two most useful languages for reconstructing this ancient tongue that he thought was spoken in Gaul. This is a crucial distinction, for it demonstrates that Lhuyd only thought it appropriate to discuss the Celts in terms of ancient times.

Finally, Lhuyd emphasised the relationship between ancient Celtic and the Irish language when he provided a definition of the very word 'Celtae' in his list of Celtic terms found in Latin sources. Starting with Caesar's description of the Celtae, Lhuyd discussed possible changes to the word during migrations to Ireland:

> Celtae, The Gauls; Caes. Goedic, Caedil or Keil, and in the Plural according
> to our Dialect [i.e. Welsh], Keilict and Keilt now Guidelod, Irishmen. And
> the word Keilt could not be otherwise written by the Romans than Ceilte
> or Celtae. Neither is there room for a satisfactory knowledge whether 'twas
> not for this reason that the more Northern part of this Island was call'd by us
> Kelidon and by the Romans Caledonia, or from woods Keliad being of that
> Signification in the Scotish-Irish to this day.[25]

Despite the novelty of Lhuyd's argument that the ancient Celtic origins of the
Irish language could shed light on the peopling of Britain, his glossography
was met with disappointment from subscribers, who had more interest in
some of Lhuyd's other antiquarian materials, including early manuscripts
and studies of ancient monuments. Lhuyd had felt that he needed to provide his readers with his cumbersome volume of word lists before
presenting manuscripts in the languages he studied. Unfortunately for his
subscribers, his premature death in 1709 meant that *Archaeologia Britannica*
did not proceed past the first volume.

Pezron's Legacy

Most eighteenth-century linguists after Pezron and Lhuyd followed Pezron
in defining the Celts as the speakers of the parent of all European languages,
though writers seeking to demonstrate the uniqueness of their home
region sometimes employed a narrower definition, as Pezron himself did
with Breton. The variation in concepts of purity in Celtic speech was as
varied as the backgrounds of writers on the topic, but virtually all agreed
with Pezron that the Celts gave rise equally to Gaelic, Welsh and Breton as
well as to English, German, Latin and Greek.

Within the variety of linguistic interpretations of the Celts in the early
eighteenth century, some works anticipated the more restricted modern
definition of Celtic languages, but these were exceptions not widely followed at the time. For example, Thomas Innes' interpretation, mainly
designed to downplay the Irish component of Scottish history, had Gaelic
speakers living in Scotland before the settlement of the Scots from northern
Ireland after Roman times:

since it appears, that the *Celtick* language, whereof the *British* is a dialect, was in use in ancient times in the furthest extremities of the north: at least the *Celtes*, or *Celto-Scyths*, were extended to these parts.

Citing Lhuyd instead of Pezron, Innes distinguished Celtic from the 'Gothish' languages like English and Dutch.[26] While Innes' work provided the foundation for later nationalist Scottish contributions to the peopling problem, its linguistic section was relatively small and did little to change the more common notion that the Celts were the ancestors of both British and Gothic language speakers.

Another Scot, the philologist David Malcolme, disagreed with Innes when he took a more universalist position in seeing Celtic as an important language in early human history, though he also saw the Scots as more ancient:

> The Ancient Scottish or Irish, is a most valuable Dialect of the Celtic, and besides its internal Beauties, is of incredible Use to illustrate the Antiquities, Languages, Laws, &c. of many other Nations; more especially these of Italy, Greece, Palestine, or Canaan, besides other Places of Asia, Europe, Africa, and America.[27]

On the other side of the debate over Scottish versus Irish origins of Gaelic was John Toland. As a Deist, Toland's main goal was to show how the Church of England retained superstitious rites and beliefs from what he argued were its Druid predecessors, and how he was uniquely positioned to shed light on the history of this ancient religion. As we will see in Chapter V, he played a significant role in connecting the ancient Celts to the Druids. In the debate over Celtic languages, however, his position was but another possibly cynical attempt to show that a particular region possessed evidence of the purest Celtic speech. He was fluent in Irish Gaelic, though he lived in virtual exile from his home in the north of Ireland. Writing to a potential sponsor, he argued that Irish was 'the least corrupted' of the 'Celtic' dialects. Lhuyd's interpretation of Irish Gaelic as the purest remnant of 'the old Celtic of Gaul' was a critical feature of Toland's argument, and Toland rejected Pezron's idea that Celtic was equally ancestral to other European tongues: 'Thus the Celtic and the Gothic, which have been often taken for each other, are as different as Latin and Arabic'.[28]

Yet another interpretation of the Celtic languages was offered to the Philosophical Society of Edinburgh in 1742 by John Clerk. In his 1742 treatise on Celtic languages, Clerk thought that 'most of the nations of Europe went sometime under the name of the Celtae', and that Celtic speakers represented the earliest group to reach Britain. He expressed the unusual theory, however, that the Celtae spoke a language ancestral to English, rather than Welsh or Gaelic, and that most of the 'Celtic nations' spoke a Germanic language.[29]

It seems that in the first half of the eighteenth century, when the peopling question mainly concerned historical and linguistic sources, most writers agreed that the Celts played an important role, though there was no consensus about who the Celts actually were or even what language they spoke. In linguistics, this situation continued into the late eighteenth century, even when a new definition of Celts was arising in the study of literature (the subject of Chapter III).

Pezron's idea that Celtic was the parent language of Europe was the foundation of a flurry of linguistic research in the mid eighteenth century. Francis Wise, a cataloguer at the Bodleian Library in Oxford, had long been interested in ancient monuments when he published a book tracing European history through the development of language.[30] He thought of the Greek tongue as one of the most ancient European languages and divided it into two successive periods, the Pelasgic and Hellenic. Pelasgic, the older dialect for Wise, he took 'to be the same which antiquaries now agree to call the Celtic,' which, as 'the first known language in Europe,' should be called 'the Universal Language of the postdiluvian world'.[31]

In the 1760s, linguists Rowland Jones and John Cleland also echoed Pezron's idea in a series of books. Jones, a Welsh solicitor living in London, saw the supposed ancient universality of Celtic as a model of world harmony and hoped to reunify world languages under English.[32] He defined the 'Cumbri-Galli-Celtes' as 'the fathers, or founders of the first nations of Asia Minor, Greece, Italy, ancient Gaul, Germany, Britain, Ireland, and most other countries of Europe'.[33] Cleland, an English dramatist and pornographer, discussed Celtic, the 'universal elementary language of Europe' and parent of 'the Greek, the Latin, the Teutonic, &c. with all their numberless subdivisions', in progressivist evolutionary terms: 'This language, which the more primitive it was, must be the stronger of the energy of nature, must also in the simplicity of its origin have been purely monosyllabic'.[34]

After living in Ireland and gaining firsthand experience of Irish Gaelic, James Parsons, an English physician, started to study the origins of European languages. Like Jones and Cleland, he used Pezron as the basis for his theory that 'the natives of *Ireland*, *Scotland*, and *Wales*' speak 'dialects of the *Japhetan* language', which he also called 'the language of the *Celts*, or rather *Gomerians* and *Magogians*'.[35] Basing his ideas on the biblical model, Parsons reasoned that there must have been two separate westward migrations of Noah's descendants. In this interpretation, Magog, ruler of the Magogians, speaking a language ancestral to Irish Gaelic, migrated from the Near East through northwestern Europe, while Gomer and the Gomerians, speaking a language ancestral to Welsh:

> spread themselves all over the South-western parts of Europe, giving the first rise to Greeks, Latins, Franks, Biscayans, and arriving in the Southern parts of Britain, by sea from the isles of Elisha, about the same time (or soon after the British islands were inhabited by their relations, the Magogians or Scythians) and long before their brethren, the Gauls or Celts, came into any part of France or Spain.[36]

Today, Parsons is celebrated for being among the first to identify connections among Indo-European languages. In fact, he found linguistic connections wherever he looked, including Mexico and Peru, which he linked linguistically to Tartary.[37] His version of Pezron's theory of Celtic migrations, while building on the close relationship between Welsh and Irish Gaelic, seemed aimed more at arguing for the primacy of the languages of Britain and Ireland than at building substantially on Pezron's results. Like Cleland, Jones and Wise, he was inspired by Pezron's synthesis of linguistics and biblical history, but did little more than tinker with the details of Pezron's model in reaffirming an image of the Celts as speakers of a Hebrew-like, post-Flood language that was ancestral to all European tongues.

Romanticism as Explanation

The most common explanation for appearance of the term *Celtic* in the eighteenth century is that it developed in association with romanticism.[38] Strictly speaking, however, the Romantic Movement started in Germany towards the end of the eighteenth century, well after the time when linguists introduced the idea of the Celtic languages. Though Pezron and Lhuyd were not themselves members of the Romantic Movement, there are ways in which their work anticipated aspects of it, thereby allowing historians to describe them using the lower-case label of *romantics*. But romanticism in itself does not explain how the term *Celtic* came to support a variety of linguistic models of the peopling of Europe.

Few who attribute the Celtic scholarship of the eighteenth century to romanticism have defined how this process might have worked. One exception is the deconstructionist Malcolm Chapman, who has referred to Pezron, Lhuyd and their successors as proto-romantics. Chapman's centre-periphery model serves as a romantic mechanism through which the concept of the Celts appeared as an ethnic term for the collective periphery in the eighteenth century.[39] For Chapman, romanticism involved an 'apparent counter-current' of fashion, in which it seemed that trends in peripheral regions moved into the centre. In reality, he argued, the ideas and styles attributed to the periphery actually developed in the centre – often through forgeries – and then moved outward, influencing the periphery to conform to the image of it that had been built in the centre. According to Chapman, the notion of the modern Celts developed in London-centred society and was subsequently taken up by inhabitants of what became known as the Celtic fringe. But Chapman never explained how the word 'Celt' was first introduced or how scholarly uses of the word changed over time.

Both Pezron and Lhuyd fit into Chapman's centre-periphery model. They came from the economic fringes of Britain and France but were eager to participate in national intellectual life. Pezron wrote *L'Antiquité de la Nation* as a general history of the nation of France, though he granted Brittany central importance by connecting the Breton language most closely with the country's first people. Lhuyd, a Welshman working in Oxford, also used his native language as a means to trace the history of his country. Instead of writing in the universal scholarly language of Latin, the two broke with their predecessors by writing in their national languages, French and English respectively. Though Lhuyd might have preferred to present his work to a Welsh-speaking audience, the economics of publishing dictated that English versions of his and Pezron's books circulated most widely in Britain.[40] By studying and celebrating life on the fringes of their emerging nation-states, Pezron and Lhuyd contributed to the aspects of romanticism that involved a growing taste for internal tourism and interest in rural landscapes, which, in turn, spurred the development of antiquarianism. Both scholars called attention to their native areas by ascribing an ennobled purity to the local inhabitants.

Despite their shared romantic motives, Pezron and Lhuyd employed the term *Celtic* in contrasting ways. Pezron cited the Breton language as the purest living descendant of the language of the Celts, while Lhuyd offered a more nuanced argument in which all of the non-English insular tongues preserved some aspects of ancient Celtic speech, with Irish Gaelic – the language furthest from the Gallic source – as the most pure. The difference in their notions of purity points to a deeper intellectual difference relating to their interpretations of the mechanisms of change. Though both cited language as the central criterion for describing a people and its history, Pezron created a model in which a linguistic group migrated into an empty land and diversified, whereas Lhuyd considered the possibility that different languages could have mixed, leaving a more complex record in which simple migrations had to be distinguished from the possible later diffusion of linguistic forms.

In the years that followed, other eighteenth-century linguists exhibited the romantic motive of elevating the status of their home regions. For them, Pezron's idea of the Celts as first Europeans flourished as they sought to show that their local language – be it Breton, Gaelic or even English – was the purest form of Celtic. But Pezron's selection of the term *Celtic* to describe the original language of Europe was fairly arbitrary. According to his own logic, 'Celtae' was just the last in a series of names by which this tribe was known. Some term was needed, however, to support the linguistic idea that all European languages branched off from a common ancestor. To name this root language 'Celtic' gave linguists a recognisable term that could then be used to support a variety of different interpretations of the historical process of the diversification of European tongues.

As linguistic ideas continued to evolve into the nineteenth century, the term *Celtic* became a permanent feature of discourse. As we will see in Chapter IV, a new leading linguistic model – that of James Cowles Prichard – soon emerged to replace Pezron's, utilising a different meaning for the term *Celtic*. But why did Prichard feel the term was unavoidable, despite his distaste for it? And why was Prichard's definition different from the one Pezron and his followers had used? It was not the study of language, but the study of literature, that produced the new idea of a Celtic language family exclusive to Gaelic, Welsh and Breton.

CHAPTER III

ROMANCING THE DRUIDS

In the mid eighteenth century, a new definition of the Celts emerged and slowly replaced Pezron's conception of Celtic as the ancestral European tongue. Increasingly, the Celts were restricted to the family of languages that includes Welsh, Gaelic, Breton, Cornish and Manx. Ironically, this new definition arose not in linguistics but in the study of literature. Echoing the romantic motives of the linguists, scholars of Celtic literature argued that Druidism was both local to their own regions and one of the oldest and purest religions in the world. To accomplish this, they linked the Druids with Pezron's Celts. It was then within literary histories of Druidism that the new definition of the Celts arose. Only in the nineteenth century, with the growth of a global perspective, contrasting with the earlier romantic one, did this definition enter the field of linguistics, when James Cowles Prichard described the Celtic languages as a branch, rather than the root, of the Indo-European tree.

Linguistic Celts and Druidical Monuments

The first step in the development of the new and more restricted definition of the Celts as one particular group in the European past was the explicit linking of the Celts with Druid priests. Despite the popular association of Celts and Druids today, there was no exclusive correlation in the classical texts between the peoples and the priests, with Celts described vaguely as living on the western end of the Continent of Europe and Druids mentioned more specifically in relation to Britain and Gaul, but with their training centres in Britain.

The Druid priests of ancient Britain had disappeared from popular memory and discourse until they became an object of British scholarship in the sixteenth century, when the ancient texts that described them became widely available. Hector Boece's 1526 history of Scotland was the first of a series of books from this period that sought to connect contemporary learning with the ancient Druids.[1] In 1618, the Druids entered the popular sphere in the production of *Bonduca*, John Fletcher's play about a British rebellion against Roman rule.

At the start of the eighteenth century, Druidism, by then widely thought of as among the world's most ancient religious orders, took on a pivotal role in debates about the peopling of the world, thanks especially to John Aubrey's theory that megaliths were Druid temples. Prehistoric megalithic monuments, dating to the late Neolithic and early Bronze Ages, are clustered across much of western Europe but are especially prevalent in the western parts of the British Isles. Stonehenge and Avebury in Wiltshire are the most famous, while smaller monuments in Britain number in the thousands. Before the seventeenth century, little notice was taken of most of these structures, which were often considered to be natural parts of the landscape. Stonehenge, on the other hand, was well known, having been mentioned in Geoffrey's history as being associated with King Arthur and Merlin the wizard. With the fall of the Brutus story by the seventeenth century, the origins of Stonehenge became the object of some debate. Leading theories about who constructed the monument named the Phoenicians, Romans, Saxons and Danes, but consensus remained elusive until Aubrey put forth his theory of Druidical origins.

In 1649, Aubrey came upon Avebury on a hunting trip and found it a remarkable monument, exceeding even Stonehenge in grandeur. When, in 1663, King Charles II heard news of Aubrey's discovery, he asked for a written description and, soon after, a guided tour. This request led Aubrey to start writing *Templa Druidum* and *Chorographia Antiquaria*, which would later be included in his *Monumenta Britannica*.[2] Influenced by the growing movement centred at the Royal Society promoting natural history and Baconian observation, Aubrey began by noting the distribution of other stone monuments in the British Isles. This evidence led him to conclude that the clustering of Britain's megaliths in western parts of the island made it likely that they were temples of the Druids, who were thought to have been based in the west. Though Aubrey never published *Monumenta Britannica*, his theory had tremendous influence thanks to its spread through his many contacts, a number of privately circulated manuscripts and excerpts pub-

lished in the 1695 edition of Camden, which was the same book for which
Lhuyd had started his collecting tours.[3] While Aubrey's idea of Druidical
origins for megaliths was instrumental in the development of theories of
Celtic migrations based on the locations of these monuments, Aubrey him-
self never thought of the builders as Celts and referred to them only as
Britons.

Inspired by the 1695 edition of Camden, a number of books appeared in
the early eighteenth century that attributed local remains to the Druids,
who could provide an area with a colourful past. In this respect, interest in
the Druids became complementary to the longer tradition of finding
remains of 'those Romantick Ages' of King Arthur and became established as
a focus of internal tourism.[4] Lhuyd, one of the first to be inspired by
Aubrey's work when he sought 'remains of Druidism amongst the Bretons',
invoked the wisdom of the Druids in the spirit of Welsh patriotism in
Archaeologia Britannica.[5] William Sacheverell, the governor of the Isle of
Man, and Henry Rowlands, a vicar on Anglesey, an island just off the north-
west coast of Wales, both wrote volumes in the first decade of the
eighteenth century claiming that their respective islands were the Mona
mentioned by Tacitus as being the original seat of the Druids. Both islands
do seem to have been called Mona at some time, though Anglesey was more
probably the island of which Tacitus wrote. In the same years, Martin
Martin began attributing stone circles and alignments in the Hebrides to
the Druids.

In Martin's 1703 account of a tour of the Scottish islands, he emphasised
that the history he was writing had the advantage of being based on actual
visits to sites of interest and on stories provided by local inhabitants.[6]
Martin's accounts of local survivals of Druidism among the standing stones
of Scotland, however, were in all probability his own fabrications inspired
by Aubrey's ideas.[7] At the many standing stones Martin found, he asked the
locals if they knew who constructed them and reported answers such as:

> they told me, it was a place appointed for Worship in the time of
> Heathenism, and that the Chief Druid or Priest stood near the big Stone in
> the centre, from whence he address'd himself to the People that surrounded
> him.[8]

In a section on 'The Antient and Modern Customs of the Inhabitants of the
Western Islands of Scotland', Martin elaborated on this supposed local
knowledge of Druidical customs: 'Every great Family in the Isles had a

Chief *Druid*, who foretold future Events, and decided all Causes Civil and Ecclesiastical'.[9] Martin did not connect these Scottish Druids to Celts, however. He called the language spoken by the islanders 'Irish' and named the Picts as 'the first Inhabitants of these Isles'.[10] The connection of these so-called Druid circles with the Celts emerged from the debate over the site of Mona.

In his book on the Isle of Man, Sacheverell left the discussion of Mona to the satirist Thomas Brown, who contributed a section called 'A Short Dissertation About the Mona of Caesar and Tacitus'. Brown did not agree with Sacheverell's claim that Man was Tacitus' Mona, the seat of the Druids, but thought it might have been another Mona, which Caesar mentioned as being at some distance from the coast.[11] Brown's chapter was mainly a critique of the ancient texts, which he challenged with a novel argument about the origin of the Druids. Brown contended that the Druids came from the east, contradicting the classical writers who described them as practising only in Britain and Gaul. In order to argue for an eastern and ancient ancestry of the Druids, Brown wrote of the Druids as Celtic priests – a connection not made explicit in the ancient texts – and then extrapolated the origin of the Druids from what Pezron argued about the origin of the Celts. Though he did not cite Pezron by name, Brown clearly employed his theory of eastern origins as well as his definition of the Celts as the parent peoples of all of Europe. For example, in disputing Caesar's claim that there were no Druids among the Germans, Brown followed Pezron in treating the Germans as descendants of the Celts, writing, 'the *Celtae*, under which name the *Germans* are comprehended', practised human sacrifice, indicating that they must have had Druids.[12] Also, Germany appears prominently in Brown's list of Celtic territories:

> I shall examine whether we of Britain had these Druids immediately from Grece [sic], or Gaul, or lastly, what I look upon to be the most probable Opinion, whether these famous Celtick Philosophers, whose Order spread itself over Germany, Gaul, Britain, Ireland, and the smaller Islands belonging to them, did not like all the other Professors of Learning come from the most Eastern parts of the World.[13]

Brown's discussion of the Druids was fairly short, and his references to the Celts restricted to the two examples cited above. The most expansive and influential work on the Druids in these years was Henry Rowlands' *Mona Antiqua Restaurata*, completed and circulated in 1708 but published posthumously. Rowlands, a vicar from Anglesey and close friend of Lhuyd, was pivotal in connecting the Celtic language speakers of Lhuyd and Pezron to the Druids. Like Sacheverell, Rowlands seems to have turned to local anti-quarianism after the 1695 edition of Camden discussed possible locations of Druidical monuments. Between Sacheverell's publication and the comple-tion of Rowlands' manuscript, Pezron's book on the Celts appeared, and its influence was clear in Rowlands' work. Far more ambitious than his Druid-hunting predecessors, Rowlands attempted to look beyond the classical texts to create an account of ancient Anglesey through a synthesis of various strands of evidence, including historical, linguistic and antiquarian. This synthesis led him to incorporate the Celts of Pezron and Lhuyd into a wider argument that used more than just the linguistic criteria that Pezron and Lhuyd used to define a people. Rowlands called his novel approach 'archaeology', though his usage of the term is not directly related to the modern discipline:

> ARCHAEOLOGY, or an Account of the Origin of Nations after the Universal DELUGE, admits of two Ways of Enquiry, either beginning at BABEL, the Place of Mankind's Dispersion, and tracing them downwards to our own Times by the Light of Records, which is HISTORY, and of Natural Reason, which is INFERENCE and CONJECTURE; or else beginning from our own Time, and winding them upwards, by the same Helps, to the first Place and Origin of their Progression; [...]
>
> A Method (I confess) very unusual, *viz.* to trace the Footsteps of Historical Actions any other way, than that of Antient MEMOIRS and RECORDS. But where those *Lights* are wanting, what shall we do? [...]
>
> There are other Things, as Analogy of Antient Names and Words: Antient *Laws*, *Constitutions*, and *Customs*: *Coins* and *Medals*: *Erections*, *Monuments*, and *Ruins*: *Aedifices* and *Inscriptions*: The *Appellations* of Places: The *Genius* and *Tempers*, and *Inclinations* and *Complexions* of People;[14]

In the second section of the book, where Rowlands addressed some critiques of his work, he defended what he called his conjectural method of uncover-ing 'the deep Obscurities of Time' before written history.[15] Using the metaphor of his various forms of evidence representing light that illuminates the darkness of ancient times, he named five 'lights' that enabled him to research pre-Roman Britain: '*Scriptural Light*' set the framework of the post-Flood peopling; '*Moral Light*' was his name for reason, which he used to deduce that the first people migrated around the world from the Ark and, later, Babel; '*Geographical Light*' pointed to the route taken by the first peoples through Europe; '*Arithmetical Light*' enabled him to calculate the time the expansion took by using the chronological method of counting genera- tions; and '*Names*' of places shed light on the language spoken by various peoples and, in cases like the town of Tre'r Drew, could point to the loca- tions of Druidical monuments by virtue of phonetic similarities with the word 'Druid'.[16] Though here he did not name the study of ancient monu- ments as one of his lights, this method was central to his argument.

In using the biblical framework as a starting point to trace the peopling of Britain, Rowlands mainly followed Pezron's argument in order to link the limited biblical text on the subject with the evidence covering Britain. In doing so, Rowlands employed Pezron's definition of 'Celtic', though he also used 'Celtish', 'Celtique' and 'antient British', to denote the name of the language of Gomer, of the first planters of Europe, 'the Mother of most of the antient Tongues of *Europe*', and 'one of the primary vocal Modes and Expressions of Mankind, after *Babel*'s Dispersion'.[17] Rowlands was aware that his use of 'Celtic' followed Pezron rather than Lhuyd. Also in contrast with Lhuyd, Rowlands argued that the Celtic language was better repre- sented by Welsh than by Irish and was closely allied with Hebrew.

The importance of the linguistic argument for Rowlands was that it enabled him to contest that Mona, or Anglesey, contained the oldest and purest form of this Celtic language, which, he argued, was one of the first to break off from Hebrew in the dispersion at Babel.[18] He then imported this linguistic argument into the religious sphere. Just as he argued that the Celtic language was one of the world's oldest and purest, he argued that the Celtic religion, Druidism, 'that true Religion, pure and untainted', preserved the knowledge of God as understood by Old Testament patriarchs.[19] Rowlands' interpretation of the Druids enabled him to focus attention more precisely on Anglesey as the purest pocket of ancient learning. His multi- source method of 'archaeology', then, was necessary for him to describe his own local area as pure, in the way Pezron had done for Brittany.

In addition to the ancient texts which called Mona the seat of the Druids, Rowlands could connect Anglesey to the Druids in another way, which was provided by Aubrey's theory that stone monuments were Druidical temples. Anglesey, like much of Wales and western England, con- tains a number of stone circles. Though smaller than Stonehenge, they are of the same type, facilitating the same Druidical attribution. Because the ancient texts described Druidical temples as being oak groves, and not stone monuments, Rowlands argued that the Druids' groves would have surrounded more permanent temple buildings like the stone circles:

And that altho' the Groves surrounding them [i.e. the stone monuments] be now quite gone and perish'd, and the antient Names of them be utterly lost, yet it may be justly expected that many of the lasting Erections (on the supposal I offer) should remain there, as standing Monuments of their long forgotten superannuated Uses.[20] (*pl. 4* and *5*)

The connections Brown and Rowlands made between stone monuments and the Druids, and between the Druids and Pezron's biblical Celts, led to two crucial results. One is that scholars began to search for Celtic monuments, as we will see in Chapter V, starting an intellectual endeavour that eventually led to the identification of Celtic art and contributed to the birth of modern archaeology. The second result is that historians began to draw a distinction between Celts, with their Druid priests, and the rest of the peoples of Europe, signalling the end of Pezron's interpretation of the Celts as the ancestors of all Europeans.

The Celtic Revival and the Distinction between Celts and Goths

Wales

In the mid eighteenth century, a literary movement that has become known as the Celtic Revival arose from the same romantic impulse that stimulated Pezron, Lhuyd and Rowlands; it was the product of thinkers from the British fringes celebrating their home regions in the context of the intellectual and social circles of London. The movement was initiated in the 1750s when the Welsh poet Lewis Morris, a surveyor whose work frequently brought him to London, helped start a rush of interest in ancient Welsh literature through his recovery and translation of forgotten manuscripts. The growing Welsh community in London had been fostering an interest in the ancient Welsh for some time. As early as 1715, Welsh newcomers to the capital had formed the Society of Ancient Britons. Then, in 1751, Welsh Londoners like Morris, seeking a more active role in promoting Welsh literature, founded the Honourable Society of Cymmrodorion. After these societies made an impact in London, similar organisations began to appear back in Wales.

Morris built on Lhuyd's pioneering work on ancient Welsh manuscripts to construct a Welsh history based on literary evidence. He was also heavily influenced by Pezron and Rowlands, whose *Mona Antiqua Restaurata* he 'corrected and improved' for a second edition.[21] Morris completed *Celtic Remains*, his study of manuscripts, in 1757, but this was not published until 1878. Nevertheless, his influence on other members of the Celtic Revival is undeniable, both through the Honourable Society of Cymmrodorion and through correspondences. The long subtitle of *Celtic Remains* illustrates Morris' goal of using the manuscript sources he uncovered to shed light on ancient Britain:

> *The Ancient Celtic Empire Described in the English Tongue. Being a Biographical, Critical, Historical, Etymological, Chronological, and Geographical Collection of Celtic Materials towards a British History of Ancient Times.* [...] *The Several Branches of that People vizt., the British or Welsh, the Irish, the Armoric, the Cornish, and Manx.*[22]

As the subtitle indicates, Morris had started using a more restricted definition of the Celts than had Pezron, though he did not make a full break from Pezron. He adhered to Lhuyd's theory that the Irish language was mixed with Spanish and echoed the common idea among Welsh linguists that Welsh represented 'the principal branch and chief remains of the ancient Celtic tongue, and that the Irish, the Ersh, and Armoric have issued from the British [i.e. Welsh]'.[23] As for early Celtic history, he followed most of Pezron's theory of Celtic descent from Gomer, but instead of seeing the Celts simply as ancestral to 'another people called *Teutons* (the ancestors of the Germans)' he argued that the Celts 'were pretty much mixed' with Teutons after the dispersion from Babel.[24] Though he described only 'the Irish, Ersh, British, Cornish, and Armoric' as 'Celtic dialects', he, like Pezron, thought of the Celts as 'ancestors of the Romans, the Sabines, and Umbrians, that inhabited Italy'.[25]

For many contributors to the Celtic Revival, the Celtic and Teutonic languages and histories were one and the same, as they had been for Pezron. The first explicit break with Pezron's theory came in the 1760s in an exchange of letters between Reverend Evan Evans, who translated Welsh bardic poetry into English, and Bishop Thomas Percy, a leading figure in the literary component of the Gothic Revival. This is the moment when the term *Celtic* began to take on its modern exclusive meaning as the non-English languages of the British Isles (plus Breton), and not as the linguistic ancestor of German, Latin or Greek.[26]

Percy initiated a correspondence with Evans in 1761 because his own work on Saxon poetry made him interested in other relatively unknown literary sources.[27] In 1764, Percy asked Evans if the 'old English Romances' about King Arthur were translated from French sources or imitations of Welsh originals.[28] In his response, Evans outlined his method of tracing ancient migrations through manuscripts that shed light on religion and language, as a way of proving that the stories were originally Welsh.[29] In doing so, he identified the Welsh language as the source of Breton, subscribing to the theory that Breton speakers came to France only after the Saxon invasion of Britain. In the history of religion, he interpreted Druidism as an indigenous Celtic phenomenon whose history could be traced through poetic forms preserved by the bards. In order to ensure British credit both for Druidism and for the Arthurian romances, he argued that the Celts and Teutons were originally distinct. While this view coincided with Percy's notion that 'the ancient Britons' were different from the 'nations of the Teutonic Race', in both their language and origins, it was Evans who linked the Britons with the Celts in making this distinction.[30] Evans first discussed the Celts in arguing that the poetic forms of the Arthurian romances dated back to the Druids:

> I think therefore that this refinement of Alliteration might more probably have made it's [sic] progress northwards in very ancient times when the Celtae were the greatest men for learning and arms in the known world. All Asia and Europe having at different periods been the scenes of their great exploits, as you may see in Pezron's antiquity of nations. [...] but still the Teutons and the Celtae are of a different origin, and their languages no ways allied.[31]

In using the history of literature as his main source of evidence for peopling, Evans adapted Pezron's theory of the ancient Celts as a widespread, primeval people, to his own theory of the origins of the Druids, but removed the aspect of Pezron's account that saw the Celts as the ancestors of all Europeans. Evans, a poet rather than a linguist, did not use language tables to justify his claim of the separateness of the Teutonic languages, but merely asserted it. Later, Evans used the diffusion of literary forms as a way to show how medieval Italian poetry had its roots in Gothic poetry which, in turn, derived from 'the Celtic bards', whose 'refined pitch', especially among the Welsh, proved their primacy.[32] For Evans, the diffusion of poetic forms – a possibility not considered since Lhuyd – proceeded separately from the movements and branchings of peoples.

Evans and Percy had been corresponding about the literary roots of the Celts for about two months when Percy began discussing his frustration with Paul Henry Mallet's work on the roots of Danish mythology. Percy objected to Mallet's assumption that the Celts and Druids were ancestral to northern European mythology and language groups. Like Evans, he argued that the Goths and Celts were distinct and unrelated peoples on account of the separateness of their languages and literary forms:

> Mallet should have intitled this piece not the *Celtic* but *Runic* Mythology. Being ignorant of all the modern branches of the real *Celtic* Language; and very little acquainted with those of *Gothic* Origin: he has every where confounded them: a mistake which I shall endeavour to rectify in my translation.—There is no foundation for his Hypothesis that these Runic fables are similar to what were taught by the Celtic Druids; I am of opinion that they were *ab origine* different. Odin the founder of the Gothic mythology, who after his death was worshipped as a God, brought all these fables with him from the east about the time of our Saviour:† whereas the Druidical superstitions had been established in Gaul and Britain many ages before. Nor did the Saxons, Danes and other northern nations begin to make their piratical irruptions into Britain and Gaul till some ages after, (*not till Druidism was abolished*) consequently could not learn IT from either the Britons or Gauls.
>
> †As we expressly learn from the Islandic Scalds.[33]

Evans agreed with this assessment, noting that the Celts were not necessarily ancestral to all Europeans, even though 'the dominion of the Celtae reached all over Europe'.[34]

In his 1770 translation of Mallet's *Introduction a l'Histoire de Dannemarc*, Percy devoted much space to pointing out problems with Mallet's lumping together of the Celts and Goths, 'a great source of mistake and confusion to many learned writers of the ancient history of Europe'.[35] In arguing that Sarmatians (Poles, Ruffians, Bohemians and Walachians) were 'extremely different' from the Celts, Percy cited 'their character, manners, laws and language'.[36] This argument was about more than the specific interpretation of the Celts as a distinct group in Europe, but was more generally about which kinds of evidence can be used in constructing a history of ancient peoples. Percy rejected the common use of evidence of place-name etymologies, arguing that they do not always reflect the language of local inhabitants: 'So much for arguments derived from Etymology; which are so very uncertain and precarious, that they can only amount to presumptions at best, and can never be opposed to solid positive proofs'.[37] He displayed similar scepticism about the use of classical texts, which even today remain controversial because they present an ambiguous picture of the Celts in which it was questionable whether they were a unified people. Classical writers, he argued, gave the Celts 'all the general name of Barbarians, inquired little farther about them, and took very little pains to be accurately informed about their peculiar differences and distinctions'.[38] Instead of place names and ancient sources, Percy offered the evidence of religion, particularly Druidism, which he said was exclusive to the Celts, and of language, which he argued separated Celtic and Gothic groups.[39] By defining a people mainly through its literary products, Percy and Evans introduced the idea that such a group was bound, not just by a common language, but by a common mentality or character, as expressed in its religious and poetic forms. To support this view, both turned to translations of old manuscripts as the most promising source of evidence.

Ireland and Scotland

For Scottish and Irish antiquaries of the Celtic Revival, the primary debate was not whether Celts were distinct from Goths but which area, Scotland or Ireland, was the first to have been settled by this ancient people. This debate also contributed to the development of a new picture of the Celts as distinct from other Europeans. The migrations of the Scoti, a Gaelic-speaking Irish tribe, to Scotland around the fifth century AD was well documented, but a series of old poems of questionable authenticity surfaced to challenge that migration and provide evidence for the reverse. In 1760, the Scot James Macpherson produced the first of his translations of these supposedly ancient Gaelic poems, attributed to a Homer-like Gaelic poet named Ossian, in *Fragments of Ancient Poetry*. The next year he published *Fingal*, an epic poem said to be from the same source. Though the poems were a forgery, they were hugely influential, not just in Britain but in all of Europe, going through dozens of editions and influencing Goethe and other German Romantics in their assessment of the 'genius' of 'primitive' peoples.

As part of an argument for peopling and migrations, the poems derived their importance from the suggestion that they represented a peculiarly Celtic literary form, illustrative of the unchanging character of a people. An irony of the often fierce debates over the authenticity of Macpherson's poems during the century after their appearance was that both sides conceived of them as representative of Celtic poetry, whether they dated to the ancient Celts or merely to Macpherson, as an heir to the Celtic ways.[40] When the controversy ended, an important cause of the demise of the poems' reputation was that contemporary notions of Celtic character no longer tallied with what the poems represented.[41] In the late eighteenth century, however, the poems of Ossian took their place beside Evans' bardic poems and Percy's Anglo-Saxon literature as examples of what separated their authors from other peoples.

Macpherson followed the publications of the Ossian poems with a book on the peopling of Great Britain and Ireland. In this account, he turned away from the biblical framework of Pezron's model and used classical texts as the basis for examining the religion, manners and customs, government and language of what he termed the 'nations' whose history he was tracing. Europe, for Macpherson, was originally constituted by separate peoples named Celtae, Sarmatae and Slavi, speaking the languages of Celtic, Teutonic and Sclavonic, though each country contained an individual mixture of all three.[42] Macpherson similarly subdivided the British nations into Gaels (North Britain), Cimbri (South Britain) and Belgae (later invaders).[43] In describing various migrations among these three groups, Macpherson devoted the main body of the book to demonstrating that Irish Gaels descended from the Gaels of North Britain, contrary to the accepted route of this migration from Ireland to Scotland.

Unsurprisingly, Macpherson's account was met with fierce resistance, especially but not exclusively on the part of Irish antiquaries.[44] While Scottish antiquaries started to look for physical evidence of the hero Fingal described in the Ossianic poems, their Irish counterparts consolidated their long-running theory that Ireland was originally peopled by Phoenicians coming through Spain, though they adapted this idea to the growing belief in the unity of Celtic languages by describing Ireland as the source of *eastward* Celtic migrations.[45]

Charles O'Conor had outlined this model in 1753 and reaffirmed it in a second, post-Ossian, edition in 1766 when he devoted a separate section to refuting Macpherson's work as fraudulent.[46] O'Conor used Pezron's definition of Celtic as 'the original Language of the Posterity of the Patriarchs, *Gomer* and *Japeth*', and argued further that 'this, in After-ages, branched out into the various Dialects of the *Persians, Teutons, Gauls, Britons* and *Scots*'.[47] In contrast to Pezron, however, he added evidence from bardic manuscripts to argue:

> Of all the old Scythian, or Celtic Nations, the antient Spaniards were the
> most martial and free, the most humanized by Letters, and the most conver-
> sant with the Egyptians, Phoenicians, and Grecians. From that Nation, our
> Gadelian, or Scotish Colony, derive their Original.[48]

O'Conor was echoed by the Irish surgeon Sylvester O'Halloran, who described his approach to Irish history as combating the 'pain and indignation' caused by 'almost all the writers of England and Scotland, (and from them of other parts of Europe), representing the Irish nation as the most brutal and savage of mankind'.[49] Like O'Conor, he argued that 'Celtic, or primeval language of the descendants of Japhet', came to Ireland through Spain, but, unlike O'Conor, he doubted the usefulness of linguistic evidence.[50] He drew on classical authors to trace the migrations of the Druids back to a Scythian colony that settled in Egypt, moved to Crete, then to Spain, and finally to Ireland.[51] Also like O'Conor, he devoted a whole section to refuting Macpherson. The interests of O'Conor and O'Halloran in the peopling of Ireland gained an institutional base in 1772 with the founding of a committee for the ancient state of arts, literature and antiquities within the Dublin Society. In 1785, this evolved into the Royal Irish Academy, which became the central institution of Irish antiquarianism. Charles Vallancey, one of the founders of the Antiquities Committee of the Academy and a military surveyor stationed in Ireland, expanded on the ideas of O'Conor and O'Halloran, but alienated his contemporaries by making extravagant claims, leading to a reassessment of the Phoenician origins story.[52]

Romanticism as Explanation Again

The historian T.D. Kendrick described romanticism as 'the ultimate cause of the revived interest in the druids that we have witnessed in the 18th century'.[53] As in the case of the first appearance of the term *Celtic* in relation to the British Isles, romanticism is also commonly invoked as a catch-all explanation for the linking of the Druids with the Celts and for the new, more restricted definition of the Celts that evolved in the mid eighteenth century. But this new concept of the ancient Celts as one of many European peoples, contradicting Pezron's model of them as the ancestors of all Europeans, cannot simply be attributed to the same romantic trend that influenced Pezron. The innovative ideas of Evan Evans and his followers were not a logical continuation of Pezron's thinking.

Romanticism did play a role, however, in the formulation of the new definition of the Celts, primarily by helping to add Druids to the equation. During the eighteenth century, interest in the Druids broadened as a part of a romantic celebration of local regions, and writers began to search for ancient Druidical temples in the landscape. The very word 'romantic' entered into popular usage as a part of this enterprise in two senses: ancient manuscripts that could be used to trace the history of Druidism were referred to as 'Romances'[54]; and writers from Aubrey onward described landscapes themselves as 'Romantick'.[55] In these cases, Kendrick is correct in linking renewed interest in the Druids with the same romantic trend that helped reintroduce the Celts into models of the peopling of Britain.

Once the Druids were accepted as a part of the ancient Celtic package, Pezron's model of the Celts as equal ancestors of all Europeans was at risk. In classical texts, the Druids are not given the kind of vague and contradictory treatment as the Celts. They are described specifically as having inhabited Gaul and Britain, with their training ground on the island of Mona, off the west coast of Britain. Despite the fact that Thomas Brown and Henry Rowlands first linked these Druids to the Celts by conceiving of Druidism as an ancient, eastern religion, the association survived into the Celtic Revival when Druidism was again seen as local to the British Isles. During this movement, writers like Morris, Evans and Macpherson described a literary tradition encompassing Welsh and Gaelic sources, which they traced back to Druid roots. They needed a term for this perceived unity, and *Celtic* was a name already associated with the Druids and with the languages themselves (though under Pezron's definition). Thanks mainly to this renewed interest in the Druids during the Celtic Revival, the Celtic branch of the human tree began to be perceived as one that had separated from the European stem at an early date, rather than as forming its very root.

CHAPTER IV

THE GROWTH OF ETHNOLOGY

By the end of the eighteenth century, at least two definitions of the ancient Celts were in circulation. The first was Pezron's idea that the Celtic language was ancestral to all European tongues. The second was the notion that the Celtic literary tradition, as understood from early Welsh and Gaelic manuscripts, was entirely distinct from other European sources. Both of these conceptions of the Celts had arisen as part of a romantic drive to link a particular local region to a larger historical model. The followers of Pezron, for example, tended to argue that their local language represented the purest remnant of the original Celtic. Literary historians likewise wrote that their local tradition was uniquely Celtic. While differing widely on the details, all of these scholars agreed that the ancient Celts, in one form or another, were central to the peopling of the British Isles.

At this point, a more universalist approach to the problem of human diversity began to emerge, opening a new era in Celtic research. Researchers without a romantic interest in a home region explored new ways of tracing ancient migrations, soon leading to the birth of ethnology, the first discipline dedicated to the problem of the peopling of the earth. Within this global program, however, the terminology of the romantics was adopted, cementing *Celtic* as the label for the non-English peoples of the British Isles and elevating the more popular literary definition of the term over Pezron's linguistic definition.

By the last quarter of the eighteenth century, linguists and contributors to the Celtic Revival had reached an impasse. Despite the introduction of literary evidence into the problem of Celtic origins, no one had been able to build substantially on Pezron's work. Agreement seemed beyond reach over the details of how the Celts arrived. Aside from the posture of confidence taken by romantics and nationalists, a mood of despair seemed to preclude the formation of a new consensus.

For writers looking at the problem of peopling from a global perspective, research into the Celts led to more questions than answers. One of the most prominent of the globalists from the late eighteenth century was Jacob Bryant, who based his world chronology on a combination of biblical history and mythological sources. He included an extensive discussion of Pezron, but argued against Pezron's 'Celtic system'.[1] Bryant also considered monuments and languages, but formed his conclusions primarily from the biblical–mythological sources. In staying grounded in texts, Bryant was sceptical that he could distill a clear picture of the Celts. Discussing Britain's stone monuments, he wrote, 'All such works we generally refer to the Celts, and to the Druids; under the sanction of which names we shelter ourselves, whenever we are ignorant, and bewildered. But they were the operations of a very remote age; probably before the time, when the Druids, or Celtae, were first known'.[2]

Jones and the Indo-European Languages

This mood of despair was soon broken, thanks in part to a growth in the knowledge of world languages which accompanied the expansion of European empires. The key figure in this regard is William Jones, who first made the case that Sanscrit, the ancient scholarly language of India, was related to most European languages, leading to the identification of what is called the Indo-European language family. This idea had grave implications for Pezron's notion of the Celtic language as the common European root. Under the Indo-European theory, the ancestor language was pushed back in time and given a more easterly location. As the language family was recognised as extending beyond a single continent, there was no longer a need for a term for an original European language. There was, however, a need to name the westernmost branch of the Indo-European tree. At this point Pezron's definition of the Celts began to give way to the more restricted definition that had arisen during the Celtic Revival.

Jones proposed his Indo-European theory in the context of an entirely new way of approaching the problem of human diversity. When he took the post of judge of the supreme court of Fort William (Calcutta) in 1783, Jones brought with him his extensive experience in studying languages, including Latin, Greek, Persian and many modern European tongues. After arriving in

India, he turned his attention to Sanscrit in order to base his interpretation of the law on local traditions and to satisfy his curiosity about the characteristics of the peoples of Asia. This led Jones to undertake a long-term study of Asia with the goal of identifying of the cradle of humankind and the major races that dispersed to people the world. His use here of the term 'race', which had previously not appeared in scholarship on the peopling of Britain, reflected the influence of the global program of classification which Jones adapted from French and German comparative anatomists.

In February 1784, Jones delivered the first of a series of annual discourses to the Asiatick Society to commemorate its founding and update its members on the progress of his research. In studying the peoples of Asia, he divided the continent into five main national divisions, Indians, Chinese, Tartars, Arabs and Persians, and dedicated a separate discourse to each nation, starting with his 1786 speech, 'On the Hindus'. He added to these discourses one 'On the Borders, Mountaineers, and Islanders of Asia', a summary one in 1792 'On the Origin and Families of Nations', and two additional general discourses before his death in 1794. The researches of the Society began to reach Europe with the 1789 publication of the first volume of *Asiatick Researches*, and Jones' work was later published in an anthology.[3]

Jones first outlined his methods in his Third Anniversary Discourse, 'On the Hindus'. He saw his work as being part of the tradition of research into 'the History of the Ancient World, and *the first population of this habitable globe*', epitomised by Bryant's *Analysis of Ancient Mythology*.[4] He disagreed with many of the etymologies on which Bryant based his analysis and sought, with a wider ranging collection of evidence, to present a surer picture of humanity's earliest days and confront the intertwined questions of human diversity and unified origins. Jones proposed to investigate four main aspects of each nation: 'first, their *Languages* and *Letters*; secondly, their *Philosophy* and *Religion*; thirdly, the actual remains of their old *Sculpture* and *Architecture*; and fourthly, the written memorials of their *Sciences* and *Arts*'.[5] Though Jones was utilising a scheme of racial classification and a research objective borrowed from comparative anatomy, he made little use of physical form in reaching his conclusions.

In the first section of his analysis of the Hindus, Jones put the 'Indo' in 'Indo-European' by arguing that Sanscrit is closely related to Latin and Greek. To this he added, 'there is a similar reason, though not quite so forcible, for supposing that both the *Gothick* and the *Celtick*, though blended with a very different idiom, had the same origin with the *Sanscrit*'.[6] By distinguishing 'Gothick' from 'Celtick', it is clear that Jones was using Evans'

definition of the term and not Pezron's. Though Jones' argument was based
on a brief acquaintance with Sanscrit, and though he was by no means the
first to see a connection among the Indo-European languages, his work
inspired a great deal of interest in Sanscrit, especially among German
philologists who gave flesh to the skeleton of his hypothesis.[7] Consensus
that 'Celtick' was definitely a part of this group, however, would have to
await the detailed linguistic work of Prichard in the next century.

In Jones' other three categories of evidence, he drew similar connections
between India and ancient Europe as part of his general argument that
many widely separated peoples in the world were in fact closely related. He
noted a relationship between the myths of ancient India and those of pagan
Greece and Rome. He also found traces of these myths in Scandinavia,
China and Peru. In the realm of architecture, the main connection he noted
was between the Hindus and Ethiopians, who, he felt, also shared physical
traits, 'particularly their lips and noses'. Citing their knowledge of science
and art, he argued that the Hindus shared a common ancestor with various
races but left the question of the location of this ancestor to later discourses.[8]

Despite confining his analysis to five nations of Asia, Jones envisaged his
project as forming the basis of a general inquiry into the peopling of the
world, for he felt that Asia was the cradle of humanity. Jones' general model
of world migrations emanating from Asia had implications, therefore, for
the peopling of the British Isles. In this model, the Arabs, the subject of his
Fourth Discourse, and the Tartars, the subject of his Fifth, assumed equal
importance to the Hindus. Jones argued that the Arabs, who 'must have
been for ages a distinct and separate race' and spoke 'unquestionably one of
the most ancient [languages] in the world', and the Tartars, whom he distinguished by their facial features, both comprised distinct races from the
Hindus.[9] Having described these three separate races, he turned his attention to finding a possible common origin point and then outlining how the
other nations of the world arose from an elementary threefold division. For
Jones, all European peoples arose mainly from the Hindus.

In Jones' Sixth Discourse, 'On the Persians' in 1789, he finally answered
his three-year-old mystery of the origins of the fundamental three races,
and, by extension, all the world's people. Citing the ancient existence of
three races in Persia within the short biblical chronology, he placed the origins of humanity in that area, specifically in Iran:

> The three races, therefore, whom we have already mentioned, (and more
> than three we have not yet found) migrated from Iràn, as from their com-

mon country; and thus the Saxon chronicle, I presume from good authority, brings the first inhabitants of Britain from Armenia; while a late very learned writer concludes, after all his laborious researches, that the Goths or Scythians came from Persia; and another contends with great force, that both the Irish and old Britons proceeded severally from the borders of the Caspian; a coincidence of conclusions from different media by persons wholly unconnected, which could scarce have happened, if they were not grounded on solid principles. We may therefore hold this proposition firmly established, that Iràn, or Persia in its largest sense, was the true centre of population, of knowledge, of languages, and of arts.[10]

Having satisfied himself with his examination of all the races of Asia, Jones moved on, in the Ninth Discourse in 1792, to synthesise his results and apply them to world racial history. He divided all the peoples of the world into three main races, or mixtures of these three. Like the literary historians of the Celtic and Gothic Revivals, Jones thought of literature as a fundamental characteristic of a people and did not think that such cultural traits could spread from one race to another through diffusion. While Jones explained world racial diversity ultimately as the product of three fundamental branches of humanity, he did not challenge the monogenism of the Mosaic account of creation. He reconciled monogenism (the notion of a single origin for humanity) with his racial divisions by arguing that the three branches of humanity separated quickly from one stem in early post-Flood Persia. For later racial history, he admitted a degree of uncertainty, especially concerning the homogeneity of the Tartars, the third original race, but he held firm to the connection he first drew between Hindus and Europeans, that:

> the first race of *Persians* and *Indians*, to whom we may add the *Romans* and *Greeks*, the *Goths* and the old *Egyptians* or *Ethiops*, originally spoke the same language and professed the same popular faith, is capable, in my humble opinion, of incontestable proof.[11]

Over the next few decades, the connection Jones postulated between Sanscrit and European languages formed the foundation for the idea of a large, closely related family of languages, later termed Indo-European. Many philologists, including the influential German thinkers who started studying Sanscrit at the turn of the nineteenth century, looked to Jones as the father of this idea and, indeed, of their field.[12] The combination of

Jones' discovery of the similar structure between Sanscrit and European languages and his critique of Bryant's 'conjectural etymology' helped establish
the methodological foundations of the new philological system in which
Indo-European linguistics arose, bringing linguistics to the forefront of the
human sciences concerned with human origins and peopling.[13] And within
linguistics, Jones' methods soon came to dominate, steering the discipline
towards historical questions and away from philosophical investigations that
investigated grammar to understand the workings of the human mind.
These developments, however, took a generation before they became clear.

In the meantime, Jones' overall project, of which the study of language
comprised just one aspect, provided a blueprint for researchers interested in
integrating linguistic, archaeological and historical evidence into a picture
of the peopling of the world that would explain observed diversity. Jones'
work was related to a new movement, particularly strong in Central Europe
where it was known in German as *Volkskunde* or *Völkerkunde*, that provided
the roots of what would later become known in English as ethnology and
ethnography, a composite discipline dedicated to the question of peopling.
The initial impact that Jones' research had on this movement was mainly
confined to Central Europe, however, and only touched Britain decades
later through the influence of the Continental researchers.

Religion and Language in Romantic Histories

The years around the turn of the nineteenth century witnessed a return to
romantic local histories, contrasting sharply with the global system Jones
helped to develop. During this period, the Celts appeared almost exclusively in books whose main purpose was to elevate Celtic history in respect to
particular regions of the British Isles, continuing the romantic tradition that
dated back to Pezron, but with the history of religion, rather than language,
as the most favoured source of evidence. These works generally eschewed
ancient remains in contrast to historical sources and tended to focus on the
Druids. Researchers in Wales extended a tradition of looking to the Celts
for national origins. Researchers in Ireland did likewise while combating
the rival origins story involving Phoenicians. In Scotland, meanwhile, the
turn to the Celts marked a departure from searches for national origins
from a few decades earlier, when Fingal and other characters from the songs
of Ossian had constituted the focus of origins research. With the growing
acceptance that Ossian had been a forgery, the Scots looked to the Celts and

the Highlands to fill the void. A parallel growth in interest in the Celts occurred in these years in France, where Jacques Cambry published his *Monuments Celtiques* in 1805, attributing great scientific advances to the Celtic ancestors of the modern Breton, and where Napoleon set up the *Académie celtique* in the same year to celebrate France's Celtic past, justifying imperial expansion to what he claimed to be the former extent of Celtic territories.

In Ireland, William Webb wrote *An Analysis of the History and Antiquities of Ireland, Prior to the Fifth Century. To Which is Subjoined, a Review of the General History of the Celtic Nations*, published in 1791. Here he argued against the bardic version of Irish origins, advanced by Vallancey and O'Halloran, which claimed that the Irish derived from a single voyage of Phoenicians who made a series of stops on their way through the Mediterranean, past Spain, up to Ireland. Webb viewed such ideas as a kind of 'romance and fiction' often put forward by nations to 'conceal the insignificance of their real origin'.[14] In place of fables, he suggested the sources of 'language and religion' to discover 'those nations, between whom and the Irish a resemblance, in these respects, can be proved'.[15] Vallancey's Phoenician hypothesis, however, continued to garner support despite Webb's critique. In the 1830s, William Betham revived the Phoenician connection using a combination of historical sources and outdated philology.[16] The issue was finally resolved in the early 1840s thanks to the attacks of George Petrie, with support from the Royal Irish Academy.[17]

Webb's use of philology echoed that of Jones in that he was against excessive etymological claims based on 'a few trifling and accidental coincidences'.[18] Webb did not know Gaelic, however, and did not offer any of his own etymologies.[19] Given this limitation, he could not use language as a positive source for showing affinities, but only as a source of scepticism of supposed resemblances between Irish and Phoenician. He did incorporate language into his romantic position 'that the Irish language is the most pure and unmixed dialect of the Celtic that now exists'.[20] This point, however, was part of an argument based on the spread of religion, his primary source for tracing Irish origins.

Webb viewed the Celts as being exclusively linked with the religion of the Druids. Tracing the Celts, then, became an exercise in tracing the origin and spread of Druidism. Arguing, as O'Halloran had in 1772, that Druidism actually started in Ireland, Webb rejected the notion that the Celts had spread westward through the Continent and Great Britain before reaching Ireland. He reversed this traditional view, writing:

The most early colonies which were settled in this island, we may with confidence suppose to be of the grand nation of the Celts, by whom the
western regions of Europe were inhabited.[21]

These original Celts, he thought, were a colony of eastern peoples who
came directly to Ireland without stopping in Europe along the way.[22]
Finally, his section titled 'A Review of the General History of the Celtic
Nations' was an extended argument against the *Dissertation* of John
Pinkerton, who had described the Celts as inferior savages.

In Wales, the last decade of the eighteenth century marked the start of a
new Celtic cultural revival, spearheaded by Edward Williams within the
circle of London Welsh. Williams emerged from debtors' prison in the late
1780s with a passion for a Welsh culture. As a personal first step toward rein-
vigorating Welsh life, Williams took on the bardic name of Iolo Morganwg.
By 1791, he had moved to London, where he introduced the local Welsh
community to an elaborate historical argument, based mainly on materials
he had forged, that the dying Welsh bardic tradition was the direct descendant of the Druidical tradition of the ancient Celts. Williams' ideas drew
immediate support, and in 1792 he created an intricate Druidical ritual,
called the Gorsedd, in London. The Gorsedd proved popular, eventually
becoming an annual Welsh event that continues to this day.

Williams' publications included *A Vindication of the Celts*, which was an
extended attack on Pinkerton, and *Myvyrian Archaiology of Wales*, which was
a vehicle for disseminating many of his forged documents.[23] Williams' forgeries did not fool everyone, however. Among his chief intellectual rivals
was Edward Davies, who disagreed with a number of Williams' technical
points but took a similar approach in looking to the history of religion and
language to investigate the Celts in Wales' past. Reverend Davies was a
school teacher with interests in theology and ancient history. His two main
works on the Celts were *Celtic Researches*, in 1804 and *The Mythology and
Rites of the British Druids* in 1809.

Celtic Researches was basically an updated and expanded version of
Pezron's argument. Davies used lists of root words to connect Celtic languages with Greek, Latin and Hebrew to show 'that all of them sprung
from one parent'.[24] He argued that the Celts, 'the original possessors of
the British Islands', led by their Druid priests, were best 'amongst the hea-
thens' at preserving 'the history and the opinions of mankind, in its early
state'.[25] In this model, Davies used both language and religion to argue
that the Celts were a well-preserved pocket of Old Testament peoples.

Because Davies rejected the idea of human progress from savagery, the notion that the Celts had changed little from the dawn of humanity implied that they were not an undeveloped holdover, but an enlightened group that preserved an original version of ancient wisdom and theology.[26] Davies further argued for this connection of the Celts to ancient peoples with a Pezron-style genealogy tracing the Celts back to Gomer, a grandson of Noah.[27]

In *The Mythology and Rites of the British Druids*, Davies elaborated on the Druidical tradition, linking classical sources on their rites with stone structures such as cromlechs and circles, especially Stonehenge. Like Williams, he connected the Druids to the modern Welsh by drawing on the bardic tradition and he reproduced a number of songs of the bards in the book. For Williams, Davies and members of the Welsh social clubs that supported the Druidical revival, the investigation of the peopling of Britain provided an opportunity to rebuild a Welsh culture under the threat of assimilation. The Celts provided a suitable outlet for this need, for they gave a noble ancient lineage to the Welsh bardic tradition and language, elevating Welsh culture by ascribing to it worldwide significance in ancient history. As the nineteenth century progressed, many Welsh scholars remained focused on the bard-Druid connection while those in the rest of Britain moved on to other means of investigating peopling.[28]

In Scotland, researchers were trying to fill the gap left by the exposure of forgeries. Following Macpherson's *Ossian*, another infamous forger, John Pinkerton, had controversially argued in his *Dissertation* that Europe was mainly peopled by Goths descended from Scythians and that the Celts, devoid of mythology, were inferior savages. Pinkerton was an Edinburgh-born historian who relied on written sources, place names and philology to construct a history for Scotland.[29] He agreed 'that the Celts were the ancient inhabitants of Europe', but compared them to 'savage' peoples such as 'Fins' and 'Laplanders' and concluded that the Caledonii and Picti, the pre-Roman inhabitants of Scotland, were descended from Scythian Goths, who, he argued, were totally distinct from Celts and formed a superior race.[30] Like *Ossian*, Pinkerton's sources for his anti-Celtic writings were exposed as forgeries, removing them as a basis for defining Scotland's origins.[31]

Despite the declining status of *Ossian*, its role in claiming for Scotland an ancient Celtic past preceding the fifth-century Irish invasion, was not abandoned. This project was furthered by the new invention of Highland dress as a supposed pre-invasion, uniquely Scottish aspect to Celtic culture.

The arrant invention of Highland culture in the late eighteenth and early nineteenth centuries culminated in Walter Scott becoming president of the newly founded Celtic Society of Edinburgh in 1820, two years before he engineered a Highlander-style reception for George IV's royal visit.

As a part of this Highland movement, the notion that Scotland's first inhabitants were Celts became incorporated into topographical surveys of the region. In 1807, George Chalmers published the first part of a mammoth three-volume work titled, *Caledonia, Or, An Account, Historical and Topographic, of North Britain*. Publication of this series continued until 1824. At the beginning of the first volume of this mainly observational work, Chalmers included an extended discussion of the peopling of Scotland. On the basis of historical sources, he argued that '*the Celtae* were the aboriginal people of Europe'.[32] With the addition of place-name evidence and linguistics, Chalmers arrived at 'a moral certainty, that the British islands were originally settled, by the same Celtic tribes'.[33] He then delved into the issue of Druidism and the 'Druid remains' such as standing stones, which are visible throughout Scotland.[34] The rest of the four volumes are more descriptive, proceeding, in Camden-like fashion, shire-by-shire through Scotland. Like the works of Grose and Gough in the previous decades (see Chapter V), Chalmers' topography took its understanding of the Celts from historical sources about religion and language and treated remains and monuments descriptively.

Prichard's *Researches*

A generation after Jones, a Bristol physician named James Cowles Prichard published *Researches into the Physical History of Man*, a comprehensive historical investigation into human diversity in which he sought to prove, without reference to the Bible 'that all mankind constitute but one race or proceed from a single family'.[35] Prichard's argument about human diversity combined evidence of physiology, history and languages to trace all the world's peoples back to a point of origin. The novelty of this project, whose methods and goals were clearly inspired by Jones, but with a more extensive look at human physical diversity, came mainly from Prichard's ability to synthesise the many traditions of inquiry into the peopling of the world and from his comprehensive overview of the world's peoples. His global approach and encyclopedic classification scheme place him outside of the romantic tradition. In his synthesis, Prichard relied on languages as the best indicator of racial affiliation and considered physical characteristics to be variable.

While Prichard's interest in diversity was global, he had a special interest in what he, like the romantics, came to call the Celtic nations. His mother was Welsh, and, living close to Wales himself, he had an affection for the Welsh language. He also had an interest in Druid histories. During his years of study in Edinburgh (1805-8), a friend reported an incident when Prichard came upon a Highlander at Loch Katrine and 'poured out a most splendid dissertation on the history of the Celtic nations – the dark, fearful, gloomy and savage rites of the Druids'.[36] In *Researches*, Prichard's section on the 'Celtic race' was central to his model of the peopling of Europe, for he considered the Celts to be the first inhabitants of the Continent because they could be found furthest from the putative origin point in the Near East.[37]

Prichard used three central strands of evidence for his model of Celtic migrations: ancient monuments, languages and historical sources on the Druids. Through the existence of 'circles of stones which are called Druidical' he connected the Celts in the British Isles to earlier occupations in Scandinavia and the Continent:

> That these wherever found were Celtic erections I have no doubt. They are chiefly observed in those parts of Britain which were never inhabited by any but Celtic people, and they are found connected with the cromlechs or Celtic altars. And they have never been observed in those countries in which the Gothic tribes were aboriginal, as Iceland, the eastern parts of Germany, &c. Besides, they are destitute of the sculpture and runic inscriptions which are always found on the rude monuments of the latter people.[38]

Through comparative linguistics, Prichard connected the Celts with peoples even farther to the east. He had not yet prepared a comparison of Celtic languages with Sanscrit, Persian and Latin, though he hoped to be able to 'supply the deficiency' soon.[39] It was not until 1831 that Prichard published this comparison in *The Eastern Origin of the Celtic Nations*. In the meantime, he linked Celtic to other European languages that he had given an eastern origin based on historical arguments: Celtic, Sclavonian, German and Pelasgian:

> the four principal departments of dialects which prevail in Europe, are yet so far allied in their radical elements, that we may with certainty pronounce them to be branches of the same original stock.[40]

Finally, Prichard connected Druidism with aspects of eastern religions:

> The Celtae under their Druids, a branch of the eastern hierarchy, advanced
> into the furthest West, where perhaps some vestiges of previous colonists may
> be found. They carried with them the mysteries, the doctrine of metempsy-
> chosis, the rites of polytheism, the philosophy and language of the East.[41]

In 1826, Prichard published a vastly expanded second edition of his
Researches in which he changed some aspects of his model of human origins, probably reflecting a growing awareness of the complexity of the evidence
as well as the influence of rival polygenist (or multiple origins) ideas.
Nevertheless, his argument that the Celts were the first inhabitants of Britain
remained basically the same, retaining monuments, languages and history as the
key sources. After acknowledging that the Celtic origin of the pre-Roman
Britons 'is no where asserted by Caesar, or positively stated as an historical fact, as
far as I know, by any ancient author,' he realised that the limitations of historical
sources on the Celts forced him to rely more heavily on the other two sources.[42]

He then looked to linguistics as the strongest argument for Britain's
Celtic origins, though this evidence left considerable gaps and was beset by
controversy. Prichard had yet to publish his work connecting Celtic with
Indo-European languages, and the language family's affiliations remained in
dispute. Without proof of Celtic's eastern origins, the main argument that
Britons migrated from Gaul was the close relationship between Welsh and
Breton. However, there was a growing realisation that Breton speakers
might have come to Brittany from southern Britain during the Saxon invasions, meaning that the Breton language was not proof that a 'Celtic'
language was spoken in Gaul during Roman times. Prichard acknowledged
the tenuousness of relying on the Breton connections and partly supported
his theory with the evidence of place names.[43] A second controversy concerned the origins of Scotland. The first historically named groups living
there were the Caledonians and Picts, whose languages had not been established, leaving their linguistic and racial affiliations open.[44]* To close these
gaps, Prichard turned to the evidence of Druidical monuments.

In the second edition of *Researches*, Prichard's expanded argument made it
clear that the Druids were indispensable to his model of Celtic migrations.
Of his three main reasons for arguing that the aboriginal Britons were

---

*Now scholars link the Pictish language with Welsh.

Celts, the first was based on linguistics, while the other two both concerned the Druids:'2. The Druidical religion and institutions were probably common to the Celtic and Belgic Gauls', and '3. Another argument may be derived from the abundance of those rude erections, commonly termed Druidical circles, cromlechs, and dolmins, both in Armorica and Wales, as well as in other countries belonging to the aboriginal Britons'.[45] Point number two was crucial for Prichard because the race of the Belgae, whose early migration to Britain was chronicled by Caesar, was in dispute; some researchers argued they were Germanic. The historically attested practice of Druidism among the Belgae and native Britons was Prichard's main evidence that both were Celtic. He then integrated the Belgic invasion into his linguistic model by assigning Welsh, Cornish and Breton to Celtic Gauls while assigning Irish Gaelic, Scottish Gaelic and Manx to the Belgae. Meanwhile, citing Chalmers, he argued in point number three that the 'many circles of dolmins, in connexion with cromlechs and sepulchral cairns' in the Scottish Lowlands, proved the Celtic origins of ancient Caledonia.[46]

The Growth of Linguistic Ethnology

By the 1830s, Prichard sought to replace his Druid-based argument of the Celtic origins of Britain with one grounded in linguistics. Before this time, Jones' historical philology had few followers in Britain beside Prichard. Alexander Murray, as chair of Oriental languages at the University of Edinburgh, had completed *A History of the European Languages; or Researches into the Affinities of the Teutonic, Greek, Celtic, Sclavonic, and Indian Nations* in 1813, but he patterned this book as much after the philosophical work of Horne Tooke as the philology of Jones. The reintroduction of Jonesian philology to Britain occurred mainly through the influence of the Saxonists Benjamin Thorpe and John Mitchell Kemble, who studied with Rasmus Rask and Jacob Grimm. The subsequent revolution in Saxon studies was paralleled by one initiated by Prichard in Celtic studies. Though Prichard had long followed developments in Continental philology, the 1830s marked his first application of comparative philology to his long-standing concern with the place of the Celts in the European past. In this study, Prichard produced a linguistic argument for the island's peopling that eclipsed the long-running Druid-based historical model, which seemed increasingly flawed to Prichard. Both Celtic and Saxonist philology earned institutional support in the 1840s with the establishment of the Philological

Society of London in 1842 and the founding of the Ethnological Society of London a year later.

Rising interest in comparative philology in Britain coincided with the first English appearances of the word 'ethnography', which had long been used in Central Europe with its partner 'ethnology' to describe the study of nations and their histories. Prichard himself was among the first – if not the very first – to use the term in English when he presented 'a survey of the progress of knowledge in relation to ethnography, with a critical account of the attempts which have been made to distribute the human species into departments constituting what are termed families of nations', to the British Association for the Advancement of Science in 1832.[47] When Prichard helped set up the Ethnological Society of London, philology was at the centre of this newly named field of study.

In his 1832 paper, Prichard outlined the methodology of his ethnographic *Researches* to the British Association in order to establish an institutional base for his work within this generalist scientific society. The British Association had formed in 1831 under the leadership of liberal Anglicans dedicated to objective science unfettered by social and moral concerns. Prichard's science did not meet these ideals because the 'ethnography' he described proved too controversial, both in its strong monogenism and classificatory impulse, and it contained unwelcome implications for the expanding colonial encounters between Europeans and indigenous peoples. Prichard's was the last paper on the topic to be accepted by the Association until he used it as a platform to distribute queries to travellers in 1839. Only after the Ethnological Society formed in the 1840s as a less political version of the Aborigines Protection Society did the Association accept the field as scientific.

In the 1832 paper, Prichard launched an attack on the 'physical researches' of Blumenbach and Cuvier, who classified humankind into a number of races based on skull forms. As an alternative, he promoted his own linguistic program. Prichard argued against Blumenbach's practice of naming skull types (Mongolian, African, Caucasian) 'not from their characteristic forms, but from some nations, in whom they in a conspicuous manner occur'.[48] And he cited the case of Africans and Papuans, whose dark skin placed them in the same physical category, but whose differing languages offered clearer evidence of their long separation. Finally, he reiterated his conviction that linguistics proved the common origin of all humankind and that races represented changing human varieties, not permanent categories. While Prichard initially failed to secure the institutional support of his colleagues at the British Association, his work on Celtic languages made an immediate impact. In 1831, Prichard published *The Eastern Origin of the Celtic Nations Proved by a Comparison of their Dialects with the Sanscrit, Greek, Latin, and Teutonic Languages* as a 'Supplement' to *Researches*. In the book, Prichard distanced himself from the 'wild conjecture' which he said characterised a good amount of philological research.[49] In allying himself with Edward Lhuyd, members of the Asiatic Society and the German philologists, he argued that the study of languages, 'if properly applied, will furnish great and indispensable assistance in many particular inquiries relating to the history and affinity of nations'.[50]

Prichard's guiding principle for employing linguistic evidence was that 'use of languages really cognate must be allowed to furnish a proof, or at least a strong presumption, of kindred race'.[51] His challenge was to demonstrate systematically that languages are cognate without turning to the superficial resemblances exploited by those he accused of conjecture. Following the German philologists, he proposed two criteria that must be met for languages to be called cognate: they must contain similar vocabulary, especially of certain words more likely to remain stable over time, like 'the most natural and universal objects and ideas, terms for family relations and for the most striking objects of visible nature, as likewise verbal roots of the most frequent and general occurrence'; and they must show similarities in grammatical construction.[52] This test ensured a higher degree of certainty than that provided by a mere comparison of words which happened to sound similar.

Having outlined his strategy, Prichard began to address the relationship of the earliest European races to those of the east, by which he meant central Asia and the Indian subcontinent. Here he reiterated his principle that philology provided the key. He argued against the usefulness of material remains, writing, 'we can discern scarcely a trace, even in the oldest memorials, of those wanderings of tribes which may be supposed to have filled this region of the world with inhabitants'.[53] He also argued against the history-of-religion method, on which he had previously relied so heavily and which could document, on the basis of incomplete historical sources, only the diffusion, or spread, of traditions and not necessarily of peoples:

It would be vain to attempt, merely from traits of resemblance in some customs or superstitions, or even from the doctrines of druidism and the mythology of the sagas, to ascribe a common origin to the nations of Europe and those of the East. By a similar mode of reasoning, we might per-

haps as well deduce the Turks and the Tartars from Arabia, and the Buddhists
of northern Asia from India or Ceylon. Nor can historical traditions fill the
void. We can only hope by an analysis of the European languages to obtain a
proof, that these races of people, having preserved common elements of
speech, were connected in origin with the nations of Asia.[54]

The problem, also recognised by Lhuyd, of distinguishing between diffusion
and migration, was critical to models of peopling that utilised the evidence
of religion or literary products. Though Evan Evans had considered diffusion in his theory of the spread of Druidism, later romantic regionalists
tended not to do so, preferring to use Druidism as a simple marker of Celtic
migrations. Jones was similarly quiet about the possibility of diffusion,
though he did consider racial mixing. Prichard's proposal that religions
could spread through diffusion while languages tended not to do so, though
ignoring Lhuyd's own concern about the diffusion of language, marked an
important step towards selecting the most appropriate among the expanding sources of evidence available to address the peopling problem.

After arguing that the speech of a race provides the best indicator of its
origin and affiliation, Prichard began to address the issue of whether the
Celtic languages belong to the Indo-European family, a question with 'particular bearing on the origin of nations of Western Europe, including the
British isles, as well as a more extensive one on the physical history of
mankind'.[55] In the 1830s, opinion among philologists was divided. Prichard
had felt since the first edition of *Researches* that Celtic was closely related to
other European languages, but a number of scholars, including Frederick
Schlegel, saw Celtic as an independent family. With the extensive linguistic
analysis in *The Eastern Origin of the Celtic Nations*, which proceeded through
examinations of vocabulary, grammar, pronouns, inflections of verbs and
conjugations of verbs, Prichard hoped to settle the issue. For the most part,
he was successful in obtaining a consensus for his view.[56]

In his newer model of Celtic origins and the peopling of Britain, Prichard
argued that this use of philology supplanted his former reliance on the Druid
connection. In the European volume of the third edition of *Researches* in
1841, Prichard retained the history of religion as a component of his peopling
theory, but made it clear that linguistics was his best argument:

> The unity of religion is certainly a strong argument, for it is scarcely credible
> that two distinct races should be found subject to such a hierarchy as the
> Druids, and to such a system of rites and superstitions as is known to have

been maintained by them. But the Druidism and Bardism said to have belonged both to the Celtae and the Britons, afford not so strong an argument of kindred origin as the possession of one common speech, if this only can satisfactorily be proved.[57]

Prichard's growing scepticism about the history-of-Druidism argument was a first step in the general decline of the role of the Druids in models of the peopling of Britain. As linguistics gained scientific prestige in the 1830s and 1840s, it overshadowed historical sources on the Druids. Attempts to integrate Celtic linguistics into history based models, as in L. Maclean's *The History of the Celtic Language* in 1840, had little influence. Similarly, in the antiquarian movement, attributions of monuments to the Druids began to seem outdated in the 1840s and 1850s.

As linguistics and, later, archaeological methods began to challenge the authority of ancient writings in models of peopling, the name of Britain's first people nevertheless remained the one taken from historical sources more than a century earlier in the work of Pezron. Prichard himself was uncomfortable with the traditional name of 'Celtic' for the family of languages he defined, because it had no firm connection with the six dialects ('Cornish', 'Welsh', 'Armorican', 'Erse', 'Highland Scottish' and 'Manks') that he identified:

> It may be doubted whether the term Celtic languages is the most proper epithet for the class of idioms generally designated, and which I shall continue, in compliance with custom, to designate by that name. The Celtae, properly so called, were a people of Gaul. Of their language we have no undoubted specimen. There are, indeed, strong grounds for believing that it was a kindred tongue with the dialects of the British isles; but it would be better to take the general name of a whole class of languages from something that actually remains.[58]

Starting with Robert Gordon Latham, who became a leading figure in linguistic ethnology upon Prichard's death in 1848, a number of researchers, continuing to the present, have followed Prichard in expressing discomfort about the Celtic name. But this collective unease has led to no serious challenge of the label.

By the 1840s and 1850s, when new definitions of the Celts arose in craniology and art history, the appellation caused a great deal of confusion, for the word came to represent several categories whose relationship to one another has still not been completely worked out. Prichard himself pointed the way toward managing the proliferation of methods of tracing Celtic migrations with his notion that some characteristics were more likely than others to spread through diffusion. As subsequent researchers debated – and continue to debate – the question of diffusion versus migration in the British past, the wider question of what constitutes a Celt, or, indeed, a collection of peoples by any name, lies at the heart of the controversy.

In the coming decades, new forms of evidence, notably material remains, would rise to challenge language as the central means of researching the Celts. In order to understand this development – the focus of Part Two – we must first return to the time of Pezron and Lhuyd, when the idea of ancient Celts in Britain first appeared.

PART TWO
MATERIAL REMAINS

When William Stukeley described the megalithic monument of Avebury as a Celtic temple in 1721, he extended Pezron's linguistic idea of ancient Celts to material remains. From this moment, ruins and artefacts became part of the evidence that researchers used to trace the Celtic peoples. Today, the study of material remains, or archaeology, is one of the central disciplines concerned with defining the ancient Celts. The path from Stukeley to twenty-first-century archaeologists is by no means a direct one, however.

During the eighteenth century, when Pezron's definition of the Celts was dominant, few antiquaries other than Stukeley looked for Celtic remains in the landscape. To the extent that these researchers contributed to an understanding of the Celts, it was mainly illustrative of the linguistic ideas. By the end of the century, excavation presented a new avenue for identifying Celtic material. The opening of burial mounds, or barrows, became increasingly popular among country gentlemen during the nineteenth century. The potential of this activity to contribute to a more refined picture of the ancient Celts was not exploited, however, and the study of material remains continued primarily to be illustrative of the theories about Druids and Celts then in circulation. Chapter V looks at the period from Stukeley's identification of Celtic monuments to the point where Part One ended, with the creation of the field of ethnology. With the exception of the development of rudimentary survey and digging techniques, there is little from this time to indicate that archaeology might soon take a leading role in the exploration of the ancient Celts.

In the 1840s a new sense of optimism entered the study of material remains from an unexpected source. The work of Scandinavian craniologists led a growing number of British researchers to start measuring ancient skulls with the promise of identifying the Celts. For more than a generation, British craniologists used skulls to build a more complex picture of the pre-Roman past than had been produced through linguistic sources. Using this new approach, archaeologists made their first substantive contribution to the study of the Celts when they argued that the Celts were not the first peoples of Britain, but arrived in the Bronze Age. This development is the subject of Chapter VI. Though the science of skull measurement has since lost its dominant position in archaeology, many conclusions of early British craniologists have endured.

Chapter VII explores a parallel phenomenon, when museum curators began to identify Celtic art. While craniology led archaeologists to talk of a Celtic race, the study of Celtic art led to a new conception of Celtic peoples as representing a culture, defined not by its blood but by its behaviour and way of thinking. In the late nineteenth century, the generation that established professional standards for archaeology employed the idea of a Celtic culture and civilisation that arose in Celtic art studies.

Part Two concludes in Chapter VIII, which examines the birth of archaeology as a discipline that did not merely describe ancient remains but took a leading role in the exploring the question of peopling. The survey work of Stukeley, the excavations of the barrow-diggers, the measurements of the craniologists and the typology of the museum curators all contributed to the birth of archaeology. Despite the many turns and dead ends on the path from the first identification of a Celtic monument to today's theories about Celtic ways of life, students of material remains across the centuries (at least until recently) have been united by their naming of a particular ancient peoples as the Celts. Though this concept ultimately derived from the linguists we examined in Part One, it is archaeologists who have since moulded the idea into something that every British schoolchild can recognise. And, ironically, today it is archaeologists who are trying to undo the work of their predecessors and remove the term from discussions of the British past.

CHAPTER V

CELTIC MONUMENTS

Between 1703, when Pezron introduced the Celts into the question of the peopling of Britain, and the 1840s, when Prichard argued that the study of Celtic languages was central to the study of British origins, research into monuments and artefacts contributed little to the debate and had no significant impact on the meaning of the term *Celtic*. However, this period was a dynamic one for the study of material remains, and developments over this century-and-a-half set the stage for the birth of the discipline of archaeology and the subsequent dominance of this field in research into the ancient Celtic presence in Britain.

The first material remains to be labelled as Celtic were monuments described in the course of general surveys. William Stukeley, considered by his followers to be 'the father of British antiquities', was the first to apply Pezron's term for the original inhabitants of Europe to British monuments.[1] His definition of Celtic monuments held sway for most of the eighteenth century. Towards the end of the century, however, James Douglas revolutionised the study of material remains by excavating burials and using material evidence to assign sites to particular peoples, including the Celts. Sir Richard Colt Hoare continued Douglas' work and expanded his excavation methods, setting the blueprint for regional studies of barrows as a way to find evidence for ancient Celts and Druids. Colt Hoare's work, in turn, inspired generations of barrow-diggers in the nineteenth century. These three pioneering yet somewhat eccentric individuals are the focus of this chapter, which documents the evolution of studies of the material remains of the Celts from surveys of monuments to excavations of burials.

Stukeley

As outlined in Chapter III, it was Aubrey, Sacheverell, Brown, Martin and
Rowlands who first attributed stone monuments to the Druids. Even
though these researchers connected the Druids to speakers of the Celtic
languages, as described by Pezron, the term *Celtic* for them applied only to
the supposedly ancient European parent language (of which many thought
of Welsh as the least corrupted survival) and not to the material remains of
this ancient people. As they tended to use 'Celtic' only in reference to this
language, they did not write of the 'Druidical' monuments themselves as
Celtic. The practice of describing monuments as Celtic was introduced a
generation later by William Stukeley, based on an unfinished project of John
Toland. While previous researchers into the Celts and Druids had pursued a
romantic agenda in describing the language and monuments of fringe
regions as 'pure' in the context of national histories, Toland and Stukeley
relied primarily on a theological definition of purity. In doing so, they
expanded the definition of 'Celtic' to include monuments from all over the
countryside, building upon the existing criteria of language and religion.
This new use of 'Celtic' inspired later antiquaries to look more deeply at
material remains when researching the first inhabitants of the British Isles.

Stukeley's Early Tours

In 1710, William Stukeley, a young doctor fresh from completing his medical studies in Cambridge and London, returned to his native Lincolnshire
where he began a series of tours around Britain. Between 1710 and 1725, he
conducted up to a dozen such journeys. During this period, he became
more and more interested in Roman and pre-Roman Britain. A shift in his
approach occurred after he moved back to London in 1717 and took the
first of his many trips to the megalithic monuments of Avebury and
Stonehenge in 1719. His 1722 tour, the *Iter Romanum*, was the first oriented
toward ancient antiquities, in contrast to his earlier journeys in which he
more casually documented curiosities, natural landscapes and buildings
from all British periods. Stukeley's account of the *Iter Romanum* also contained a number of references to 'Celtic' monuments, which was a
departure from his earlier practice of calling pre-Roman monuments
'British'.[2] In the 1724 publication of *Itinerarium Curiosum*, which contained
the diaries from all of his tours, Stukeley had a long section in the index
titled 'Celtic Antiquities', but with one ambiguous exception (see below),
and with the exception of a drawing he made in 1721, he never used the

term *Celtic* in the text of his tour diaries before the *Iter Romanum*. By the time he completed the *Itinerarium Curiosum*, however, Celtic monuments had become so important to Stukeley that he was seeking subscribers for a series of books on the Celts:

> What I shall next trouble the reader withal, will be my intended work, of the history of the ancient Celts, particularly the first inhabitants of Great Brittan, which for the most part is now finish'd. by what I can judg at present it will consist of four books in folio. I. The history of the origin and passage of the Celts from Asia into the west of Europe: particularly into Brittan. of their manners, language, &c. II. Of the religion, deitys, priests, temples, and sacred rites, of the Celts. III. Of the great Celtic temple at Abury in Wiltshire, and others of that sort. IV. Of the celebrated Stonehenge.[3]

In order to understand why Stukeley suddenly started using the word 'Celtic' in the drawing of 1721 and then more regularly in 1722, it is necessary to review his activities in the years leading up to the *Iter Romanum*.

In Stukeley's first tour in 1710, he visited the Rollright Stones, a well-known stone circle near Oxford. As with other similar pre-Roman monuments, he thought of this as an example of the 'temples of the antient *Britons*'.[4] Just before this stop, however, 'at *Souldern*' he had found 'a curious barrow neatly turned like a bell, small and high', and wrote, 'I believe it *celtic*'.[5] The barrow at Souldern is the only example of Stukeley, or anyone else, calling a British monument by that name before 1721. While he might have written this in 1710, conflating the name of the language commonly thought to belong to the first European people with a monument attributed to that people, it is possible that he added this remark while preparing his manuscripts for publication in 1724, for its appearance in 1710 does not fit with his other writing on the topic from this time. Towards the start of his account of his first tour, Stukeley had written, 'We may be assur'd that this whole country was well inhabited by the antient *Brittons*'.[6] And in discussing tumuli 'of a very considerabl [sic] bulk', which showed no affiliation with Roman material, he mentioned 'our *Cimbrian* predecessors', whom he traced to Holland and Zealand.[7]*

---

*The Cimbrians appeared in Pezron's list of names by which the Celts used to be called.

In the *Iter Cimbricum*, the account of Stukeley's 1712 tour to Wales, Stukeley's stated intention was 'to hear at least a language spoke soon after the deluge', which Pezron and Rowlands had called Celtic.[8] Yet Stukeley never employed the term *Celtic* in this account. He had written about 'the old *Britons*', found an 'old *British* ax', and even discussed the derivation of British words in Wales.[9] His not using the word *Celtic* in this account, which would be the most appropriate place to do so considering what had previously been written about the Celts, casts further doubt that his attribution at Souldern was written in 1710. Even if he had written it in 1710, it was not until after 1721 that the attribution was noticed or echoed by anyone else, so this early example is an isolated one.

Stukeley's thinking on ancient Britain entered a new phase around 1714 when a fellow member of the Gentlemen's Society of Spalding sent him a list of antiquarian books, including Caesar and Tacitus. That same year, Stukeley was busy compiling a British king list based on Geoffrey of Monmouth's Brutus story. Two years later, Stukeley created a model of Stonehenge based on a drawing he had seen. Stukeley did not really develop his ideas, however, or come into contact with key sources and other researchers until his return to London in 1717.

In London, Stukeley befriended Roger and Samuel Gale, the sons of Thomas Gale, who had known Aubrey during the writing of *Monumenta Britannica* and who had prepared a commentary on the Antonine Itinerary, a useful source on the place names of Roman Britain. Through the Gale brothers, Stukeley entered the world of London learned societies. Soon after his arrival, Stukeley helped the Gales take what had been an informal weekly pub meeting to discuss antiquarian topics and formalise it as the Antiquarian Society of London. Six months later, Stukeley became a fellow of the Royal Society, which was then under the leadership of another native of Lincolnshire, Sir Isaac Newton, who kept antiquarian topics out of the scope of the Society, but who later wrote his own contribution to the problem of peopling.[10]

Through the Gales, Stukeley was able to study a copy of John Aubrey's unpublished *Monumenta*. Like Aubrey, the Gales thought of Stonehenge and Avebury as pre-Roman, British monuments. This was still a minority opinion, however, and Stukeley had a number of acquaintances who disagreed. When Stukeley arrived in London, for example, Johann Georg Keysler, also a fellow of the Royal Society, was spending time in the city during his antiquarian travels through Europe. After returning to his native Hanover, Keysler published *Antiqvitates Selectae Septentrionales et Celticae*, in which he argued that, because megalithic monuments also exist in northern Europe, they are not Druidical, but Anglo-Saxon.[11] When Stukeley finally decided to visit Stonehenge and Avebury for himself in 1719, he had probably not yet settled on an answer to the question of who built them. In the antiquarian and linguistic sources that he had read up to this point, the Celts hardly figured in the debate and were virtually absent from discussions of the British context.[12] Instead the question was whether the megalithic monuments belonged to the Druids or a later people.

At the end of 1720, Stukeley had already started to connect Pezron's concept of the ancient Celts with the stone monuments that Keysler, Martin, Rowlands and others had surveyed in the British Isles and on the Continent. In a description of a Roman temple that Stukeley had seen only from a drawing, Stukeley wrote:

> The *Etruscans* were the Progeny of the *Celts*, as is admirably well shewn in Monsieur *Pezron's* Antiquities of that Nation, the first, at least most considerable Inhabitants of the Body of *Europe*, who brought along with them the Manner of building Temples open at Top, suitable to the Conceptions of the *Persians* and more *Eastern* Nations, from whence they came into the Infancy of Mankind [...] It is observable that the ancient *Celtic* Nations, of which the Inhabitants of these Countries are Part, erected all their Temples in a circular Form, and of dry Stones, whereof innumerable Examples are still to be seen in all the *British* Islands, as well as upon the Continent.[13]

Stukeley became enthralled by the Wiltshire megaliths, especially Avebury, and from 1719 to 1724 he made an annual excursion to survey the monuments. By 1721, he was clearly leaning toward the Druids as the builders of Stonehenge and Avebury, as shown by his describing different parts of Avebury as solar and lunar temples, an idea proposed by Martin and adopted by Toland.[14] Also, in his 1743 publication of Avebury, a drawing of the site dated August 16, 1721, is titled, 'View of the Cell of the Celtic Temple' (*pl. 6*).[15]

Toland's Influence

By this point, Stukeley had read Aubrey, Pezron and Rowlands, but the greatest influence on the development of his idea of Celtic monuments seems to have been John Toland, whom he probably met around this time and who was working on a major treatise on the Druids using a combination of linguistic and textual evidence. Toland's interest in the Druids dated back to the early 1690s, when he met with both Aubrey and Lhuyd and corresponded with Gibson during the making of the 1695 edition of *Britannia*, but he waited more than 20 years to proceed with his own investigation of the Druids. Toland's fascination with the ancient Druids came about in the context of his status as a Dissenter. In 1696, he had sparked a religious controversy with his Deist treatise, *Christianity Not Mysterious*, in which he challenged Church of England doctrine in arguing for a rationalist interpretation of the Bible. Toland sought to show that the Church of England retained superstitious rites and beliefs from what he argued were its Druid predecessors.

In 1718 and 1719, Toland wrote a set of three lengthy letters to Robert Molesworth, a Member of Parliament and fellow of the Royal Society, asking for financial backing for a book titled *The History of the Druids, Containing an Account of the Antient Celtic Religion and Literature*.[16] Toland never received his sponsorship and died in 1722, leaving these letters as the only record of his project. Toland presented himself as being uniquely positioned to write on the Druids, because, as a fluent speaker of Irish Gaelic, which he described as 'the least corrupted' of the 'Celtic' dialects, he could access the 'numberless monuments [i.e. literary sources] concerning the Druids, that never hitherto have come to the hands of the learned'. Toland's emphasis on 'Celtic Religion and Literature' in reference to the Druids seems to be intended to emphasise his linguistic qualifications to undertake the task and his novel contribution in the form of old Gaelic textual evidence. Lhuyd's interpretation of Irish Gaelic as the purest remnant of 'the old Celtic of Gaul' was a critical feature of Toland's argument, and Toland rejected Pezron's idea that Celtic was equally ancestral to other European tongues.[17]

In constructing a picture of the ancient Druids, the Gaelic manuscripts provided Toland with just one form of evidence. In addition to these and classical texts, he argued for the use of languages themselves, traditions still evident among the Irish and stone monuments.[18] The last of these was, of course, the greatest influence on Stukeley. Toland's second letter to Molesworth was largely a discussion of the stone monuments visible in Wales, Ireland, Scotland and the Isle of Man, places where spoken 'Celtic' dialects were in evidence. Toland first discussed cairns, or piles of stones, often found on the tops of mountains in 'all the Celtic countries'.[19] He then turned to standing stones, like the Rollright circle and Avebury, which he described as Druidical temples. In surveying these monuments, Toland again argued that Celtic traditions were restricted to the British Isles and

France, and that other European areas did not have Druids: 'The Druids were onely coextended with the Celtic dialects'.[20] When Toland died before he was able to complete this survey of Druidical monuments in Celtic areas, Stukeley had a ready blueprint for his proposed book on Celtic monuments. Stukeley also drew on Toland's theory of the role of Hercules in the peopling of Britain.

Stukeley the Druidophile

By 1722, Stukeley's growing interest in ancient Britain became more than just a focus of research. In July of that year he founded, along with some antiquarian friends, the imaginative Society of Roman Knights. In the Society, each member adopted the name of a Roman or non-Roman contemporary. Stukeley chose Chyndonax, the name of a Gallic Druid described as a Celt in an excavation from a century earlier.[21]

The Society of Roman Knights was founded on July 23, 1722, the same day Stukeley set out for his annual trip to Wiltshire. He then spent a few weeks making plans of Stonehenge and Avebury before returning to London by way of the Roman town of Silchester. From London, he set out on the *Iter Romanum*, a tour designed to follow Roman roads from London northward to Lincolnshire and then back southward through London to Kent.[22] Soon after setting out, he found a field of saffron near a Roman town and thought the local place name derived 'from the *Celtic* word [for] a field or enclosure'.[23] Here, for the first time in his itineraries, Stukeley referred to the ancient British language as Celtic, though on the same journey, he wrote that he was looking for place names in 'the *british* or *saxon*', and made repeated references to British remains.[24] After Stukeley passed Leicester on his way southward, he came upon an ancient barrow which reminded him of the Rollright Stones and their surroundings. He wrote of the barrow, 'I doubt not but this is of great antiquity and *celtic*'.[25] A few days later, near Dunstable, he found another barrow and wrote, 'I have no scruple in supposing it *celtic*'.[26] On the Roman roads of Britain, 'Prince Chyndonax' had found his Celtic subjects. And for the first time, a British researcher described as Celtic material remains that were not stone monuments associated with Druids.

In 1723, Stukeley's work on the Celts widened to become his primary research interest. The results of his itineraries for 1723-5, including an extensive discussion of the site of Stanton Drew (not published until the second edition of *Itinerarium Curiosum* in 1776), are filled with references to Celts and Celtic monuments.[27] Back at Avebury in July, 1723, meanwhile, he wrote *The History of the Temples of the Antient Celts*, the book for which he solicited subscriptions in the preface of *Itinerarium Curiosum*. He failed to garner enough interest, however, and it was never published, though parts of it appeared in his later books on Avebury and Stonehenge. In this work, Stukeley interpreted megalithic monuments as Druidical, often as the sites of human sacrifice, and saw them as providing key evidence for tracing early Celtic migrations through Europe. Stukeley's definition of the Celts followed that of Pezron and Rowlands in that he described them as the original people of all of Europe, including the Scandinavian countries.[28] This usage was not 'in default of the concept of the word "prehistoric"', nor was it 'a quite reasonable non-committal word for "Pre-Roman"', as Stuart Piggott argued in a biography of Stukeley, but it closely followed the linguistic model of peopling then in the ascendancy.[29] With this book, Stukeley incorporated evidence of megalithic monuments into the history-of-religion approach to reconstructing Celtic migrations and the peopling of Europe:

In many parts of our Islands are these Circles of Stones, & some in Scotland calld as this kind Druids Temples from long continued tradition. & without doubt the Druids were their authors, being the priests of that vast people which we generally call the Celts that overspread the whole Continent of Europe & consequently peopled Britain in the earlyest Ages after the floud. I observe in the remains of these Antient Temples there are generally some or all of these parts, 1. an Avenue or Walk leading up to them, for State as well as divershon [?], sometimes hou [?] 2. an Area or plain before or around 'em where the people assembled & the Sacrifices probably were prepared.[30]

What is then of so common & universal a nature that from the very slender memoirs we yet have such works, we can be able to trace 'em from the Britannic Isles all the way to Persia, but Religion & the worship of the Gods, in which all nations & people agree, & these were their temples, the constant tradition of the simple vulgar in the most barbarous parts, the form, the manner, the salvation, the identitys & [?], the nature & reason of things nay the very stones themselves speak it sufficiently. [...] but in general I assort 'em to be temples of our Ancestors the Celts. I doubt not but infinite numbers of them have been destroyed, & without question there is or has been many in France, Spain, Tuscany, & all over the vast Continent which this people inhabited.[31]

With this study, combining historical evidence with the study of monuments, Stukeley hoped to make the question of the peopling of the world
an integral aspect of antiquarian scholarship, which he thought would
'become a necessary qualification for a Scholar & a Gentleman'.[32] His failure to sell the book, however, shows that the antiquarian community was
not yet willing to support this endeavour, though part of his problem
derived from the poor reputation he had gained through factual errors in
Itinerarium Curiosum.[33] Stukeley soon found a way to continue his work,
however, by looking to another source for his income.

In 1726, Stukeley moved back to Lincolnshire, and, three years later, was
ordained in the Church of England. From this position, he had time to
write his books, while his research into the Druids became relevant in light
of Toland's inclusion of their history within the theological debate over
Deism.[34] In this context, Stukeley moved away from the observational style
of *Itinerarium Curiosum* and became immersed in imaginative theories about
the Druids and even attempted to revive Druidical ceremonies. In 1726
Stukeley built a Druidical folly at his home in Grantham, pre-dating the
fashion for such follies by more than 30 years, when architects of the stature
of Capability Brown became involved in designing similar megalithic constructions.

In 1729, after his ordination, Stukeley wrote of his hopes to continue
studying 'our Celtic ancestors and their religion' by expanding on Toland's
image of Druidism as a predecessor to Christianity, though in a positive
light in contrast to Toland's idea that Druidism represented a shameful
superstition.[35] From this time onward, Stukeley's emphasis on ancient Celts
became muted as he focused his energies on the Druids. This shift is evident
in his changing of the title of his manuscript, *The History of the Temples of the
Ancient Celts*, to *The History of the Religion and Temples of the Ancient Druids*, at
some point before 1733. By the time Stukeley was able to publish his prom-
ised books on Avebury and Stonehenge, the Druids had taken centre stage
in his research and the Celts received but a few mentions.

Stukeley's books on Stonehenge and Avebury finally appeared more than
two decades after he began studying the monuments. This delay was principally a result of his finances and the changing market for antiquarian books.
After Stukeley's first wife died in 1737, he married a sister of the Gales, who
brought him a substantial dowry. Having moved to Stamford, Stukeley constructed a 'Hermitage' like the Druidical folly he had built in Grantham,
and, soon after, used some of his new wealth to publish *Stonehenge: A Temple
Restor'd to the British Druids*. Three years later, he published *Abury: A Temple of*

the British Druids, with Some Others Described wherein is a More Particular Account of the First and Patriarchal Religion; and of the Peopling of the British Isles. These books represented two of the four volumes he had proposed in 1724. The posthumous, enlarged 1776 edition of *Itinerarium Curiosum* finally made available much of the information he had hoped to include in the other two.

Part of the reason that Stukeley hardly discussed the Celts in *Abury* and *Stonehenge* is that they were no longer central to the model of peopling he then favoured. In maintaining relevance to contemporary Church of England debates, Stukeley made the histories of languages and monuments subservient to the history of religion, which he reconstructed through an idiosyncratic combination of historical sources, the Bible and deductions based on religious principles. In *Stonehenge*, Stukeley envisioned his work on the monument as part of a larger study he titled, 'Patriarchal Christianity: Or, A Chronological History of the Origins and Progress of True Religion, and of Idolatry'.[36] His purpose was to trace 'the fundamentals of revelation' back earlier than they had previously been traced, 'to the fountain of Divinity, whence it flows; and shew that Religion is one system as old as the world, and *that* is the Christian Religion'.[37]

In turning to the history of religion, Stukeley had become less interested in the movements of entire peoples or tribes and focused mainly on the movements of the Druids, who, he argued, practised 'the first, simple, patriarchal religion', which 'undoubtedly is true, as coming immediately from God'.[38] Stukeley's reconstruction of the arrival of the Druids involved Phoenician colonists led by the Tyrian Hercules, who, he wrote, 'had a considerable hand in peopling Britain', and who possessed significant astronomical knowledge.[39] He also argued that Abraham himself had built stone temples before imparting that knowledge to Phoenician sailors.[40] Though seemingly eccentric and different from much of what had been written on peopling, Stukeley's argument had precedent in the work of Toland, and, before him, Bochart and Sammes.[41]

The Celts did not disappear completely from Stukeley's story, however. He noted that people speaking 'Celtic dialects' were present when the Phoenicians constructed Stonehenge and other Druidical temples:

> The old Britons or Welsh, we find, had a notion of its [i.e. Stonehenge] being a sacred place, tho' they were not the builders of it; for I take them to be the remains of the Celtic people that came from the continent, who chiefly inhabited England, at least the south part, when the Romans invaded the

island, they are more particularly the remains of the Belgae. [...] The most ancient inhabitants, the remains of the old Phoenician colony and primitive Celts who built Stonehenge, were the Picts, Scots, Highland and Irish, all the same people, tho' perhaps differing somewhat in dialect, as in situation: no otherwise than a Cumberland-man and one of Somersetshire now. The Cornish, I suppose, some remains too, of the old oriental race.[42]

In this, as in other passages in *Stonehenge* (there are fewer in *Abury*), the Celts simply denote an 'old oriental race' from the Continent, and Stukeley made no effort to elaborate on exactly who they were. His interest in the Phoenician connection seems to have precluded any need for him to say at this point whether he still subscribed to Pezron's model of Celtic migrations or to any other. In short, as the Celts lost their importance in Stukeley's model of peopling, there was little need to define them precisely. And in Stukeley's later work, such as *Palaeographica Britannica*, a series published in the 1740s and 1750s, his attention drifted toward later periods.[43]

Surveys Reach an Impasse

During the mid eighteenth century, as Stukeley appeared to lose interest in the material remains of the ancient Celts, no one arose to continue his earlier work. Though gentlemen like Stukeley still produced surveys of ancient monuments, these kinds of works became merely descriptive and no longer addressed questions like the origins of the remains.

The only major study of Celtic monuments from this period was produced by William Borlase, a Cornish vicar hoping, like Pezron, Lhuyd and Rowlands, to draw attention to the historical importance of his home region. In 1753, Borlase journeyed to Oxford to publish his work on local megaliths, a study he thought was of value 'where there were few Grecian or Roman remains to be met with'.[44] The following year, this study appeared as *Observations on the Antiquities Historical and Monumental, of the County of Cornwall*.

Borlase followed Pezron in his understanding of Celts as the group, 'anciently of great extent', responsible for peopling 'all Europe' and for speaking a language 'suppos'd to have contributed largely towards forming the Greek, Latin, and most European tongues'.[45] He disagreed with Stukeley's theory of the Phoenician origins of Druidism and with the prevailing view of Druidism as an Old Testament religion, while, like Toland, he saw the religion as a corrupt one.[46] Like both Toland and Stukeley, however, he put a great deal of emphasis on the history of the Druids, following Rowlands in connecting local megalithic monuments with Druidism and eastern idolatry.

Borlase's approach was one of synthesis, combining 'the authority of Monuments and Histories, to throw light upon the manners, arts, languages, policy and religion of past ages'.[47] He complained that many writers on the Druids failed to include enough evidence from the monuments themselves and he tried to fill this gap with illustrations not only of 'Rude Stone Monuments in General' but of associated artefacts (*pl. 7*).[48] He also compiled language lists, particularly of the Cornish language. For Borlase, Cornwall, with its supposedly uncorrupted Celtic language and megalithic monuments, was well suited for providing evidence complementary to written history in investigating Britain's first inhabitants:

> Cornwall being one of the two places to which the first inhabitants of this island who surviv'd the Roman and other conquests chiefly retir'd, in order to preserve the little remains of British blood, and liberty, and having retain'd the very language of the ancient Britans down to the present times, we may safely conclude, that the history of Cornwall must principally depend on that of Britain in general, however imperfect.[49]

In a sense, Borlase's book marks the end of a period, started by Aubrey, in which megalithic monuments provided a focus for antiquarian research into the Druids and Celts. The study of ancient remains continued, but it revolved more around particular areas than historical problems, which tended to be seen as either unsolvable or solved already by Stukeley. Even at the Society of Antiquaries, where ancient objects were frequently exhibited during this period, papers on the peopling problem tended to follow the linguistic and biblical framework of Pezron and contained little on artefacts or monuments.[50] By the 1770s, the optimistic mood fostered by the work of Pezron and Lhuyd was at an end, and simple description overshadowed historical narrative in antiquarian writing.

In surveys during this period, pre-Roman Britain was either ignored or dismissed. To take a famous example, in Samuel Johnson's celebrated trip to remote parts of Scotland, following a similar route to Martin's, Johnson found traces of 'the tongue of the first inhabitants', but said nothing about Druidical monuments.[51] And a few years later, he said, 'All that is really *known* of the ancient state of Britain is contained in a few pages. We *can* know no more than what the old writers have told us'.[52] Also in the 1770s, the artist Francis Grose started publishing a series of large volumes on antiquities, but included little on megaliths, preferring to focus on castles, abbeys and Gothic architecture. When he did include Stonehenge, he simply cited Stukeley's theory that it was Druidical.[53] Only in Grose's posthumous Ireland volume did a section appear on 'Pagan Antiquities', written by another contributor, Edward Ledwich, who argued on the basis of language and religious history that these remains belonged to 'Celtes' who lived 'in an age far beyond the reach of history or conjecture'.[54] Richard Gough's expanded 1789 edition of *Britannia*, which took more than 30 years to prepare, also concentrated on medieval Britain with little on ancient times, saying only that the nation is 'under a cloud of darkness, error and ignorance' about the origin of its first inhabitants.[55]

One new development in the late eighteenth century was that burials increasingly drew the attention of antiquaries. For Aubrey, the many barrows found across Britain had represented the graves of fallen soldiers. Later, fellows of the Society of Antiquaries like Cromwell Mortimer, Samuel Pegge and Hayman Rooke opened barrows as a part of their antiquarian research. Few researchers, however, did more than describe the objects they unearthed. As early as 1726, in the context of a travel diary, Roger Gale had considered the possibility of distinguishing tumuli among 'Celtick or British, Danish or Roman' times, but it took another 50 years for anyone to do more to address this question.[56] In a study of sepulchral monuments presented to the Society of Antiquaries in 1770, Thomas Pownall used etymology to attribute these monuments to the Celts, but this had little impact. The monuments were located near the woods, he argued, and the word 'Celt' could be traced to a root meaning 'woods'.[57] In 1773, Reverend Bryan Faussett completed his survey of barrows, which he attributed to Roman-era battles, but these later turned out to be Saxon.[58] In 1774, John Hutchins published a two-volume survey of history and antiquities in Dorset; its brief introduction cited the various 'opinions concerning the original inhabitants of this country', siding with the predominant Celtic/Gallic theory but expressing confusion about the makers of barrows.[59] After more than 50 years of research into ancient monuments, from Gibson's edition of Camden to Borlase's work in Cornwall, a sense of pessimism about the contributions these studies could make to the peopling problem seems to have led researchers simply to report their observations of monuments and grave contents.

Douglas and Excavation

Optimism returned suddenly to antiquarian work on the peopling problem when James Douglas started excavating tumuli. With this optimism, there was still no new meaning for the term *Celtic*, but the approach heralded a new means of defining the Celts. In this sense, the torch of Stukeley's early work was finally carried by another researcher. Douglas came to his interest in antiquarianism through the military. While building fortifications in chalk downs, he became involved in fossil-collecting, which, in turn, brought him in contact with antiquities dealers in the course of his travels. As a boy in Manchester, he had collected natural history specimens with Ashton Lever, who, in 1780, supported his application to the Society of Antiquaries of London. And by that year, Douglas had befriended Henry Godfrey Faussett, who inherited his father Bryan's substantial collection of grave goods.

In the next two years, Douglas wrote a large portion of what was to become *Nenia Britannica: Or, A Sepulchral History of Great Britain; From the Earliest Period to Its General Conversion to Christianity*. The publication of this book began a few years later, in 1786, and continued in series until 1793. Douglas' goal in *Nenia* was 'to draw a line between all speculative fancies in antiquities and on Hypothesis founded on reason and practical observations'.[60] He modelled his work after the chorographical and topographical traditions, especially in the work of Stukeley, whom he called 'the father of british antiquities'.[61] Yet he disapproved of how Stukeley saw 'our antient monuments with the magnifying lens of Celtic optics'.[62] In an attempt to avoid such biases, Douglas treated the 'many specific distinctions' of ancient funerary monuments as being of problematic origin and argued for a classificatory scheme to discover 'the identity of a people' based on a detailed analysis of their contents.[63]

Douglas' method of viewing antiquities as a source independent of the written word arose partly from the characteristically Anglican viewpoint that the scriptural account of human and world history could be supplemented through the exercise of reason. Religious faith constituted a strong motivation for Douglas, who was Chaplain in Ordinary to the Prince of Wales from 1787. The year before the start of *Nenia*'s publication, Douglas read a paper to the Royal Society in support of the very ancient, pre-Flood status of fossils. In examining fossil shells, whose antiquity had long been a point of controversy, he noted that shells found in ancient barrows showed no fossilisation, indicating that fossil shells must be significantly older than the barrows, which he thought were built by colonists soon after the Flood.[64] When Douglas focused his attention on archaeological remains in *Nenia*, he turned to this same method of using observations to build up a picture of the past that might stretch beyond what was known through written history, but would nevertheless be in accord with a certain interpretation of the Bible. In using this method, Douglas became one of the first British antiquaries to articulate the idea of a prehistoric human past, or a past that existed before written history.

Douglas used written history as a launching point for separating funerary monuments among the Celts, Britons, Romans, Saxons and Danes, a list of peoples derived from written sources. Yet assigning remains to these groups was far from straightforward. Written sources, often conflicting, were not always clear about burial practices; and, as modern archaeologists now know, the British past was more complex than this list of peoples implies. In Douglas' time, however, the study was quite novel, and Douglas felt he could forward scholarship this way: 'The uncertainty of applying the sepulchral relics found in this kingdom to their true owners has chiefly arisen from the neglect of careful discrimination'.[65] After he began his program of separating burials among past peoples, Douglas gained confidence in the potential of antiquarian research to serve as a test among different historical sources and as a confirmation of the truth of the Bible, which was fairly vague about the post-Flood peopling of the world and silent about the peopling of Britain:

> The Antiquary, on this striking discovery of durable monuments, with similar customs in other regions of the globe, enters into a profound and critical investigation of the early peopling of our island; he attempts to discriminate the race of men from the general mixture, and he thus finds these monuments to be more certain guides than history itself. His comparisons have proved them to have existed before the doubtful records of profane history; and his authorities are rendered presumptive by the testimonies of Holy Writ. They are thus rendered the unerring witness of the truth of the Sacred Text, and the ground tenable on which the historian moves for the history of all ancient colonization.[66]

As he turned to ancient monuments as a source of evidence independent of written history, Douglas made an important contribution to the history of field archaeology by identifying Saxon remains. The Anglo Saxons had been a subject of much interest since the overthrow of the Brutus story of

English origins, but they were only known through written sources. While isolated Saxon objects had previously been identified, no archaeological site had been shown to be Saxon before the publication of *Nenia*. This identification also cleared up the confusion about Bryan Faussett's collection, which Douglas showed also to be Saxon. Douglas' reasoning in identifying 'small barrows in clusters' as Saxon was based on the coins he found within them and on comparisons with similar barrows found in northern Europe.[67] This identification, still considered basically correct, launched the field of Anglo-Saxon archaeology.

His identification of Celtic barrows, however, has not withstood the developments of the 200 years since his publication. As with Saxon barrows, Douglas sought to identify Celtic barrows through comparisons with materials known from outside Britain:

> By contemplating the relics discovered in our antient sepultures, the historian may have an opportunity of comparing them with similar relics found in different places, and on which arguments have been grounded by authors who have written on the antient inhabitants of Britain.[68]

Unlike the Saxons, who were known to be a Germanic tribe, the Celts had no clear or widely agreed source area outside Britain. Douglas filled this gap in knowledge through an argument, based on comparative mythology and religion, that the Celts were a branch of Scythians, a people described by Strabo and other ancient authors as living to the east of Greece. In writing about Celtic mythology, he disputed John Pinkerton's assertion that Europe was peopled mainly by Goths descended from Scythians and that the Celts were devoid of mythology:

> But Mr. Pinkerton, in his Dissertation on the Scythians, says, 'of the Celtic mythology we know nothing.' I should perfectly agree with him, had he remarked they were an extreme early race of people; and, when the Greek and Roman authors began to write, were almost extirpated; but they seem to have been, at a remote period, a people who had over-run the whole continent of Europe and Asia; and to these very early people the monuments, which have been here discussed, may with great reason be attributed.[69]

In *Nenia*, Douglas was at pains to rescue the Celts from Pinkerton's attack, citing the history of the Druidism, which Pinkerton argued was 'a late

invention in the south of Britain' rather than an early and important development in the history of world religion.[70] Claiming that even savages have
priests, Douglas argued that the Druids arose as a Celtic priesthood just
after the Celts split off from the Scythians, thereby retaining many features
of eastern religion.[71] Among the monuments and artefacts he ascribed to
Scythian religion, making them good indices of the presence of Celts in
Britain, were symbols of the 'brazen bull' and megaliths:

> The Cimri being conclusively a branch of the old Celts, the Celts must have
> retained this worship in all the countries they visited; hence the rocking
> stones and other stone erections already discussed, being peculiar to this old
> Scythic worship of Bacchus or Brouma, are found in those regions where
> this universal and very antient conquest extended. The old Celtic mytholo-
> gy was therefore Scythic, and the Celts a branch of these people, from
> whom all the European and other polished nations arose.[72]

One of Douglas' biggest challenges was separating Celtic material from
Belgic. The Belgae were a tribe known through written sources to have
invaded Britain soon before Caesar's conquest. Douglas argued that the
Belgae were a separate group from the Celts, because they worshipped
Mercury.[73] In assigning barrow types to these groups, Douglas constructed
a hierarchy of barbarism, in which the Celts were a primitive branch of
Scythians, while the Belgae were more civilised than Celts, but not as
advanced as the Scythians from whom he thought they also descended. He
then provided illustrations of grave contents in order to assess their level of
barbarism:

> Several specimens of arms have been selected in this plate to connect those
> that are demonstratively applied to a barbarous people with those which
> have been found in our detached and large barrows. From the known fact,
> that familiar arrow-heads as are found in our antient sepulchres are used at
> this day by the barbarous natives of the globe, it is a natural and a reasonable
> inference that they were used by a barbarous people who were, at a certain
> period, the inhabitants of this island.
>
> Admitting this argument, which common sense must assent to, the
> reader may expand his thoughts on the period in which these barrows were
> raised. If he should be inclined to suppose these arms were Celtic, they may
> have exceeded the period of the arrival of the Belgae, who passed into the
> South of Britain about 300 years before Christ, and who are supposed to

have driven the Celtae, or other barbarous clans, to the remote and distant parts of the island, to the West and to the North.[74]

The picture of the Celts that emerged from Douglas' study was little different from what had come out of earlier antiquarian research. For Douglas, the Celts were a relatively primitive early people who colonised much of Europe from the east. They were distinguished by their religion, which was Druidical, and their language, which could still be heard in isolated corners of the British Isles. While these attributes were sometimes contested by researchers like Pinkerton, alternative views of the Celts were not based on ancient monuments, but relied almost exclusively on written sources carefully selected to construct a national history that celebrated one race at the expense of others. Douglas broke with this romantic tradition. Although he drew most of his evidence from the region around his home, he did not highlight any particular part of the British Isles, preferring to present his work as a sepulchral history of the nation's entirety. The novelty of Douglas' work came not from his view of the Celts, but from his method of distinguishing among various ancient remains. He set in motion a tradition of research into monuments that proved both popular and stable over the next half century, and which led to no significant changes in thinking about the Celts until the 1840s.

In the decades after *Nenia*, few antiquaries took up Douglas' method of sorting remains among past races in Britain. One who did was John Milner, who opened barrows in Dorset and reported his finds to the *Gentleman's Magazine* in 1790. But Milner's project was comparatively small and his reasoning less complex than Douglas', for he judged barrows as Celtic based merely on the 'rudeness' of the urns.[75] As Douglas' ideas failed to garner immediate interest, there was a temporary return to the descriptive chorographical tradition in the publication of substantial volumes by topographical artists like Grose and Gough. At the Society of Antiquaries, one of the only papers from this period to address the question of the Celts, whom 'foreign writers have agreed to call the first inhabitants of Britain', did not consider 'the more usual objects of antiquarian pursuits', but turned to classical texts, Welsh and Irish sources, and languages to clear up the fact that researchers 'differ widely on the meaning of that name'.[76]

Soon, however, another individual arose to follow Stukeley and Douglas in looking to material remains as a key means to track the Celts. And despite the common misconception that early research into the ancient Celts was mainly the concern of the 'Celtic fringe', this researcher, like Stukeley and Douglas before him, was English.

Ancient Wiltshire

Like the early nineteenth-century romantic regionalists in Ireland, Scotland and Wales, Sir Richard Colt Hoare argued that the Celts were the first peoples to have arrived in Britain, yet he alone used Douglas' method of basing his argument on excavated remains while relegating historical sources to a supplementary role. In 1810, publication began for Colt Hoare's *The Ancient History of Wiltshire* (also known as *Ancient Wiltshire* thanks to the pseudo-archaic title page calling the book 'Auncient Wiltescire'), which documented the results of a decade of barrow-digging. This work was the product of collaboration among a variety of antiquarian researchers, and Colt Hoare was the ultimate financial sponsor. The involvement of so many people in this endeavour reflected a general growth in domestic antiquarian activities, of which barrow-digging was one aspect. William Cunnington was the primary excavator, who alone remained part of the project from the outset. From the last few years of the eighteenth century, he had various sponsors who paid him to dig so that they might publish his results. Among these were his friend John Britton, who feuded with Colt Hoare over access to Cunnington's material, published a series of topographical books and expressed his interest in the area's ancient monuments through the 'Celtic cabinet' he made for his London home in the 1820s: H.P. Wyndham, a local politician with an interest in barrows; and Colt Hoare's friend William Coxe, who started working on a history of Wiltshire, but turned the project and financial responsibility over to Colt Hoare in 1804.[77] A final key character in the book's creation was Cunnington's classicist friend and advisor Thomas Leman.

One of Colt Hoare's great achievements in *Ancient Wiltshire* was to apply the results of excavations to the problem of pre-Roman chronology. Both Colt Hoare and Cunnington used Baconian language, echoing Douglas' goals in setting out to write *Nenia*. The beginning of *Ancient Wiltshire*'s introductory section is subtitled, 'we speak from facts, not theory'.[78] Colt Hoare followed this subtitle with a statement that has a modern resonance for archaeologists:

I shall not seek amongst the fanciful regions of romance, an origin for our Wiltshire Britons, nor, by endeavouring to prove by whom, and at what

period our island was peopled, involve myself in a Celtic or Belgic controversy; neither shall I place too much reliance on the very imperfect
traditions handed down to us by former antiquaries on this subject.[79]

This was merely a rhetorical ploy by Colt Hoare, who hoped to show that
his work marked a significant break from that of his predecessors. Colt
Hoare was not removed from contemporary debate, however, and devoted
his entire introductory section to reviewing what had been written on the
peopling of Britain. Far from rejecting the endeavour, he used historical
sources, linguistics, studies of monuments and a notion of the progress of
civilisation to arrive at the conclusion:

> I have no doubt but that the greater part of our Wiltshire barrows, and more
> particularly those in the neighbourhood of Abury and Stonehenge, were the
> sepulchral memorials of the Celtic and first Colonists of Britain; and some
> may be appropriated to the subsequent colony of Belgae who invaded our
> island.[80]*

---

*Colt Hoare's work has been widely misunderstood, thanks largely to Glyn Daniel's assess-
ment of the role of the book in his *A Hundred Years of Archaeology* (London: Gerald
Duckworth and Co., 1950), 30-31. This misreading has yet to be addressed, so it is worth
describing it in some detail. For Daniel, *Ancient Wiltshire* represented 'a great step forward
from antiquarianism to archaeology' because of its emphasis on excavation and because of
Cunnington's and Colt Hoare's Baconian approach in concentrating on facts and rejecting
the Druidophiliac musings of Stukeley. To illustrate this Baconian approach, Daniel wrote,
erroneously, that Colt Hoare declined to assign remains to a particular ancient people.
Compounding this misreading, Daniel noted a significant shortcoming in Colt Hoare's supposed inability to separate archaeological material chronologically, when, in fact, one of
Colt Hoare's most significant accomplishments was to do just that. In Daniel's interpretation, Colt Hoare's failure to identify the makers of ancient monuments nevertheless
reaffirmed his Baconian approach of not theorising beyond what his observations allowed.
   In addition, Colt Hoare's studies of monuments and his theory of the gradual progress of
civilisation contradict the interpretation put forward by Daniel, *The Idea of Prehistory*
(Cleveland and New York: The World Publishing Company, 1962), 56, that pre-Roman
chronology was, for Colt Hoare, wrapped in a 'despairing fog'. Daniel seems to have based
his flawed understanding of the text on a misreading of Colt Hoare's statement in a footnote in Colt Hoare, *The Ancient History of Wiltshire*, vol. 1, 20: 'After the result of ten years'
experience and constant research, we are obliged to confess our total ignorance as to the
authors of these sepulchral memorials: we have evidence of the very high antiquity of our
Wiltshire barrows, but none respecting the tribes to whom they appertained, that can rest
on solid foundations'. When Colt Hoare, *The Ancient History of Wiltshire*, vol. 2 (London:
Lackington, Hughes, Harding, Mavor and Lepard, 1821), 2, declined to assign a particular
tribe to the barrows, he meant one of the 'Celtic' tribes, such as Bibroci, Segontiaci,
Durotriges and so forth, known through historical sources. Colt Hoare was, in fact, keenly

In arguing forcefully for the Celtic origin of ancient monuments, Colt Hoare's legacy was to set a pattern for county histories in which descriptions of excavated remains were integrated into attempts to present a pre-Roman chronology. In this sense, he owed a huge debt, which he acknowledged, to *Nenia Britannica*. Many of his followers had difficulty – more difficulty than either he or Douglas – in relating excavated remains to ancient chronology, but they nevertheless followed his example of excavating barrows to shed light on the country's ancient past. As the enterprise of barrow-digging spread, based on Colt Hoare's example, it became routine to ascribe most ancient material to the Celts. Given the influence of Colt Hoare's model, it is worth examining in detail his own reasoning for calling Britain's ancient remains Celtic.

Colt Hoare's interest in pre-Roman chronology pre-dates the publication of *Ancient Wiltshire*. Before turning to the monuments of Wiltshire, he had taken the Grand Tour to the Mediterranean and then pursued tours in Ireland and Wales when the Napoleonic Wars prevented him from returning to the Continent. He based his Welsh trip on a well-known medieval

---

interested in the question of who built the monuments, and his answer of the 'Celts' was neither obvious nor did it represent the absence of an answer. Daniel, *The Idea of Prehistory*, 36, made a similar misreading when he took the following passage from Colt Hoare's *Journal of a Tour of Ireland, A.D. 1806* (London: W. Miller, 1807), 257, to mean that Colt Hoare refused to speculate on the peopling of Ireland: 'I shall not unnecessarily trespass upon the time and patience of my readers in endeavouring to ascertain what tribes first peopled this country; [...] for, I fear, both its authors and its original destination, will ever remain unknown'. Here again, Colt Hoare used the word 'tribe', by which he meant a historically named tribe, not a people or collection of tribes, like the Celts. Daniel seems either to have missed or to have discounted the section of the book where Colt Hoare, *Journal of a Tour in Ireland*, xxiv, wrote, 'As to its original inhabitants, it is most probable, that IRELAND, as well as ENGLAND, were peopled from the neighbouring Continent of GAUL; first by the CELTIC, and afterwards by the BELGIC tribes'. Daniel also missed the page preceding the quotation he did cite, where Colt Hoare, *Ibid.*, 256, wrote, on the basis of parallels between ornaments in the New Grange passage tomb and Wiltshire urns, 'I am inclined therefore to attribute this singular temple to some of the Celtic, or Belgic tribes, who poured in upon us from the Continent of GAUL, and peopled England, together with WALES, SCOTLAND, and IRELAND'.

By focusing solely on Colt Hoare's reluctance to overextend his synthesis of historical and material evidence, Daniel overlooked the argument about pre-Roman chronology in which Colt Hoare did engage, and Daniel mistook his argument about pre-Roman Britain for the absence of an interest in chronology. In fact, Colt Hoare did construct a chronology of pre-Roman migrations and attempted to integrate that chronology into what he knew about the monuments. Finally, Colt Hoare's importance did not derive simply from his Baconian approach to ancient remains and certainly did not come from his reticence in linking particular Celtic tribes with particular monuments, for virtually all of his followers attempted to do just that.

tour, and so did not devote much attention to Welsh history before the arrival of Caesar's troops.[81] His book on Ireland, however, contained a section on ancient antiquities and considered the problem of peopling. Here he adopted the idea of two waves of invaders: the Celts followed by the Belgae, coming to Britain and Ireland from Gaul.[82] While he did not explore this question in detail, he did mention place names and languages as the main evidence supporting this theory.

In *Ancient Wiltshire*, Colt Hoare expanded on this place-name argument with a presentation of excavated barrows:

> [in order] to throw some new light on the history of those Britons who formerly resided on our hills; to point out the sites they selected for habitation, and to mark their gradual progress from the bleak hill to the fertile valley, and from barbarism to civilization.[83]*

Based on readings of classical texts and the work of William Jones, Colt Hoare echoed Douglas in starting with the notion that a people called the Scythae were the first to expand westward from Tartary. Upon reaching western Europe, this group became known as Celts and became the original inhabitants of Gaul and, afterwards, Britain: 'The inhabitants of Gaul and Britain were originally the same people; they had the same customs, the same arms, the same language, and the same names of towns and persons'.[84] Up to this point, Colt Hoare's argument was Pezron's standard model, by then a century old, based on the history of language and religion. From there, however, he entered into a discussion of how one can separate ancient remains into various epochs. He used a survey of the geographical extent of megaliths and barrows to argue that, even though Britain was peopled originally by Celts from Gaul, advances in civilisation came from Cornwall, thanks to early commerce there between the locals and Phoenicians seeking Cornish tin:

> Numerous remains of stone circles, cromlechs, rocking stones, and tumuli still exist in the Scilly islands, and are continued along the coasts of Cornwall and Dorset to the widely extended plains of Wiltshire; all, from their rudeness, bespeaking a very ancient, and I may pronounce, a Celtic

---

*Despite the stereotype that it is only Americans, rather than the British, who spell 'civilization' with a 'z', the British almost always used this spelling as well, at least until the late nineteenth century.

origin, and corresponding in a very striking degree with those on the opposite shores of our mother-country, Gaul.[85]

Having identified the source (Cornwall) and types of Celtic remains, Colt
Hoare presented some common characteristics:

> When we find these works irregular in their form, simple in their construc-
> tion, and with single and slight banks and ditches, we may, I think, safely
> pronounce them to be of genuine British origin, and the works of a bar-
> barous and uncivilized people; and when we find the intrenchments
> multiplied and distinguished by the vastness of their banks, the height of
> their keeps, and extreme depth of their ditches, we may suppose these to
> have been the works of people better versed in the art of castrametation.
> But whenever we meet with works of a square or oblong form, bounded by
> straight lines, and with rounded angles, we may indubitably pronounce
> them the work of the Romans.[86]

After discussing general traits of Celtic, as opposed to later, remains, Colt
Hoare turned to pre-Roman chronology in a section about 'Modes of
Burial'. Here he cited both ancient and modern writers to conclude that
full body interment was more primitive, and therefore generally earlier,
than cremation.[87] He also looked at the materials found in barrows and
argued, as many others would in the mid nineteenth century, that iron was
the latest pre-Roman technological development in Britain:'Hitherto our
researches have furnished very few instruments of iron, and those denote a
much later period. Gold and brass [i.e. bronze] were known before iron'.[88]

While Colt Hoare did construct a chronology for pre-Roman Britain
based, on the one hand, on the notion of successive Celtic and Belgic
migrations, and, on the other hand, on the idea of technological progress, he
was hesitant to synthesise these ideas in a grand plan in which he could
identify a barrow as definitely Celtic or Belgic. Nevertheless, the method he
constructed held the promise of achieving this some day, and he hoped that
a visit to France (which was never politically possible for him thanks to the
Napoleonic Wars) might clarify the British sequence.[89]

Though Colt Hoare was the sole author of *Ancient Wiltshire*, the roots of
his innovative chronological ideas and his use of the evidence of objects lie
with the ensemble of researchers involved in the book's creation. As the primary excavator, Cunnington spoke out against reliance on written records,
preferring to base his ideas on remains. His understanding of pre-Roman

chronology, however, was less complex than Colt Hoare's, for he placed less emphasis on the Belgic invasion and thought of most of the early British material as Celtic, derived entirely from Gaul without direct Phoenician contact in Cornwall. He outlined these ideas in a letter to Thomas Leman:

> I contend that the information to be gathered from the Roman & Greek Historians will afford little information as data for illustrating Abury, Stonehenge Marden etc. etc., the Works of an ancient people like the Celtic Britons.* The information to be gathered from Caesar and Tacitus relate to the Britons in their times – therefore all theories drawn from such sources in regard to our Celtic Britons are ever at war with facts.†
> *Perhaps no more than the manners & customs of the Otaheitians.
> †The Book which best illustrates British Antiquities is the Bible.[90]

Leman, a classicist, agreed with Cunnington to the extent that one could learn about pre-Roman Britain without relying wholly on ancient writers. On a blank sheet in one of Cunnington's manuscripts, Leman proposed a version of the three-age system – apparently unrelated to the three-age system developed in Denmark (see Chapter VI) – in which the Celts were Britain's Stone Age inhabitants, while the Bronze Age was marked by the Belgic invasion, bringing long-distance commerce to Britain:

> I think we distinguish three great eras by the arms of offence found in our barrows. Ist those of bone and stone, certainly belonging to the primeval inhabitants in their savage state, and which may safely be attributed to the Celts. 2nd those of brass [i.e. bronze], probably imported into this island from the more polished nations of Africa in exchange for our tin, and which may be given to the Belgae. 3rd those of iron, introduced but a little while before the invasion of the Romans. The Britons on the coast from Essex to Lands-end at the time of Caesar's invasion were Belgae, a nation totally distinct from the Celts.[91]

The primary attraction that brought together so many researchers in the production of *Ancient Wiltshire*, with its novel approach to understanding the Celts, was, to a large degree, Wiltshire's two most famous monuments, Stonehenge and Avebury. Most of the contributors to *Ancient Wiltshire* argued over the origins of Stonehenge, and the question brought James Douglas into contact with the Wiltshire group. Cunnington's original interest in Wiltshire's ancient monuments was partly inspired by the collapse of one of Stonehenge's trilithons in 1797 and a subsequent excavation that supported the idea that it was pre-Roman. By 1806, Leman argued that most of the structure was Celtic with a few later Belgic additions. In 1809, Douglas contacted Cunnington about Stonehenge and visited the monument. While Douglas suggested a number of religious uses for Stonehenge, from a Phoenician shrine to a Roman mithraeum, he thought the structure pre-dated the Druids. Finally, at the conclusion to the second volume of *Ancient Wiltshire*, Colt Hoare attributed the 'stone temples' of Wiltshire to 'primitive Celtic and Belgic tribes' whose masons constructed them for use by the Druids.[92]

The prestige of Colt Hoare's *Ancient Wiltshire* precipitated an increase in barrow-digging in the British Isles. And his conclusions influenced others to report primitive finds as belonging to the Celtic period.[93] Part of the appeal of exploring the past through excavation was that barrow-digging was accessible to almost anyone with access to land, for the pursuit required little training or specialised knowledge. As a gentlemanly activity, barrow-digging remained popular through a number of changes in antiquarian method and theory until excavation became a more professionalised activity in the late nineteenth century. For much of this time, excavators tended to work within the boundaries of a single county. In this respect, Colt Hoare and his followers differed from Douglas' Britain-wide approach to sepulchral history and paralleled the romantic regionalists in focusing on the history of their home counties in relation to that of the whole country. The romantic impulse among barrow-diggers is also reflected in their fascination with the Druids.[94] The identification of Druidical monuments could serve as an effective pretext for long, imaginative descriptions of Druid sacrifices, like that offered by William Augustus Miles in *A Description of the Deverel Barrow, Opened A.D. 1825*.[95] Druidophilia also led to increased interest in megalithic monuments, like Stonehenge and Avebury in Wiltshire and Carnac in Brittany (*pl. 8*).[96] Just as the Druids constituted the focus of inquiries into the peopling of Britain based on the history of religion, the ancient priesthood provided much of the motivation for antiquaries who integrated the evidence of monuments into their theories. For the first three decades of the nineteenth century, the Druids remained at the centre of inquiries into the peopling of Britain, regardless of which source of evidence was most highly esteemed.

Over a 100-year period, three individual researchers, Stukeley, Douglas and Colt Hoare, were instrumental in introducing ancient remains as a new source of evidence for researching the ancient Celts. But their work did little

to change perceptions of the ancient Celts that had arisen in linguistics and
the study of literature. Early antiquarian research merely cemented the by-
then common understanding that the Celts and their Druid priests were
part of an inseparable unit. Soon, however, this new means of researching
the ancient Celts would lead to an entirely new definition of them. By the
1840s, with the growth of Prichard's version of linguistic ethnology, research
into the Druids started to become marginal activity, marking particular
researchers as unprofessional. In the study of material remains, research into
the Celtic settlers of the British Isles was about to undergo a revolution that
would displace Prichard's linguistics as the new primary source of evidence.

CHAPTER VI

CELTIC SKULLS

At the beginning of the 1840s, the same time that James Cowles Prichard helped establish the field of ethnology with a language-centred approach to tracing the first inhabitants of Britain, an alternative means of researching early peoples emerged in Scandinavia, based on measurements of crania. Prichard himself was the first to import this craniological method to British ethnology, and it quickly rose to challenge the study of language as the most promising form of ethnological inquiry. As the supposed character of Celtic skulls came to dominate the peopling debate, researchers for the first time began to consider that the Celts may have been preceded by others in the pre-Roman sequence of Britain's peopling. Also around this time, the idea of Celtic art (the topic of Chapter VII) entered into the discussion. In the second half of the nineteenth century, with growing interest in the bones and artefacts of the ancient Celts, the study of material remains dislodged linguistics as the most fertile area of research.

The popularity of research into Celtic skulls was inextricably linked with the emergence of ethnology as a discipline. In 1841, the British Association for the Advancement of Science began to recognise 'the importance of Ethnological researches' when it distributed queries to travellers.[1] The next year witnessed the founding of the Ethnological Society of London. Over the subsequent quarter century, ethnology grew as a synthetic discipline, incorporating disparate strands of research to address the question of peopling, but with craniology dominating the debate. This dynamic period is often seen as the beginning of modern archaeology in Europe, and, in many ways, ethnology was archaeology's parent discipline. Archaeology was not the only child of ethnology, however, and the period after 1865 is characterised by fragmentation, as art historians, linguists, craniologists and others went their separate ways, bringing different definitions of the Celts with them. By 1865, however, when craniology was in the ascendancy, most researchers did agree that – in a radical departure from 150 years of consensus – the Celts were not Britain's first inhabitants, but entered the island during the Bronze Age.

Craniology and the Three-Age System

The emergence of craniology in Scandinavia came about in the context of introduction of the three-age system. This system divides pre-Roman, or prehistoric Europe into three successive epochs – the Stone, Bronze and Iron Ages – distinguished by the predominant material of tools and weaponry. The development of this system, which remains the basic ordering principle in European archaeology, is normally counted among the key moments in the birth of the discipline and is associated with the idea of gradual technological progress. When the Danish curators and anatomists who developed the system first introduced it to British researchers, however, it was a non-developmentalist system whose importance derived mainly from its potential as a new tool for addressing the ethnological problem of tracing the earth's races from their biblical origins to their current diversity. For the first generation of scholars working with the system, its chief function was to provide a means of identifying skeletons with a particular race in a particular period, giving impetus to a craniological approach within ethnology.

The main consequence of the three-age system for research into the ancient Celts was that it added a new depth and variety to the pre-Roman period. Combined, the three-age system and craniological ethnology had profound implications for the position of the Celts in models of the peopling of Britain. The Celts continued to be connected to more eastern peoples through arguments about Indo-European languages, Druids, ancient monuments and artefacts, but they were no longer widely considered to have been Britain's first inhabitants. Prichard is a transitional figure in this regard. While he was one of the first British researchers to recognise the importance of the three-age system and to use craniological evidence, he nevertheless clung to his belief that the Celts were the first people to set foot on British soil. For Prichard's followers, the main ethnological question about Britain changed from a tracing of Celtic migrations to the fitting of the Celts into the Stone–Bronze–Iron sequence of British prehistory. In the

1850s, as the Celts began to be regarded as a later arrival in this sequence, generally at the beginning of the Bronze Age, craniology became the primary tool for differentiating between Celts and possible earlier races in Britain.

The Three-Age System in Scandinavia

By the early nineteenth century, the idea of three ages already existed as a literary model for human development. As a theory based on the extensive analysis of artefacts and their find-contexts, however, the three-age system was born in the Museum of Northern Antiquities in Copenhagen in the 1810s and '20s. The main impetus for the system's development came from Christian Jürgensen Thomsen, a numismatist whose first 20 years of curating the Danish collections led to the 1836 publication of *Ledetraad til Nordisk Oldkyndighed*, translated into English in 1848 as *Guide to Northern Archaeology.**

According to the 1848 translation of Thomsen's *Ledetraad* by Lord Francis Egerton, the first Earl of Ellesmere, Thomsen's interests resided in artefacts rather than peoples, and he did not use his evidence to trace migrations. In discussing the Bronze Age, for example, he wrote, 'It would seem that an earlier culture, long before iron came into general use, was diffused over the greater part of Europe, the produce of which was in great measure alike in regions very far apart', but he did not offer a theory as to which race this might have been or even if the culture, as he called it, was comprised of a single race.[2]† Thomsen's goal with the collection was, 'by a careful comparison and by accurately noting what sorts are generally found together', to 'ascertain the order in which the successive changes took place, and thus determine the periods to which a mere inspection of the ornaments will authorize us to assign the object'.[3]

This program initially appealed not only to museum-based researchers, but also to anatomists with ethnological interests. Both kinds of scholars relied mainly on opening barrows for their materials, the difference being whether they focused on the skeletons or on the objects buried alongside.

---

*Daniel, *A Hundred Years of Archaeology*, 41, mistakenly called this translation *A Guide to Northern Antiquities*, and this error has found its way into numerous articles and text books.
†This quotation contains one of the earliest instances of the word 'culture' to describe an archaeological people tied together by their characteristic artefacts. It is noteworthy that, when defining a people in this way, Thomsen discussed their spread in terms of diffusion, rather than migration or invasion.

Among curators, the Swede Bror Emil Hildebrand trained under Thomsen in Copenhagen before reordering the Historical Museum at Lund University and the Museum of National Antiquities in Stockholm according to the system. In the museum in Christiania (Oslo), Rudolf Keyser was using Thomsen's system by the mid 1830s. Perhaps the most influential of Thomsen's protégés was Jens Jacob Asmussen Worsaae, who worked in the Museum of Northern Antiquities with Thomsen in the 1840s and readily adapted the system to ethnology. During Worsaae's nine-month tour of Britain and Ireland in 1846-7, he introduced the system to museums in Edinburgh, Dublin and London, though his reception was mixed.

Among the first anatomists to use Thomsen's system were Daniel Friederich Eschricht, Sven Nilsson and Anders Retzius. Eschricht, Professor of Physiology at the University of Copenhagen, unearthed barrows to find crania which he then ordered according to the three ages. Though many of the early British advocates of the system cited Eschricht, his work on human bones was never translated into English. Nilsson, Professor of Zoology and Director of the Zoology Museum in Lund, published his *Skandinaviska Nordens Urinvånare*, which focused on ethnographic parallels to the Scandinavian Stone Age, in series from 1838 to 1843. This was translated into English in 1868. Nilsson's cranial analyses in this volume were first made available in Britain when he presented the paper, 'On the Primitive Inhabitants of Scandinavia', to the British Association in 1847. In 1842, Retzius, also a Swedish anatomist, developed the enormously influential cephalic index, which soon replaced the facial angle, the index developed by the Dutch anatomist Pieter Camper in the 1760s, as the leading racial index in European craniometry. The cephalic index gave a relative measure of head form, separating brachycephalic (short-headed) from dolichocephalic (long-headed) types. According to Nilsson, it constituted the major step forward that established the ethnological potential of craniometry.[4] Retzius presented his work to the British Association in 1846 in his paper, 'On the Ethnographical Distribution of Round and Elongated Crania'.

Prichard and the Three-Age System in Britain
Though Thomsen had developed the three-age system by the 1820s, neither he nor any of his Scandinavian followers published English accounts of it until the late 1840s. Before this time, knowledge of the system filtered to a handful of British researchers through personal contacts, mostly through the Royal Society of Northern Antiquaries of Copenhagen. David Laing, an officer in the Society of Antiquaries of Scotland from the 1820s, had

friends in Denmark and initiated an official correspondence with the
Danish Royal Society in 1829. Yet the Scottish Society did not adopt the
system in its displays or publications until Worsaae's visit in 1846. Thomsen
himself had written a letter about the system to the Society of Antiquaries
of London in 1828, but it received little notice. The Earl of Ellesmere was a
British member of Denmark's Royal Society and heard briefly of some
aspects of the system in a communication from the Society in 1836, but
waited 12 years to publish his translation of Thomsen's *Ledetraad*.[5] And on
the first anniversary of the Ethnological Society of London in 1844, when
the Secretary, Richard King, indicated that the Society in Copenhagen was
engaged in 'highly-interesting' activities, he did not mention the three-age
system specifically.[6] Whether on account of a lack of appeal or difficulty in
reaching a British audience, Thomsen's own writings on the three-age system had little influence in Britain. By the time *Guide to Northern Archaeology*
was finally published in 1848, British antiquaries and ethnologists had
already learned of the system through the anatomists.

One of the earliest published references in Britain to the Danish three-
age system came from Prichard, highlighting the fact that in Britain the
primary appeal of the system before the 1860s was its potential application
to the emergent science of ethnology. In 1841, in the European volume of
the third edition of his *Researches*, Prichard quoted at length from
Eschricht's work on skulls and included drawings of skulls in Eschricht's
collection among the plates (*pl. 9*). While Prichard did not mention the
three ages specifically at this point, his quotation of Eschricht certainly indicated the chronological potential of assigning excavated tumuli to various
ages depending on the materials found with the skeletons:

> in the most ancient times the [burial] ornaments were generally of amber,
> and the weapons and implements of stone or bone; seldom, perhaps never,
> of metal. This circumstance furnishes the ground for distinguishing the
> sepulchral remains of the northern land as belonging to different chrono-
> logical eras.[7]

Because the three-age system spread to Britain through the work of
Scandinavian anatomists, it soon became linked with the growth of craniology in British ethnology. In the same volume where he first showed
familiarity with the three-age system, Prichard expressed increased optimism about the potential contributions of craniology to ethnology. In both
the first and second editions of *Researches*, Prichard had paid careful attention

to skull shape, calling it the 'most important instance of diversity in the human form'.[8] Yet in neither case did he consider tracing racial movements through the use of excavated crania. Though Prichard still used language history as his primary source of evidence in the third edition of *Researches*, he added a short discussion of ancient British skulls, which he described as having narrow foreheads.[9] His limited use of cranial evidence, however, derived only partly from this preference for linguistic and historical data. He did not yet have access to a significant number of crania and lamented the lack of a 'national collection of the sepulchral remains of our ancestors', of the kind that existed in Scandinavia, where Retzius had access to hundreds of skulls, and in Ireland, where William Wilde was setting out on a program of studying ancient Irish crania (see below).[10] Instead of arguing against a form of evidence that might contradict his ethnological theories, Prichard sought to incorporate cranial evidence into his work and hoped that someday he would have more than a handful of ancient skulls at his disposal. The work of craniologists like Daniel Wilson, Joseph Barnard Davis and John Thurnam, who succeeded Prichard, can be seen, therefore, partly as an extension of his program in light of new evidence. In the weeks before his death in 1848, Prichard told Thomas Hodgkin at a meeting of the Ethnological Society that he was planning a volume similar to what was soon to become Davis' and Thurnam's master work, *Crania Britannica*.[11]

In 1843, Prichard further explored the implications of Eschricht's work in *The Natural History of Man*, in which he presented his results to a more general readership. Here, Prichard described Eschricht's work as that of fitting burial evidence into the three-age framework, possibly marking the first published reference to the Danish system in English.[12] By this point, the Scandinavian craniological approach to ethnology had produced results significant enough that Prichard felt the need to address in detail their implications for his model of the peopling of Europe:

> The purpose for which I have been induced to offer these observations is to point out the series of osteological remains which may be established by means of them. There seems to be good reason to believe that, by a collection of skulls and skeletons from these different sets of barrows, an historical series may be established, each set displaying the remains of the races of people by whom they were erected.[13]

In the 1840s, Prichard was leaning more and more toward craniology as a crucial source of ethnological evidence, yet he retained his belief that linguistics

provided the key for tracing the movements of races. He was able to recon-
cile these two strands of evidence by viewing physical form as highly
variable – a notion evident since the first edition of *Researches* – and determined by environment. This view had the added benefit of allowing him to
explain ancient writings which conflicted not only with each other but also
with his own observations of physical characteristics.[14] So, while he considered physical forms to be helpful in illustrating racial affiliation, he
continued to rely on language as the most stable racial indicator. He reiterated this point in 1847 in a speech on the methods of ethnology for the
Ethnological Society: 'The most important aids to historical researches into
the origin and affinity of nations is undoubtedly the analytical comparison
of languages'.[15] This thinking guided his incorporation of the Scandinavian
craniological program into his own interpretation of the three-age
sequence in Britain.

Eschricht had argued that the Celts' arrival marked the beginning of the
Bronze Age in Europe and that they were responsible for introducing metal
technology. This matched Nilsson's argument, which Prichard may have
learned about when Nilsson visited both London and Prichard's native
Bristol during a research trip in 1836.[16] Prichard was also in touch with
Retzius, who subscribed to the Danish philologist Rasmus Rask's 'Finn
hypothesis', which held that a Finn-like group occupied Europe before the
Indo-Europeans.[17] In the leading Scandinavian model, shared by Eschricht,
Nilsson and Retzius, the Stone Age population of Europe was made up of
non-Indo-European groups, like modern-day Basques, Finns and
Laplanders. When Prichard began addressing these results in the third edition of *Researches*, he became receptive to the notion that there were races –
which he termed collectively as Allophylians – that reached Europe before
the Indo-Europeans (*pl. 10*).[18] In an 1844 paper on crania, he supported the
notion that such peoples had skull forms different from later European
types.[19] Yet he never accepted that Allophylians preceded Celts in Britain,
despite the fact that he considered Britain's earliest inhabitants to have had
'something of the Mongolian or Turanian form of the head'.[20] Prichard jus-
tified this loyalty to his long-standing theory of the peopling of Britain, in
light of the new cranial evidence, by upholding his belief in the superiority
of linguistic data.

Evidence for Prichard's proposed Allophylians came from both linguistic
and craniological research. While the key evidence for Allophylians came
from the presence in Europe of non-Indo-European languages like Basque,
Finnish and Lappish, he believed that the corresponding races were only

traceable into ancient times by means of craniological measurements. Historical sources were silent about these groups in the distant past, and one of Prichard's central methodological principles was that classical writings should be used merely to complement linguistic data and that the Bible be used sparingly. Scandinavian ethnologists had no trouble fitting Allophylians into a local three-age sequence, for the presence of modern Lapps, who were less technologically developed, had already been explained by the notion that they were once dominant and were pushed to remote regions by the subsequent intrusion of more advanced peoples. In Britain, however, Prichard had no evidence for early linguistic groups other than the Celts. Though the ancient Picts in Scotland showed ambiguous linguistic affiliations, he did not think they provided convincing enough evidence for Allophylians in Britain.[21] For Prichard, therefore, languages remained the primary source of evidence for the peopling of Europe, while craniology and the three-age system offered the potential to illustrate local sequences in mixed areas.

One of the key problems in using primarily craniological criteria for defining Allophylians – or Celts for that matter – aside from Prichard's conception of Allophylians as comprising a number of different races, was the disagreement among craniologists about which head forms corresponded to particular races. When Retzius first presented his analysis to the British Association meeting in Southampton in 1846, he described Celts as dolichocephalic and Finns as brachycephalic.[22] A year later, when the Association met in Oxford, Nilsson sent in a paper that described Basque, Lapp and various other 'very ancient' Europeans as brachycephalic, historical-era Gothic races as dolichocephalic and Celtic races as 'longer than the first and broader than the second'.

[23] Davis and Thurnam later addressed this multiplicity of views on various head types in *Crania Britannica* and echoed the prevailing interpretation that not enough skulls had yet been collected in order to locate a definite type for each race.[24] In retrospect, the enterprise of distinguishing European races by means of the cephalic index was doomed to fail, but this would not become clear until large numbers of skulls were collected and measured. Meanwhile, Prichard, who had only studied a handful of skulls, seems to have avoided reliance on skull types for the pragmatic reason that he was better equipped to use other forms of evidence.

In the absence of an unambiguous Celtic head type, Prichard assigned racial affiliations to ancient British crania by continuing to rely on his proven mixture of linguistic and historical evidence. His notion that Stone Age tumuli in Britain were Celtic was supported, not by the shape of the crania within, but by his observation that the ancient Indo-Europeans 'were probably ignorant of the use of iron and other metals, since the terms by which these are denoted are different in different languages; and must, it would appear, have been adopted subsequently to the era of separation'.[25] Probably because he thought of physical forms as being more variable than did his Scandinavian counterparts, who tended towards the polygenist idea of the permanency of racial types, Prichard did not need to explain the three-age sequence in terms of racial replacements. This also explains his view of craniology as mainly illustrative of local developments rather than as a primary means of reconstructing racial movements.

Because the Scandinavian ethnologists themselves did not visit British scientific meetings or send English versions of their work to Britain until 1846, Prichard was the main outlet for their ideas in the early 1840s, and the more limited role he ascribed to craniology held sway in British ethnology in that period. For example, at the British Association meeting in 1845, a local vicar addressed Celtic migrations in a paper that followed Prichard in attributing skull variability to short-term environmental influences.[26] Prichard's dominant position, both in the ethnology sub-section of the British Association and in the Society of Ethnology, meant that his mono-genist framework and particular use of craniology in reconstructing racial movements faced little challenge within Britain. This was not the case on the Continent, however, nor in America, where Samuel Morton had pub-lished a section on the Celtic type in his polygenist *Crania Americana*, in which he argued for the superiority of craniology over language history as ethnological evidence.[27] With the arrival of the Scandinavians, this chal-lenge reached Britain as well.

Wilde

Before the Scandinavians came to the British Isles, there was one other researcher who imported the new craniological method. This was the Irish physician and ethnologist William Wilde, better known as Oscar Wilde's father. Wilde entered ethnological circles through the British Association, where he contacted Prichard as early as 1839 about skulls he had examined on a Near East trip that led to his bestselling travel book, *The Narrative of a Voyage*.[28] In the 1840s, Wilde turned his attention to ancient Irish skulls, a series of which he presented in a speech on ethnology to the King and Queen's College of Physicians in Dublin in 1844. In 1849, he incorporated this speech into an ethnological chapter in his Irish travel book, *The Beauties of the Boyne, and Its Tributary, The Blackwater*, which was also a bestseller.

After Wilde became interested in ancient skulls on his trip to the Near East, he contacted Retzius and Eschricht, 'two of the most distinguished northern philosophers', to discuss his views on ancient Irish examples and he enlisted a colleague to translate articles of the Scandinavian anatomists.[29] Following his contact with Prichard and the Scandinavians, Wilde became the second researcher in the British Isles to utilise the three-age system:

> [as a part of] the science of Ethnography, or the natural history of man, including his physical character – his form and stature – the colour of his skin – his hair and his complexion – his physiognomy – his habits and moral condition – together with his geographical distribution, but more particularly than all the rest, the form of his skull.[30]

Though Wilde saw physical ethnology as just one of four avenues for investigating Ireland's past – along with linguistics, the study of art and architecture and history – he regarded it as the most reliable.

Wilde did not share Prichard's reluctance about arguing for a pre-Celtic race. Combining the system with what he knew from early Irish literature, he argued that Ireland's first inhabitants were Stone Age 'Firbolgs', a 'simple pastoral people' who, following Rask's Finn hypothesis, were non-Indo-European.[31] The Firbolgs were then replaced by a Bronze Age 'globular-headed, light-eyed, fair-haired, Celtic people', known as the 'Tuatha De Dannan', who, in turn, brought metal technology to Scandinavia.[32] Wilde's sequence ended at AD 900, which he thought marked the start of the Irish Iron Age thanks to the arrival of northern races. While Wilde considered that the modern Irish, deriving from all three waves of advance represented by the three ages, were racially mixed, he felt he could locate past racial boundaries by looking at modern physical types. In this way, he claimed to find traces of Firbolgs and Celts across the country.

Worsaae's Arrival

In the mid 1840s, the Scandinavian proponents of the three-age system began reaching the British Isles in person, helping spread their craniological methods and lending support to Wilde's new theory of the place of the Celts in the nation's racial sequence. Of these Scandinavians, the most outspoken was Worsaae, who had worked closely with C.J. Thomsen. Worsaae had just published *Danmarks Oldtid*, an ethnological examination of Denmark's past structured around the three-age system. Worsaae shared Prichard's distrust of 'uncertain and imperfect' historical sources, which, in any event, were not of much use for learning about the ancient past of a part of Europe virtually untouched by classical civilisations. Instead of turning to languages as an alternative, however, Worsaae proposed, 'it is clear that we are enabled, by means of the antiquities and barrows, to form much clearer ideas, as to the peopling and civilization of Denmark, in primeval times'.[33]

In the spring of 1846, Denmark's King Christian VIII, who had commissioned *Danmarks Oldtid*, asked Worsaae to visit Great Britain and Ireland to look for traces of Danish monuments there. Though Christian VIII did not live to see Worsaae fulfil this request, his successor Frederick VII, himself an avid archaeologist, supported the idea and, by the autumn, Worsaae had arrived in Britain. At this point, *Danmarks Oldtid* was available in a German translation. To Worsaae's surprise, when he reached Britain, he learned that it had already been translated into English. The translator was William Thoms, who reviewed the German edition in 1846, the same year that he coined the word 'folk-lore'. Thoms celebrated Worsaae for allowing antiquaries to divide barrows among various races and for showing 'the gradual progress of civilization'.[34] Thoms' translation, which he had enlarged from the original, was eventually published in 1849 as *The Primeval Antiquities of Denmark*. Worsaae's activities on his research tour did as much to spread the three-age system as did the English publication of his book, which happened afterwards.

Worsaae's visit brought him in personal contact with the major museums and archaeological societies in Edinburgh, Dublin and London. Though he only spoke about the three-age system in two formal lectures, both to the Royal Irish Academy, he was able to win converts through informal discussions. Though today we tend to think of Worsaae as an important early archaeologist, he presented his work as part of ethnology, 'a most important branch of science'.[35] Like Prichard, he contrasted his new approach with a reliance on written records. But eschewing Prichard's favoured linguistics, he argued that 'it has become possible to enter upon an entirely new inquiry into the history of the earliest state of the European nations, by means of the antiquities alone'.[36] Thanks in large part to Worsaae's influence, this new kind of ethnology, revolving primarily around antiquities and the three-age system, challenged Prichard's linguistic ethnology and became the basis for the emergent discipline of archaeology.

Both in his second speech to the Royal Irish Academy and in *Primeval Antiquities*, Worsaae argued that craniology provided the key to ethnology. In his speech, he outlined his three-age understanding of Danish and Irish antiquities. Describing the Stone Age, he said:

> It is only through a careful examination and comparison of the skeletons
> and skulls found in the tumuli just mentioned, that we can get information
> concerning the races to which this aboriginal people belonged.[37]

In *Primeval Antiquities*, he reiterated this position. In attempting to figure out
which race was represented by the Stone Age, he lamented the dearth of
cranial evidence, which he thought would provide a definitive answer with
the collection of more skulls.[38]

For Worsaae, the Stone Age was the period which most needed cranial
evidence in order to be incorporated into an ethnological history of
European races. Until the mid 1850s, when Worsaae began to regard the
Iron Age in northern Europe as starting shortly before Roman times, he
saw iron technology as becoming widespread only after the fall of Rome,
meaning that he took all the 'barbarian' peoples in classical texts to be part
of Bronze Age Europe.[39] For the Bronze and Iron Ages, therefore, he could
more easily turn to historical and linguistic sources.

In Worsaae's interpretation, race replacement was the major explanation
for change from one age to the next: 'All facts, for instance, seem to shew
that Europe was not peopled at once, by a race of mankind who bore in
themselves the germ of all future progress, but that this race has gradually
received the addition of others, who continually supplanted the former, and
laid the foundation for a more advanced civilization'.[40] The fact that
Worsaae considered that the three ages represented not just the presence of
different races, but also the 'state of civilisation' in which they existed –
reinforced by Thomsen's citing the 'resemblance to savages' of Stone Age
Europeans – indicates the polygenist leanings of ethnology based on craniology and the three-age system.[41]

Despite Worsaae's reliance on craniology for investigating the Stone Age,
he used a different ethnological approach for the later ages. In his picture of
the European past, the Celts entered the scene in the Bronze Age, for he
interpreted their degree of civilisation as too high for the Stone Age.[42] He
did not equate the Celts with the entirety of European Bronze Age civilisation, however, and he did not think of them as a unified tribe. Instead, he
combined a host of different sources of evidence – historical texts, traditional songs, place names, languages and artefacts – to ascertain the
geographical extent of Celtic occupation. While he concluded that the
Celts were widespread in Europe in the Bronze Age, he thought that the

oldest runic inscriptions in Denmark provided convincing evidence that Bronze Age Denmark was home to a Gothic race, rather than a Celtic one.[43] For the Celtic past, he looked especially to Ireland, Wales and parts of Scotland.

With this focus on degrees of civilisation and race replacement, it is not surprising that even Worsaae's contemporaries described him as being 'national to the backbone' and accused him of bias in his examination of the Danish presence in the British Isles.[44] He concluded his book on the insular Danes with a celebration of 'the ancient power' of the Scandinavian race:

> The North sent out the flower of its youth and strength, not merely to destroy and plunder, but rather to lay the foundations of a fresher life in the western lands, and thus to impart a new and powerful impulse to human civilization.[45]

Just as he thought of Denmark as the heart of ancient Gothic power, he saw Ireland as occupying the same position for the ancient Celts:

> Ireland has an immense advantage over Scotland, England, and all other countries, which are now partly, and were once completely inhabited by a Celtic people, in that it has preserved an entire literature, whilst other countries have preserved little or none at all. All nations of Celtic descent will, therefore, be obliged to turn their eyes to Ireland, when seeking information concerning the ancient manners and institutions of the genuine Celtic people.[46]

Worsaae reiterated this sentiment in the published results of his 1846–7 research visit. Because of Ireland's later literary tradition and because he felt Ireland was not as racially mixed as areas on the Continent, he wrote, 'Ireland may still be justly called the chief land of the ancient Celtic tribes'.[47] In discussing Wales' Celtic character, Worsaae wrote in the same terms, reflecting the fact that despite his reliance on craniology for early periods, the linguistic definition of the Celts continued to pervade his thinking:

> This little mountain tract, which, in comparison with England, is poor as regards fertility, but all the richer in natural beauties, contains the last remains of the former masters of England, the Celtic Britons. By its remote situation, its rocks and narrow mountain passes, the characteristics of its former

inhabitants have been preserved in our times. The people speak the ancient Welsh language, a branch of the Celtic stock; and have also inherited no small share of that burning hatred which their forefathers nourished against the English, who gained possession of their original fatherland by force [...] The people, whose scanty remnant thus spend the last days of their old age among the Welsh mountains, formerly belonged, both by possessions and kinship, to the most powerful in Europe. Not only were the Scotch and the Irish of the same origin with them, but on the other side of the channel, throughout Gaul, or France, Spain, and the middle and south of Europe, dwelt tribes of the Celtic race. Until about the time of the birth of Christ, there was no people north of the Alps, which, with regard to power, agriculture, commerce, skill in the arts, and civilization in general, could equal, much less surpass, the Celts.[48]

In associating the study of a nation's ethnological past with a patriotic interest in celebrating that nation's supposed character, Worsaae struck a chord with local researchers:

A nation which respects itself and its independence cannot possibly rest satisfied with the consideration of its present situation alone. It must of necessity direct its attention to bygone times, with the view of enquiring to what original stock it belongs, in what relations it stands to other nations, whether it has inhabited the country from primeval times or immigrated thither at a later period, to what fate it has been exposed; so as to ascertain by what means it has arrived at its present character and condition.[49]

William Wilde, for example, was soon echoing some of Worsaae's comments about the Celts and Ireland. By 1849, when Wilde put his ethnological results into *The Beauties of the Boyne*, he underlined the contribution of the Celts to Ireland's past by calling attention to the early Irish literature that impressed Worsaae:

It may be regarded as a boast, but it is nevertheless incontrovertibly true, that the greatest amount of authentic Celtic history in the world, at present, is to be found in Ireland.[50]

He also celebrated Ireland for being able to produce, under the patronage of the Royal Irish Academy, 'a museum of Celtic and early Christian antiquities, unexampled on the British isles'.[51] In spite of the importance Wilde attached to Ireland's Celtic past in these comments from the book's preface, his racial sequence, which was consistent with his 1844 version, did not place special emphasis on the 'Celtic' Bronze Age. He did make a case for Celtic technological superiority, however, by claiming, in reverse of the prevailing view, that Irish Celts brought knowledge of metalworking to Scandinavia.

Though it is tempting to exaggerate the connection between ethnology and patriotism or nationalism, the relationship between this young science, interest in the Celts and any political project, can be complex. Worsaae's association of ethnology with patriotism helped to win him favour in Denmark, where he was sponsored by the king. The spread of his methods, however, was not strictly correlated with patriotic or nationalist ideologies elsewhere. Though Worsaae associated the three-age system with a celebration of the pre-Anglo-Saxon races of Ireland and Wales, the system did not appeal primarily to scholars from the purportedly 'Celtic' fringes of the British Isles. William Wilde and Daniel Wilson (see below), hailing from Ireland and Scotland respectively, were two early adherents to the Scandinavian program, though both emphasised the phenomenon of racial mixing and neither advocated separatism. In Wales, no prominent scholar used the system to explore that region's past, while a host of English researchers did. By the 1860s, there were far more English than Irish scholars practising craniological ethnology within the three-age framework. The growth of this ethnological program cannot be tied to a particular national movement or ideology within Britain and Ireland. Though it had the profound effect of dislodging the Celts from their recognised position as first inhabitants of the islands, the program seems not to have become popular because of this result, but because it was associated with what were considered to be advanced scientific techniques.

In Ireland, the 1840s were a fertile decade for the development of Irish antiquarianism as well as for a brand of nationalism that focused on the Celtic past, but it was not until the 1850s that the term *Celt*, which was also the title of a magazine put out by the Celtic Union, became firmly associated with separatist politics. In 1840, the topographical artist George Petrie and his colleagues founded the Irish Archaeological Society to supplement the antiquarian work they conducted within the Royal Irish Academy. As the decade progressed, various local archaeological societies sprang up, as did the conservationist Celtic Society, which later merged with the Irish Archaeological Society. In the mid 1840s, as anti-English frustration grew in reaction to England's failure to mitigate the suffering caused by the Great

Famine, Wilde's future wife, Jane Francesca Elgee, published anonymous separatist poetry in *The Nation*, the voice of the Young Ireland movement. In this environment, Wilde's ethnological investigations were clearly related to the drive to find a unique and prestigious 'Celtic' past for Ireland. Yet Wilde's public loyalty to Queen Victoria, his rejection of the activities of Young Ireland, and the fact that, as Lady Wilde (from 1851), Jane Francesca stopped writing potentially treasonous poems, challenge the notion that Wilde's interest in Celts was part of a separatist, rather than a merely local patriotic, ideology.[52] And his particular approach to ethnology, with its strong emphasis on craniology, seems to reflect more of a desire to investigate Ireland's past with prestigious new methods than any political conviction.

The Celts as Bronze Age Invaders

By 1847, when the three-age system had become known among British ethnologists and when Worsaae and other Scandinavian researchers had either visited Britain or published English versions of their work, Prichard finally tempered his almost career-long confidence that the Celts were the first Britons, highlighting the impact of the Scandinavians' arrival. Under the growing weight of craniological evidence that Stone Age Europe was inhabited by non-Indo-Europeans, Prichard wrote, 'Whether the oldest tombs were the sepulchres of a Celtic race, is a question not yet decided'.[53] And, in discussing the possibility that Europe was first peopled by 'Ugro-Tartarians' (part of Prichard's Allophylians), he wrote:

> I must here observe that many modern writers seem disposed to believe that the Celtic nations, at least the original people of the British Isles whose descendants are the Welsh and Irish, were in part of Finnish or Lappish descent and sprang from a mixture of this race with a tribe of Indo-European origin.[54]

It is notable that he recognised the growing popularity of this rival theory, which gave more weight to craniology than to linguistics. Prichard died in 1848, during this moment of change. With his passing, most younger researchers, like Wilde, subscribed fully to the notion that the Celts were Bronze Age invaders.

Wilson

Just as Wilde brought craniology and the three-age system to Ireland, the Scottish antiquary Daniel Wilson did the same for Scotland, though he used a slightly different mixture of ethnological evidence. Wilson joined the Society of Antiquaries of Scotland shortly before Worsaae's 1846 visit and was appointed Secretary soon after. Wilson's response to Worsaae was swift. In 1849, he organised his *Synopsis of the Museum of the Society of Antiquaries of Scotland* according to the system, with both the Stone and Bronze Ages – the two pre-Roman periods according to Worsaae – labelled as Celtic. Despite using the new Scandinavian system, Wilson's catalogue dated the arrival of the Celts on the authority of Godfrey Higgins' *The Celtic Druids*, which was a late version of the Genesis-based history-of-religion approach to the peopling of Britain.[55] In 1850, when Wilson presented his work to the British Association during its summer meeting in Edinburgh, he had completed his conversion to the Scandinavian model, in which non-Indo-Europeans were the first inhabitants of Europe, and he stopped basing his work on Druidical histories like that of Higgins.

The title of Wilson's paper, 'Inquiry into the Evidence of the Existence of Primitive Races in Scotland prior to the Celtae', clearly reflected the influence of the Scandinavian approach for his picture of Britain's past. He wrote the paper as an argument, not just for the existence of pre-Celtic inhabitants of Britain, but for the very practice of craniological ethnology: 'It is to be regretted that this branch of physical archaeology has heretofore been so little esteemed in this country in comparison of the contributions afforded by philological researches to ethnology'.[56] His regret was echoed by other British Association ethnologists, who 'repeatedly commended' his results 'as the first steps in an entirely new course of scientific investigation'.[57]

In outlining his evidence, Wilson mainly followed Sven Nilsson's work, and added his own data to illustrate the particular sequence of races in Scotland. For the first inhabitants of Scotland, Wilson departed from Nilsson's sequence for Scandinavia.[58] Instead of Nilsson's model of a brachycephalic race followed by a dolichocephalic one, Wilson argued that the earliest Scots were 'Cymbocephalic' (meaning 'boat-like') and were followed by a brachycephalic race, although larger-brained than the Scandinavian brachycephalic race.[59] Nilsson and Wilson agreed that the next race in the sequence, which arrived with bronze technology, had 'the true Celtic type of cranium' and exhibited 'an intermediate form, shorter than the true *Dolicho-cephalic*, and longer than the *Brachy-cephalic*'.[60]

Wilson had not determined the cause of the physical differences among the races in the three ages. He did, however, associate the technological progress of the three ages with a social and intellectual progress echoing the four-stage theory of the Scottish Enlightenment:

> Whether by the gradual improvement of the aboriginal race, or by the incursion of foreign tribes, who were already familiar with the fruits of agricultural labour, the wild pastoral or hunter life of the first settlers, would of itself put an end to the possibility of finding subsistence by means of the chase.[61]

Wilson remained open to the idea that cranial forms changed because of the infusion of new blood, rather than simple race replacement, though his staunch monogenism made him less inclined than the Scandinavians to attribute all physical changes to the arrival of new races. In either case, he was able to study the process' effects in his study of Scotland's past.

A year after introducing his craniological study to the British Association, Wilson published *The Archaeology and Prehistoric Annals of Scotland* in which he classified Scotland's past into four ages: Stone, Bronze, Iron and Christian. Unlike Wilde's shorter book, *The Beauties of the Boyne*, which had just one ethnological chapter, Wilson's book was a monumental study, entirely dedicated to outlining and illustrating the past peoples of Scotland. The importance of this book for the history of archaeology has generally been understated, and it is usually noted simply for its relatively early uses of the three-age system and of the word 'prehistoric'. With *Prehistoric Annals*, Wilson set out to draw together various research traditions – the county history genre of Colt Hoare, object-based antiquarianism and linguistic and physical ethnology mixed with historical and biblical analyses – to address the peopling of Scotland.[62] In his vision of how these traditions fitted together, antiquarian objects were useful in providing a context for interpreting human skeletal remains in order to construct, with the help of written sources, a racial sequence. This vision did more than establish a methodology for what he termed 'scientific antiquarianism'.[63] It defined the field's central subject, which was the time period that had previously been subsumed under the general term *Celtic*. To do this, he brought a new critical perspective to the use of any historical ethnic name to categorise antiquities.

Wilson understood the novelty of his project and made an effort to explain its usefulness. He couched the argument for his brand of archaeology in terms of the struggle to gain recognition as a section at the British

Association for ethnology, which he defined as the study of 'the origin and progress of the human race'.[64] Archaeology, for Wilson, deserved similar recognition for its special qualities:

> It rests, however, with the archaeologist to assert for his own study its just place among the essential elements of scientific induction, and to shew that it not only furnishes valuable auxiliary truth in aid of physiological and philological comparisons, but that it adds distinct psychological indices by no other means attainable, and yields the most trustworthy, if not the sole evidence in relation to extinct branches of the human family, the history of which possesses a peculiar national and personal interest for us.[65]

Wilson went on to set out his argument for the central importance of 'Physical Archaeology' in his project:

> To this branch of evidence it is probable that much greater importance will be attached when it has been thoroughly investigated, since to it we may look, with considerable confidence, for a distinct reply to the inquiry, which other departments of archaeological evidence suggest as to the existence of primitive races in Britain prior to the Celtae.[66]

This confidence that further evidence and analysis of human skeletons would lead to an archaeological answer to the ethnological question of the peopling of the British Isles echoed Prichard's call for more research into skulls, and both Wilson and Prichard based their confidence on the work of Eschricht, Nilsson and Retzius.[67] Wilson's collection of skulls was quite small, on the order of dozens, though it was more than the handful that Prichard had at his disposal and, presumably, more than the unspecified number Wilde examined.

Wilson's newfound critical perspective in assigning ethnic names to antiquities is traceable to the influence of another Scandinavian visitor to Scotland, Peder Andreas Munch, who arrived in Edinburgh toward the end of 1849. Munch convinced Wilson that the practice of attributing certain remains to a Danish influence merely masked the complexity of ancient society, and, in any case, was not always faithful to actual Danish artefacts. In arguing against literature-based interpretations of antiquities, Wilson wrote, 'The name of Dane has in fact for centuries been one of those convenient words which so often take the place of ideas and save the trouble and inconvenience of reasoning'.[68] For the most part, Wilson turned to crania in order to do more than merely separate remains 'between Northman or Dane and Celt or Saxon' and form a 'consistent arrangement of our archaeological data'.[69] In seeking to establish a new chronology for what had previously been considered a homogenous Celtic period, Wilson recognised that he was contradicting previous usages, in which 'the term Celtic is loosely applied in contradistinction to Saxon or Teutonic, and in accordance with the pre-conceived idea that the Celtae are the primeval colonists of Britain'.[70]

Despite arguing against Prichard's characterisation of the Celts as the original inhabitants of Britain, Wilson owed a great deal to Prichard's influence. He retained Prichard's monogenist framework and emphasis on demonstrating the truth of the Bible and he followed Prichard in extending the traditional 6,000-year biblical chronology by between 1,000 and 2,000 years in order to allow enough time for the observed human diversity to develop.[71] Wilson endorsed Prichard's conception of the Celts as a historically early wave of the many 'successive migrations' of 'races from the same eastern centre, to which we refer the origin of the whole human family', and, like Prichard, he supported this model with linguistic, historical and place-name arguments.[72] His only major deviation from Prichard's model was his attributing the Stone Age and the construction of 'Druidical' monuments to 'Allophylians', marking one of the first attempts by a British researcher to decouple Druids and Celts.[73] Wilson's choice of Prichard's word, 'Allophylian', to describe this race is indicative of the fact that Wilson saw himself as working within Prichard's ethnological program, though with an increased emphasis on Scandinavian-style craniology.

Wilson did not interpret the transitions among the three ages as disjunctions, as Worsaae did. He allowed more room for development within each race, arguing that the Stone Age people 'were abundantly capable of civilization, and possessed a cerebral capacity fully equal to that of nations which have carried the practical and decorative arts far in advance of a more archaic period'.[74] When, according to his model, the Celts arrived in the Bronze Age, Wilson argued that the Allophylians had already begun working with bronze technology.[75] And he broke with Worsaae's model by postulating the existence of a pre-Roman Iron Age, albeit a short one.[76] By this time he had resolved the causal ambiguities he had expressed in his paper to the British Association and had come down firmly in favour of race mingling, rather than replacement, as an explanation for the distinctive Scottish sequence of crania.[77]

Part of Wilson's goal with *Prehistoric Annals* was to argue against the view, forwarded by the archaeologist Thomas Wright, of pre-Roman Britons as

'mere painted savages' whose artistic achievements were 'assumed of necessity to have a foreign origin'.[78] Archaeology, for Wilson, was a science that
recognised the achievements of all the ancient peoples of Britain. The
importance of the Celts in Wilson's project is reflected in his selection of a
particular skull unearthed on the island of Iona as the archetypal example of
the Celtic form. He did not choose this skull solely for its measurements,
which fit Nilsson's criteria for the Celtic type, but for its location in 'the
venerable centre of Celtic civilization', which was becoming a tourist destination at the time thanks to its ancient church and promise of even earlier
Druidical remains.[79] For Wilson, therefore, and for tourists interested in
Scotland's past, the Celts were an accomplished and widespread civilisation
whose spiritual centre was in the Hebrides. Wilson characterised the Celts
as a valuable component of Britain's racial past, but he used craniology to
emphasise the composite nature of the island's population.

In 1853, Wilson left Scotland to become Professor of History and English
Literature at Toronto University. With the exception of the 1863 revised edition of *Prehistoric Annals*, in which he changed little other than to recognise
the recent establishment of the great antiquity of humanity, Wilson did not
pursue further original research in British archaeology. He did, however, stay
in touch with European archaeology through periodic visits and continued
to research British ethnology in Canada by measuring the head sizes of
European immigrants. In his absence, British craniological ethnology continued to grow in popularity among members of the many new
archaeological societies and among barrow-diggers.

The Barrow-Diggers

In order for craniology to have an impact on the peopling debate, more evidence was needed. The group best positioned to supply the necessary crania
was the barrow-diggers following in the tradition of Colt Hoare. Thomas
Bateman, primarily affiliated with the British Archaeological Association,
was one of the first in the barrow-digging tradition to turn to cranial evidence, but only after he felt the influence of Scandinavian craniological
ethnology and of the growing field of British phrenology. Before turning to
crania, Bateman had written a simple account of his county's material
remains in *Vestiges of the Antiquities of Derbyshire* in 1848. In this volume,
Bateman described the peopling of Britain as 'a mystery upon which conjecture or theory can throw but little light'; instead of offering an
archaeological theory, he put forth a literary version of events, which he
drew from 'the opinions of scholars and chronologists' who connected the

Celts through an ancestral tree back to Noah.[80] Bateman's approach had changed radically by the 1861 publication of his follow-up book, *Ten Years' Diggings in Celtic and Saxon Grave Hills*, in which he criticised Colt Hoare for neglecting 'ancient Celtic crania' and looked to ethnological archaeology as a way to study the 'possibly pre-Celtic' population of Britain.[81]

Between 1848 and 1861, Bateman adopted the three-age system and started to treat crania as a valuable source of evidence. From the many barrows Bateman had opened, he created a private museum, which was well known to members of the various archaeological societies. In his 1855 museum catalogue, Bateman divided his Britannic Collections into a 'Celtic Period' of 'Stone and Bronze', a 'Roman and Romano-British Period' and a 'Teutonic or Iron Period', before the more recent historical periods.[82] While this periodisation differed slightly from Wilson's, it shared the use of the three-age system as the key to creating a sequence of cranial types and the method of defining the three ages by race as well as by the materials of technology.

The shift in Bateman's thinking probably occurred in 1849. In August of that year, Joseph Barnard Davis visited Bateman's museum and noticed that Bateman had collected a large number of ancient skulls, probably one of the largest such collections in Britain at the time.[83] Before Bateman, none of Colt Hoare's followers had collected human skeletal remains, partly because Cunnington, one of the most influential of the early barrow-diggers, had left them in place as uninformative and partly because the collection of bones had been stigmatised by the 1830s scandal – which sent the Edinburgh anatomist Robert Knox into poverty – of 'resurrectionists' supplying medical courses with illegally unearthed and murdered bodies. With the influence of the Scandinavian ethnologists, barrow-diggers became more amenable to collecting ancient skeletons along with the objects buried with them. In the years after their 1849 meeting, Bateman and Davis collected skulls together, providing material for Bateman's *Ten Years' Diggings* and Davis' *Crania Britannica*.

Growing interest in skulls was also fostered by the phrenological movement, whose relevance was manifest in the subtitle of the short-lived (1848–9) *Ethnological Journal: A Magazine of Ethnography, Phrenology, and Archaeology, Considered as Elements of the Science of Race* and which captured the attention of Davis early in his career. In fact, the very word 'craniology' was often taken to be synonymous with phrenological inquiry into a person's character by examining head shape. The movement seems to have influenced at least one Prichardian inquiry into the peopling of Britain in the 1820s, but it was not until the 1840s that ancient skulls, instead of ancient descriptions of physical attributes, caught the attention of researchers.[84] Though phrenology was waning by the 1840s, it fitted well with Scandinavian ethnology in that both disciplinary traditions sought to identify the skull types of various races. George Combe, a leader of the phrenological movement, thought that phrenology 'holds good in the case of nations as well as of individuals' and presented a sample of European crania in his synthesis of the field.[85] In the 1840s, aside from Bateman's collection of ancient skulls, most British skull collections (including one in Edinburgh that provided Wilson with most of his material) were gathered by phrenologists.[86]

Davis and Bateman were soon joined in their research into British crania by the physician John Thurnam, who dated his interest in archaeology to seeing two ancient skulls in 1849 in a display at the hospital where he worked and who was familiar with phrenology through his work on the insane. Both Thurnam and Davis were members of the Archaeological Institute and used it as a forum to further their craniological program. In 1850, Thurnam presented a paper to the Institute praising the success of Worsaae's approach to the early peopling of Europe and encouraging British researchers to collect crania as well.[87] Davis followed this with a paper to the British Association in 1854 and one to the Archaeological Institute in 1856, the same year that *Crania Britannica*, his joint effort with Thurnam, began publication. In his papers, Davis argued that physical characteristics were superior to languages as a source of ethnological evidence and that the three-age system provided the key for studying crania.[88]

Like Wilson, Davis singled out a particular skull as containing 'the true *typical form* of the ancient British cranium', though he chose a different skull (*pl. 11*).[89] While Wilson's typical skull was chosen mainly for its location on Iona, Davis chose his for phrenological reasons, 'the indications of wild passions operating on the muscles of expression' and its 'savage character'.[90] In *Crania Britannica,* Davis and Thurnam identified a handful of specimens, all excavated in England, as being typically British, though these skulls belonged to the Stone Age and were not seen necessarily as Celtic.[91] Davis rejected Wilson's postulated racial sequence for Britain and argued that more crania must be studied in order to separate general trends from local variation. *Crania Britannica* was created mainly to satisfy this need.

Wilson learned of Davis' work on crania in 1852 and suggested that the physician make a general study of British crania with the title *Crania Britannica*, echoing Samuel Morton's *Crania Americana* and potentially encompassing more of Britain's past than Davis' proposed *Crania Celtica*.[92] With financial help from the Royal Society, Davis and Thurnam began publishing this study in 1856 and completed the work with the sixth instalment in 1865. While the study only included 56 skulls, which was not substantially more than the 39 Wilson examined, it was noteworthy for including life-sized illustrations of the skulls with detailed descriptions of each. The work was divided into two parts, the first volume including analyses of British ethnology and the second containing the illustrations and descriptions. Davis and Thurnam supplied separate chapters and each examined a different set of skulls.

With two authors working in parallel and publication spread out over a decade, this work had a fragmentary quality, contributing to its lack of any firm conclusion about the ancient British past. Davis' review, in Chapter II, of what the day's major ethnologists had to say about Celtic crania, made it clear that this lack of a conclusion also derived from the general disarray in craniology. Though the authors viewed skull shape as 'not transmutable in the different Races', there was no agreement among ethnologists as to which shapes corresponded with which races.[93] Davis did not go much further than to characterise Celts as '*truly native*, much more remotely than any history can ascend' in contrast to the 'entirely intrusive' Teutonic race.[94] He did tentatively suggest that long barrows tended to contain longer, dolichocephalic, crania – but with the qualification that Britain's racial past was always somewhat mixed and that deformities confused the picture.[95] Thurnam, meanwhile, had more confidence in the notion that a dolichocephalic Stone Age race was replaced by a brachycephalic Bronze Age one, and presented this idea to the Anthropological Society of London: long barrows, the earlier interment class, corresponded with long heads; round barrows, the later class, went with round heads.[96] In light of the confusion, both authors agreed that further study and collection were necessary, the goal being the identification of pure types.

Despite the primary interest of Thurnam and Davis in the evidence of skull forms in ethnology, both included multi-source ethnological analyses of the British past in *Crania Britannica*. Thurnam conceived of his chapter on the 'Historical Ethnology of Britain' as among the first attempts to treat British ethnology 'in its combined historical, antiquarian, and philological aspects'.[97] Davis took a multi-source approach to the term *Celtic*, which he recognised was 'applied by the ancient authors to Gaul in its entirety' and not to Britain, although 'the term Celtae has been further applied to the aborigines of these Islands' because 'they adjoined what was called Celtica,

in this larger sense, and used a similar speech'.[98] The two did not view craniology as a departure from linguistic research, but conceived of their work as
being an ingredient in the general science of ethnology, with *Crania
Britannica* their attempt at a synthesis.

Debates in Ethnology

Despite the growing interest in physical ethnology and the three-age system, there was a large degree of resistance to the new methods. The system's detractors, led by Thomas Wright, opposed the idea of the three ages
on the grounds that it was a generalisation not supported by enough evidence.[99] Aside from being committed Baconians who viewed archaeology
as best used 'hand-in-hand with history', the detractors were probably hesitant to adopt the system because both Thomsen's and Worsaae's published
accounts were brief, unsupported by more than cursory evidence and
appeared more as assertions than conclusions drawn from extensive examinations of finds.[100] Also, many antiquaries misunderstood the system,
wrongly thinking that it assigned objects to different ages solely on the
basis of the material of manufacture. Until the publication of John
Lubbock's *Pre-Historic Times* in 1865, there was not a sufficiently strong
argument for the three-age system in print for it to capture the over-
whelming support of many antiquaries and thereby solidify the new interpretation that the Celts were Bronze Age invaders. In the intervening time,
the system's adherents and detractors both thought of their work as relevant to ethnology, with the central difference being their varying emphasis
on historical and craniological evidence.[101]

Another reason for the variable reception to the Scandinavian approach
related to differing interpretations of the capabilities of the Celts. While
Wilson had described all of Scotland's racial sequence as 'abundantly capable of civilization', Wright characterised Celts as 'serfs, without civil
influence or even civil rights; the mere slaves of superior orders'.[102] In this
debate, the craniologists were supported by numismatists, many of whom
were members of the same archaeological societies as the barrow-diggers.
The growing acceptance of the existence of pre-Roman coinage made
more credible the notion that the Celts, whom craniologists placed in the
Bronze Age, were familiar with metal technology. It also 'heightened'
numismatists' 'national feeling' in recognising achievements of the early
Britons.[103] Among prominent pre-Roman numismatists, John Yonge
Akerman, Secretary of the Numismatic Society, defeated Wright for the position of Secretary of the Society of Antiquaries in 1848. Akerman overcame

initial reservations to argue strongly for the existence of pre–Roman coinage, and, by the mid 1840s, the Numismatic Society had formed an Ancient Numismatics section.[104] Akerman had allies in C.J. Thomsen himself, in the British Museum's Keeper of Antiquities, Edward Hawkins, who used the existence of ancient British coinage as a reason to open a room dedicated to British antiquities in 1851, and in the prominent fellow of the Society of Antiquaries, John Evans, who studied coins to challenge ancient sources.[105] Collectively, the activities of numismatists supported an institutional structure and intellectual climate in which archaeological research into prehistoric Britain could flourish.

Among craniologists too, there were challenges to the interpretation that the Celts were part of a Bronze Age civilisation. In addition to the prehistorians using the three-age system, craniology provided a home for anti-Celt racists, who did not subscribe to Prichard's monogenism. One of the earliest and most radical of the polygenist craniologists was Robert Knox, who revived his reputation – tainted by the 'resurrectionist' scandal – by citing the revolutions of 1848 as proof of his theories about the inevitability of conflict in mixed-race countries. Knox, primarily interested in colonial peoples, discussed their subjugation and slavery in terms of their supposed biological inferiority. He treated the 'Irish Celts' as inferior colonial subjects and attributed the anti-British agitation of the 1840s to the irreconcilability between Celt and Saxon.[106] While Knox's own work was too controversial for the ethnological mainstream, his extreme form of polygenism did have some supporters among ethnologists and archaeologists in the 1850s.[107]

Among the ethnologists Knox influenced was James Hunt, who played an instrumental role in precipitating a bitter split between liberal-minded, monogenist ethnology and his brand of polygenist, racialist physical anthropology. Hunt's group broke from the Ethnological Society in 1863 to form the Anthropological Society of London. The new society established a journal, *The Anthropological Review*, which, though mainly racialist in content, was open to printing opposing viewpoints. Thurnam was among the first British craniological ethnologists to use the forum to express increasingly racist views of different past races' cranial capacities, echoing ideas developing on the Continent.[108]

Wilson, meanwhile, countered this trend by sending the journal a major critique of the excessive claims of craniologists.[109] Wilson's essay revolved around two main points: he rejected the notion, then supported by Thurnam, that racial sequences show that more technologically advanced races had larger brains, writing, 'Neither history nor definite archaeology, moreover, confirms any such "natural order"', and in a departure from his earlier work, he rejected the notion that racial skull types ever existed, writing, 'A type is an ideal abstraction embracing the mean of many variations, and is not to be determined by the selection of one or two characteristic examples'.[110] Wilson had abandoned the idea of racial types by the 1863 publication of the second edition of *Prehistoric Annals*, when he lost his confidence in being able to identify 'the form of the typical Celtic cranium' and criticised the Museum of the Phrenological Society of Edinburgh for labelling a cast skull as 'the Celtic type', though he felt that 'the era of the race [of the Celts], and its order in point of time, are well known'.[111] Part of Wilson's criticism on these points came from the tendency of polygenist anthropologists, and some of the early ethnologists who preceded them, to define Celts in terms of stereotyped notions, rather than scientific theories: 'The controversies, moreover, of which the term *Celtic* has furnished the key-note, were long embittered by the narrowest spirit of national prejudices, and exposed thereby to well-merited ridicule'.[112]

Though Wilson took issue with the direction craniology had taken in the Anthropological Society, he did not temper his faith in 'physical ethnology', which by the 1860s had 'received an amount of attention in some degree commensurate with its importance'.[113] He felt this was a vindication of his radical proposal in 1850 that there had been a pre-Celtic race in Britain. Wilson still believed, 'that the form of the human skull is essentially distinctive of race', with the difficulty lying in identifying 'the ethnical significance of form, proportions, prognathism or orthognathism, and other characteristic diversities'.[114] The absence of a consensus about the head shapes of the different races, compounded by the problem of ancient skulls possibly representing mixed races, led Wilson, under the influence of Gustaf Kombst, to measure living people's head sizes as a way to help sort out the confusion. From his base in Canada, Wilson continued to collect craniological data, first by visiting world skull collections at the Smithsonian Institution and the Academy of Natural Sciences in Philadelphia (which held the Morton collection) and then by conducting surveys of the hat sizes of Canadian immigrants from Great Britain and France, working out whether they were Celtic or Saxon on the basis of their last names.[115] This survey led him to confirm the opinion of the majority of craniologists, with the notable exceptions of Nilsson and Davis, that the Celts were dolichocephalic.[116] Wilson's method of measuring living populations in order to distinguish the different races thought to have arrived in Britain at different times had already been taken up by the Scottish antiquary John Beddoe, but it did not become more widespread until later in the century.[117]

As Wilson's changing views illustrate, through the use of innovative methods, craniology in the 1860s survived both the elusiveness of identifying racial types and its possible stigmatisation as a racist science thanks to the growing prominence of polygenist physical anthropologists. And despite the departure of the more fervent racialists into the Anthropological Society, craniology remained an important aspect of the activities of the Ethnological Society in the years after the split. In 1871, when the two societies merged as the Anthropological Institute of Great Britain and Ireland, archaeology and physical anthropology were at the forefront of the organisation's activities.

Lubbock

The controversies of the 1860s about the usefulness of craniology and the place of the Celts in Britain's racial sequence, were, to a large degree, settled by John Lubbock, albeit with the qualification that more evidence was needed to confirm the results. A prominent evolutionist and neighbour of Darwin, Lubbock became president of the Ethnological Society upon Hunt's departure, just two years before the publication of his 1865 *Pre-Historic Times*, which combined the three-age interpretation of craniological ethnology with the new understanding of the great antiquity of humanity into a program of prehistoric archaeology. Lubbock's use of craniology, like Wilson's, eschewed the racialism of Knox and Hunt, and it lacked the 'moral' dimension of their anatomical program. His emphasis on using ancient crania to understand past racial sequences, however, became part of mainstream ethnology and anthropology thanks to the unmatched pre-eminence of *Pre-Historic Times* in the next half century.

In addition to the three-age system, the establishment of human antiquity in 1859 provided the key impetus to *Pre-Historic Times*. This revolution in thinking about the age of humanity had a tremendous impact on broader ethnological issues and brought about the final collapse of the biblical chronological framework, yet it had little bearing on the particular question of the peopling of Britain. Brixham Cave, in Devonshire, convinced members of the Royal Society that humans coexisted with extinct animals, meaning that humans had been in Britain thousands of years before any postulated Celtic migrations, but British ethnologists simply accommodated these early Britons within the notion of pre-Celtic Allophylians. For John Evans, Joseph Prestwich and others who studied the Brixham stone tools 'from an antiquarian rather than a geological point of view,' the tools were viewed as pre-Celtic, while 'the so-called Celtic period' was seen as coming later, with the introduction of polished stone tools and more advanced technologies.[118] Celtic ethnologists, then, could continue their research program with little change. For example, Daniel Wilson's model of the peopling of Britain in his 1863 edition of *Prehistoric Annals of Scotland* differed little from that of 1851, except in allowing much longer periods of prehistoric occupation.[119]

Lubbock's *Pre-Historic Times* was a landmark volume for a host of reasons beyond his influential treatment of the three-age system in the context of deep human antiquity. It set out to establish prehistoric archaeology as a discipline, it coined the words 'Palaeolithic' and 'Neolithic' to describe two periods of the Stone Age, it incorporated evolutionary ideas into the three-age framework and it drew extensively on ethnographic parallels to illustrate human technological development. Its discussion of the three ages and the peopling of Europe, however, shows a great deal of continuity with the craniological ethnology that developed in the previous 20 years. The first six chapters of the book amounted to an extended argument for using the three-age system as an ethnological tool. This was the first such argument to appear in print since Thomsen's and Worsaae's frankly cursory arguments for the system were translated in the late 1840s. In addressing the question of which races corresponded to the different Ages, Lubbock followed his ethnological predecessors in seeing the issue as unresolved until further collections could be made.[120]

Lubbock's argument for the three-age system revolved around the existence of the Bronze Age, which he supported with 'the testimony of the most ancient writers' as well as 'the evidence of the objects themselves', which were almost always found in caches segregated by type of metal.[121] He further supported the notion of a separate Bronze Age with the observation, 'The handles of the bronze swords are very short, and could not have been held comfortably by hands as large as ours, a characteristic much relied on by those who attribute the introduction of bronze into Europe to a people of Asiatic origin'.[122] Lubbock devoted the second chapter of *Pre-Historic Times* to a discussion of the nature of the Stone-Bronze transition. Notwithstanding the small-handled swords, Lubbock saw the Bronze Age as an intrusion of a possibly Indo-European race. Like Prichard, Wilson, Davis and Thurnam, he thought the resolution of the issue depended on further collection of crania:

> The form of the head would also be very instructive; but owing to the unfortunate habit of burning the dead which prevailed at that period, we have, as yet, very few skulls which can safely be referred to the Bronze age,

and, on the whole, we must admit that, for the present, the evidence is not sufficient to justify us in expressing any very definite opinion as to the source of the Bronze age civilization.[123]

Once he had established the existence of a Bronze Age, Lubbock could argue persuasively that stone assemblages were not simply the tools of poor or primitive people, but dated to an earlier technological age and to 'ruder races of men'.[124] He began his discussion of Stone Age peoples with an examination of their grave goods and modes of interment. He seems to have seen this as an incomplete and outdated method, however, and looked to skeletal evidence:

> Eventually, no doubt, the human remains themselves, and especially the skulls, will prove our best guides; but at present we do not possess a sufficient number of trustworthy descriptions or measurements, to justify us in drawing any generalisation from them, excepting, perhaps, this, that the skulls found with bronze in some cases closely resemble those discovered in graves containing only stone implements; from which we may infer that, even if the use of bronze was introduced by a new and more civilised race, the ancient inhabitants were probably not altogether exterminated.[125]

Though Lubbock had not yet ascertained whether the Bronze Age represented a complete replacement or merely the intrusion of new people, he generally followed the Scandinavian model of the three ages, in which the Celts arrived at the end of the Stone Age. He qualified this model, however, with appeals to more evidence and by offering the possibility that there were many different races during the long and apparently varied Stone Age:

> As regards the pre-historic races of men we have as yet derived but little definite information from the examination of tumuli. The evidence, however, appears to show that the Celts were not the earliest colonisers of Northern Europe. Putting on one side the mysterious 'kumbecephalic' skulls [identified by Wilson] which have been already alluded to, the men of the Stone age in Northern Europe appear to have been brachycephalic in a very marked degree, and to have had heavy, overhanging brows. Many ethnologists are inclined to believe that the Turanian race, now represented in Europe by the Fins, Lapps, and probably the Basques, once occupied the greater part of our continent, which was, however, even before the beginning of history, wrested from them by the Celts and the Teutons.[126]

With the publication of *Pre-Historic Times*, the Scandinavian three-age system and craniological approach to sorting out a racial sequence reached the forefront of British archaeology. The book marked the culmination of a shift from Prichard's mainly linguistic brand of ethnology to the craniological emphasis of the prehistorians. This change was accompanied by a new conception of the place of the Celts in the British past. Prichard had seen the Celts as Britain's first inhabitants, while the prehistorians viewed them as Bronze Age invaders in the context of a more complex racial past, in which simple replacements had to be distinguished from mixing. The more racialist craniologists, like Thurnam, interpreted each of the three ages as replacements of existing races by intrusive ones. Most researchers favoured the notion of mixing, especially because it helped explain the observed variety of ancient crania. While the craniologists debated Britain's racial history and the very shapes of the crania of different races, an alternative definition of the Celts emerged from the work of archaeologists studying non-skeletal remains, leading to the identification of a Celtic art style.

CHAPTER VII

CELTIC ART

The Identification of Celtic Art

Today, most of us can confidently identify Celtic art. The familiar interlace designs, stylised animals and human heads are described as Celtic, not just in specialist books, but in design manuals and even tourist art. As we look back to the middle of the nineteenth century, it can be tempting to see the first identification of Celtic art simply as the discovery of objects with these designs. But as we have seen in our story so far, there were many definitions of the Celts in circulation at this time: Bronze Age invaders, a primitive early people, speakers of particular languages and a race with distinct physical traits. When objects with what we now call Celtic art were appearing with increasing frequency in excavations from the 1840s onwards, their age and geographical extent were not yet known, and interpretations took place within existing models of the British past.

The study of Celtic art first arose within ethnology and contributed to discussions of Celtic migrations in that discipline. With the application of the study of style to the ethnology of the Celts, a new interpretation appeared in which the Celts were an Iron Age people, rather than a Bronze Age one, because much Celtic art appears on iron implements. Ultimately, this investigation led to the idea, still current in the popular imagination, that the Celts were an Iron Age people with Bronze Age roots. By the end of the nineteenth century, the study of Celtic art contributed to a new, non-ethnological research program which examined the development of culture and civilisation, rather than simple movements of peoples. This approach to ancient artefacts was an essential ingredient in the development of modern archaeology, and the study of Celtic art played a prominent role in this transformation.

The British Museum

In the mid nineteenth century, a combination of fresh discoveries and the formation of new museum collections presented researchers with the problem of creating categorisation schemes for a growing amount of ancient material. These researchers, based mainly in museums but with ties to archaeological societies and the British Association, borrowed racial categories from ethnology and connected these races with distinctive types of artefacts and art styles. One of the earliest institutions, if not the very first, in which this process unfolded was Britain's national museum, which was nearing its 100th anniversary.

Before the 1850s, the British Museum housed almost no domestic antiquities, with the exception of a room that Edward Hawkins had set up to satisfy his numismatic interests. In this decade, however, two curators, Samuel Birch and Augustus Wollaston Franks, both members of the Society of Antiquaries and the Archaeological Institute, campaigned to use the museum as a storehouse for British material from all ages. Birch joined the museum in 1836 and soon became Assistant Keeper of the Department of Antiquities. He was primarily an Egyptologist, but his duties brought him in contact with an assortment of objects in the fairly generalised department. In the 1840s, Birch developed an interest in 'Celtic antiquities', culminating in the reorganisation of the Museum's Department of Antiquities upon Hawkins' retirement in 1860.[1] In 1861, Birch became Keeper of the Oriental, British and Medieval sections. In 1866, he devoted his energies to the Oriental section, which included Egyptology, and handed the British and Medieval sections to Franks. In Birch's program, tracing the spread of art styles could compensate for the perceived limitations of linguistic models of the peopling of Britain. He outlined this strategy in two papers to the Archaeological Institute in 1846, in which he based his notion of Celtic art on recent finds in Ireland as well as on classical accounts:

> In investigating the history of our Celtic ancestors, we can place but little reliance on the traditions which have descended to us respecting them, traditions enveloped in doubt, which mere philological inquiry cannot satisfactorily resolve, and in the absence of better evidence, their remains are the chief tests of their social condition, and the place to which they are entitled among the past races of mankind. Thus the question arises, whether the art-remains of the Celts are sufficient to enable us to fix the position which that people occupied in the scale of nations?[2]

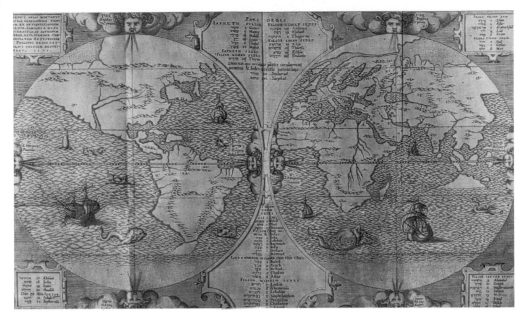

1 Map of the peopling of the world based on Berosus. Benedictus Arias Montanus, *Sacred Geography*, 1571

2 John White drawing of an 'Ancient British Man' inspired by his drawings of native Americans. © *The British Museum*

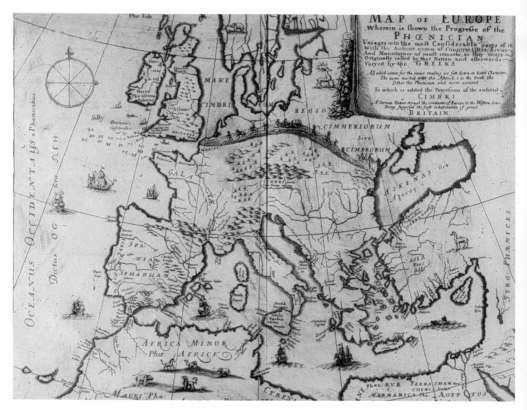

3 Map of the peopling of Britain that features Phoenicians arriving by boat and people crossing Europe on a track. Aylett Sammes, *Britannia Antiqua Illustrata*, 1676

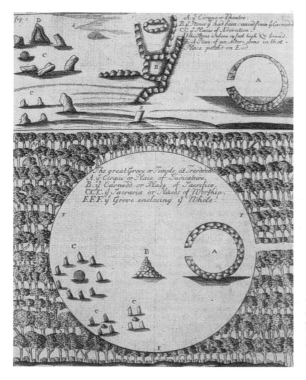

4 and 5 (Left and opposite) 4 Illustration of a megalithic monument surrounded by an oak grove. 5 A Druid. Henry Rowlands, *Mona Antiqua Restaurata*, 1723.© *Society of Antiquaries*

Dna. A: M. Delin. *The Chief Druid* from a Statue.

6 Drawing dated 1721 that is the earliest confirmed reference to material remains in Britain as Celtic. William Stukeley, *Abury*, 1743. © *Society of Antiquaries*

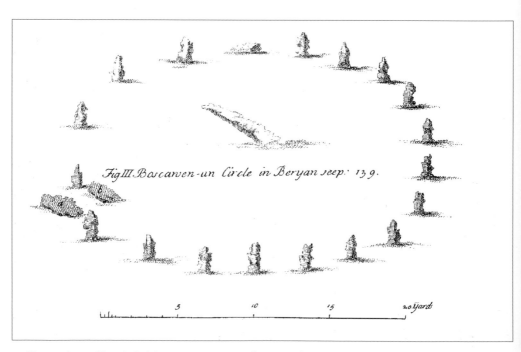

7 Illustration of local Celtic monuments. William Borlase, *Observations on the Antiquities Historical and Monumental, of the County of Cornwall*, 1754. © *Society of Antiquaries*

8 An imaginative view of a Druidical ceremony at Stonehenge. Samuel Rush Meyrick and Charles Hamilton Smith, *The Costume of the Original Inhabitants of the British Islands*, 1815. © *Society of Antiquaries*

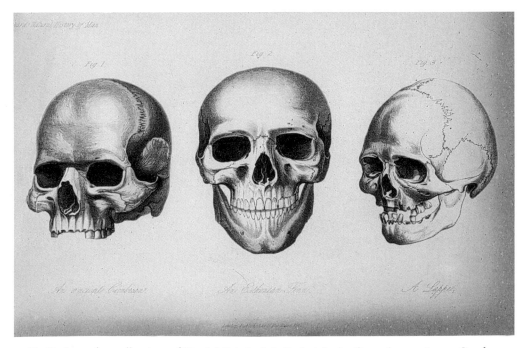

9 Skulls from the collection of Daniel Friederich Eschricht in Copenhagen. James Cowles Prichard, *Researches*, 1841

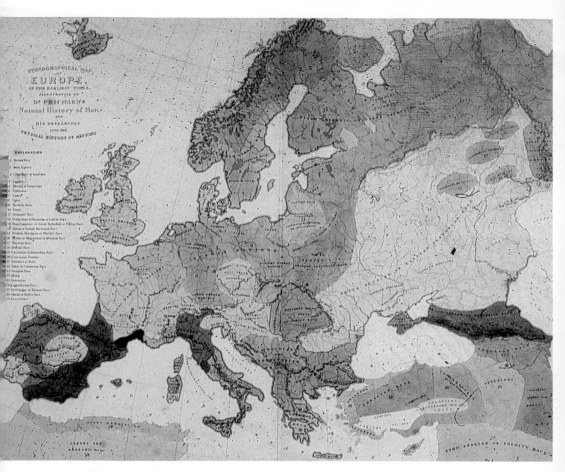

10 An Ethnological Map. James Cowles Prichard, *Natural History of Man*, 1843

11 (Opposite) A 'typical' Briton. Joseph Barnard Davis and John Thurnam, *Crania Britannica*, 1856–65

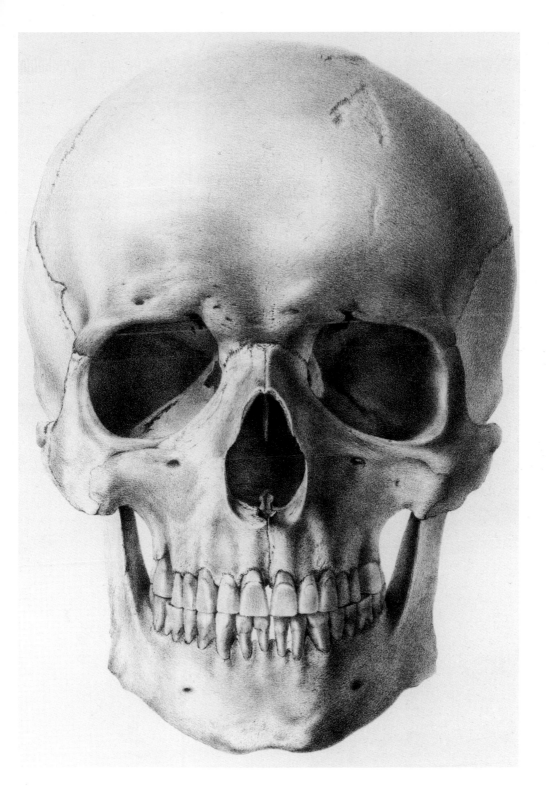

DETAIL OF ORNAMENT ON THE TARA BROOCH
IN THE DUBLIN MUSEUM

DETAIL OF ORNAMENT ON THE TARA BROOCH
IN THE DUBLIN MUSEUM

12 Detail of the Tara Brooch. John Romilly Allen, *Celtic Art in Pagan and Christian Times*, 1904. © *Society of Antiquaries*

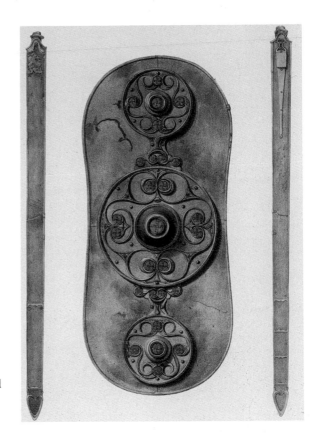

13 The Battersea Shield. John Kemble, Robert Gordon Latham and Augustus Wollaston Franks, *Horae Ferales*, 1863. © *Society of Antiquaries*

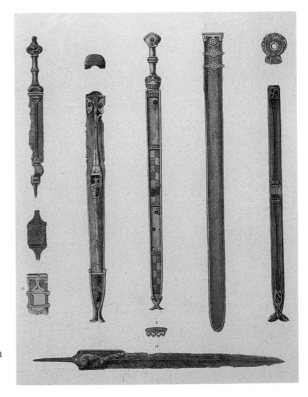

14 Examples of 'Late Celtic' swords. John Kemble, Robert Gordon Latham and Augustus Wollaston Franks, *Horae Ferales*, 1863. © *Society of Antiquaries*

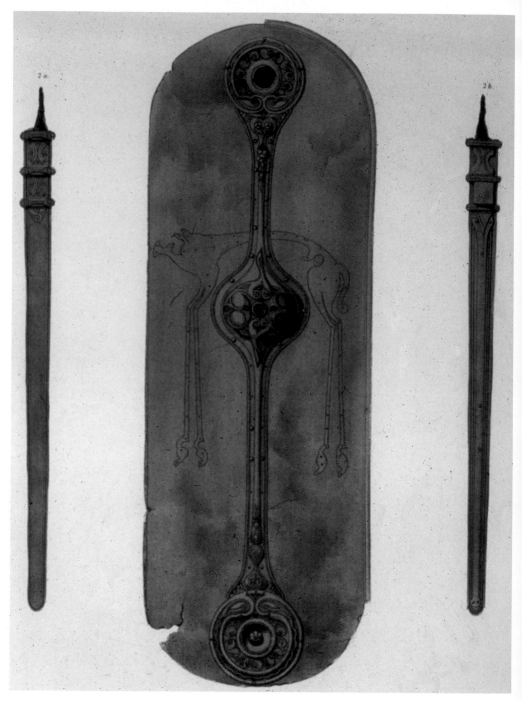

15 Shield and sword from the River Witham. John Kemble, Robert Gordon Latham and Augustus Wollaston Franks, *Horae Ferales*, 1863. © *Society of Antiquaries*

PL LXXV

MARIN *Iron.*

16 Swords from La Tène. Ferdinand Keller, *The Lake Dwellings of Switzerland and Other Parts of Europe*, 1866. © *Society of Antiquaries*

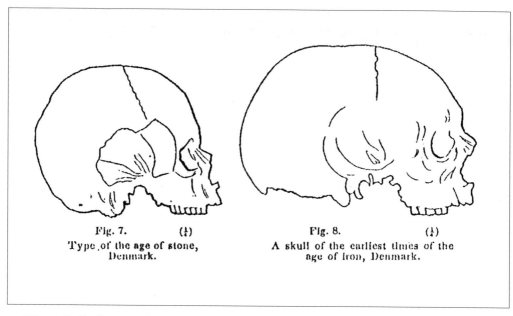

Fig. 7. (⅟)
Type of the age of stone,
Denmark.

Fig. 8. (⅟)
A skull of the earliest times of the
age of iron, Denmark.

17 These skulls illustrate the racist interpretation of the three-age system, with smaller brains correlating with earlier epochs. Adophe von Morlot, 'General Views on Archaeology', 1861

18 Bronze object illustrative of Celtic art from Scotland. Joseph Anderson, *Scotland in Pagan Times: The Iron Age*, 1883. © *Society of Antiquaries*

Symbols.	Class I.	Class II.	Totals.	Symbols.	Class I.	Class II.	Totals.
[symbol]	40	19	59	[symbol]	6	4	10
[symbol]	27	22	49	[symbol]	8	2	10
[symbol]	31	13	44	[symbol]	7	2	9
[symbol]	15	18	33	[symbol]	...	8	8
[symbol]	4	10	14	[symbol]	8	...	8
[symbol]	8	5	13	[symbol]	3	4	7
[symbol]	7	5	12	[symbol]	3	4	7
[symbol]	10	2	12	[symbol]	6	...	6
[symbol]	11	...	11	[symbol]	5	1	6
[symbol]	3	8	11	[symbol]	2	3	5
[symbol]	4	6	10	[symbol]	...	4	4

19 Table showing Anderson's typological approach to Celtic art. Joseph Anderson, *The Early Christian Monuments of Scotland*, 1903. © *Society of Antiquaries*

BRONZE ARMLET OF THE LA TÈNE PERIOD FROM GERMANY

BRONZE ARMLET OF THE LA TÈNE PERIOD
FROM LONGIROD (VAUD)

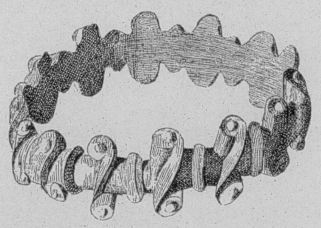

BRONZE ARMLET OF THE LA TÈNE PERIOD
FROM THE CEMETERIES OF THE MARNE

20 Examples of La Tène metalwork. John Romilly Allen, *Celtic Art in Pagan and Christian Times*, 1904. © *Society of Antiquaries*

VIEW, FROM THE S.W., OF THE RADIATING TIMBERS FOUND BETWEEN FLOORS Iii AND iv,
AT THE WEST END OF MOUND XIII.

21 Arthur Bulleid and Harold St George Gray, *The Glastonbury Lake Village*, 1911. © *Society of Antiquaries*

22 Arthur Evans,'On a
Late-Celtic Urn-Field at
Aylesford', 1890

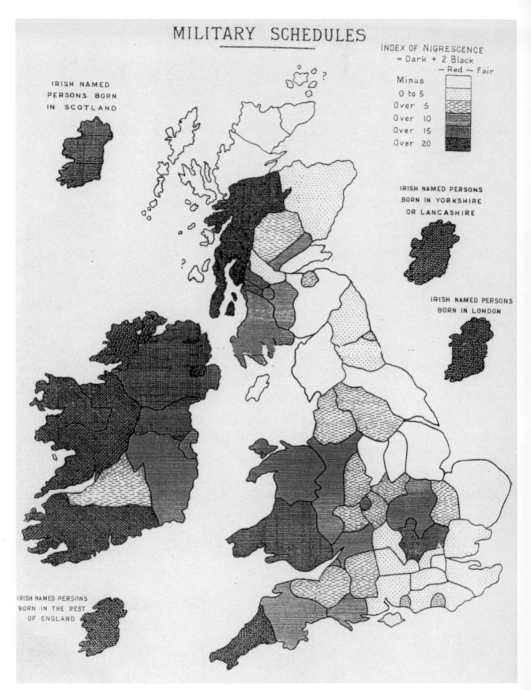

MILITARY SCHEDULES

INDEX OF NIGRESCENCE
= Dark + 2 Black
− Red − Fair

Minus
0 to 5
Over 5
Over 10
Over 15
Over 20

IRISH NAMED
PERSONS BORN
IN SCOTLAND

IRISH NAMED PERSONS
BORN IN YORKSHIRE
OR LANCASHIRE

IRISH NAMED PERSONS
BORN IN LONDON

IRISH NAMED PERSONS
BORN IN THE REST
OF ENGLAND

23 John Beddoe, *The Races of Britain*, 1885. Map of the British Isles showing the results of his physical anthropological surveys where he compiled an index of nigrescence. He found darker skin and eye colours the farther west he looked, with the exception of 'Irish named persons' in Great Britain (which were darker) and in northern Scotland, where more recent migrations from Scandinavia were thought to have led to a lighter-skinned population

This was probably the first ever reference to Celtic art in print. Birch did not follow up on his preliminary work on Celtic 'art-remains', however, and instead turned his attention to the Egyptian collection. The program Birch outlined was slowly taken up by Franks, who joined the British Museum in 1851 when Hawkins opened his mind to collecting pre-Roman artefacts after recognising the numismatists' claim that ancient Britons had coins. Franks' antiquarian interests dated to his years at Trinity College, Cambridge (1845-9), where he was a founding member of the Cambridge Architectural Society and a member of the Cambridge Antiquarian Society. Franks soon developed a good reputation in the antiquarian community and compiled exhibition catalogues in London after his graduation in 1849; the first was for an exhibition on stained glass.[3] More important was his catalogue for the Royal Society of Art's Medieval Exhibition of 1850. While preparing this catalogue, Franks contacted key members of the Society of Antiquaries like the Earl of Ellesmere, John Yonge Akerman, William Thoms and James Talbot – all committed to the three-age system.[4] His success with this project led directly to his appointment to the British Museum in 1851. In the catalogue, Franks highlighted two primary purposes of an exhibition on ancient art: first, the art supplied means 'of correcting the taste and refining the judgment', and, second, 'to the Archaeologist, materials are presented for observation and study; the very facts and *data* upon which his science is founded are spread out before him'.[5] Franks synthesised the movement, exemplified by the Cambridge Camden Society, to study ancient art in order to refine taste, with the newer movement in archaeology, spurred by the adoption of the three-age system, to study ancient art as a part of a scientific investigation of the past.

At the same time that the three-age system provided researchers with a chronological tool for studying antiquities, a movement in Anglo-Saxon research sought to use antiquities in order to establish the geographical extent of past peoples. Charles Roach Smith, co-founder of the British Archaeological Association, spearheaded this movement by extending to the regional level James Douglas' method of trying to assign burials to different peoples. Roach Smith's innovation was to put together an enormous catalogue of antiquities from different areas throughout Britain and the Continent, resulting in a picture not just of Anglo-Saxon art, but of regional differences within that category. From 1848, he published descriptions of this material in an eight-volume set titled *Collectanea Antiqua*. When Roach Smith, Wright and others sought to house such material in the British Museum in order to carry out their regional program, they failed to convince its Trustees of the value of the scientific study of artefacts. The Trustees' refusal in 1854 to accept Bryan Faussett's Anglo-Saxon collection, the largest and most important of its kind, underscored their resistance to objects unrelated to classical art. Nevertheless, Franks was sympathetic to Roach Smith's project and worked to enlarge the British collection through the 1850s. Eventually, Roach Smith's regional approach to Anglo-Saxon art influenced the Saxonist John Kemble and served as a blueprint for Franks' work on Celtic art.

Franks started his work on British materials in 1851, when Hawkins asked him to organise a new room for domestic antiquities. In Franks' description of the British collection, he noted the dearth of objects from 'those obscurer periods of our history, known as the stone and bronze periods', and highlighted the museum's deficiency in 'Celtic pottery'.[6] It is unclear from this account how he thought Celtic remains fitted into the three-age system, but it seems from his next report on the museum's British collection, which he described as being of 'Primeval and Celtic antiquities', that, like the craniologists, he thought that 'Celtic art' dated to the latter parts of the sequence.[7] In an 1855 article on bronze weapons from the Isle of Wight, however, Franks argued that such weapons were indigenous and ancient, and he did not assign them to any of the 'different tribes and even races' that had passed through Europe.[8] It seems that he was reluctant to extend evidence of Celts to 'that vast and obscure portion of our history unrelieved by any written records'.[9] A few years earlier, when Akerman had assigned 'the more primitive weapon' of the Bronze Age to Celtic tribes, he had turned to classical texts to support the point, highlighting the importance of historical evidence for relating artefacts to the Celts.[10] Franks did not substantially refine his own placement of the Celts within the three ages until the late 1850s, after a number of crucial discoveries and exhibitions which drew together large quantities of finds.

Irish Exhibitions

The discovery of impressive artefacts near Tara in Ireland in the late 1830s provided a key catalyst for the development of the idea of a Celtic art style. These finds provided Birch with some of his material for his 1846 study of Celtic art.[11] In 1850, the most famous of the finds was an early medieval penannular brooch found near Drogheda. It was acquired by the Dublin jewellery firm, Waterhouse and Co., which named it the 'Tara Brooch' because of Tara's association with early Christian Gaelic legends, and began selling mass-produced copies (*pl. 12*). Waterhouse sent the brooch to various exhibitions, including the Great Exhibition of 1851, where Queen Victoria bought two copies for herself, giving prominence to the style in London fashion.

As this art style was receiving public attention, it started to be identified with the Celts, thanks to a number of exhibitions and conferences in Ireland in the 1850s. In 1852, the Belfast Natural History and Philosophical Society prepared a catalogue of antiquities on the occasion of the Belfast meeting of the British Association.[12] The catalogue seems to have been created in order to introduce Irish antiquities into ethnological discussions of the earliest races to inhabit Great Britain and Ireland. Papers on antiquities had only rarely been accepted at the ethnological meetings of British Association conferences, while craniology and linguistics dominated discussions of the peopling of Britain and Ireland.[13] The Belfast catalogue, meanwhile, urged visitors 'to judge for themselves of the nature and extent of our ancient civilization' and employed the three-age system as an aid to drawing comparisons between Irish and other European materials.[14] For the authors, 'large quantities' of finds in Ireland from as far back as the Stone Age were taken as evidence 'that they were very anciently manufactured by the Celtic tribes of Britain and Ireland'.[15] In other words, in 1852, despite William Wilde's craniological work placing the Celts in the Bronze Age, many still considered ancient Ireland to have been unmixed and Celtic, making the identification of Celtic artefacts relatively straightforward.

In the following year, the embarrassing absence of a comprehensive antiquities display at the Dublin International Exposition motivated the Royal Irish Academy to consolidate its antiquarian holdings, which had long been considered illustrative of 'the habits and history of the Celtic tribes'.[16] The Academy commissioned George Petrie, whose work on round towers made him one of the leading Irish antiquaries of the mid nineteenth century, to write a catalogue for the new museum. Since Worsaae's visit to the Academy in 1846, Petrie had been a convert to the three-age system and organised his own collection according to the principle. He never completed the catalogue, however, and the task fell to Wilde, who finished the first volume in time for the Dublin meeting of the British Association in 1857.

For Wilde, the British Association meeting provided an opportunity to introduce ethnologists to the unique characteristics of Ireland's past. He accomplished this through the completion of the catalogue and by conducting a group of about 70 conference attendees to the Aran Islands off Ireland's west coast. Wilde chose Aran because he was trying to establish the

Islands as an Irish tourist attraction that could rival Scotland's Iona. He set up a banquet in the ruins of 'the great Firbolgic fort of Dun Aengus' and, in his after-dinner speech, spoke of the location as 'the last standing-place of the Firbolg aborigines of Ireland, here to fight their last battle if driven to the western surge'.[17] In his 1844 speech on craniology, Wilde had considered the Firbolgs and Tuatha de Dannan, two supposedly Greek tribes known through the bardic tradition, to have been the earliest inhabitants of Ireland.[18] In addition to the romantic aspects of a banquet in a cliffside ancient fort, the dinner at Dun Aengus had a patriotic theme in that Wilde seems to have been drawing a parallel between the Irish 'aborigines' defending themselves from foreign aggressors and modern ethnographers studying the Irish past to remember aboriginal culture.

In his catalogue, Wilde did not classify the Academy's materials by means of the three-age system. Instead, he used material and type of artefact as his ordering criteria. This categorisation nevertheless lent itself to a three-age interpretation, and Wilde reaffirmed his long-standing view that there had been a gradual transition to metal tools and that iron was the last metal to be discovered.[19] In contrast to Wilde's earlier ethnological work, he had now turned primarily to types of monuments and art styles to trace ancient migrations.

When Wilde traced the spread of 'the Celtic race' in his 1857 catalogue, he connected the ancient Irish with source points in Great Britain and on the Continent through the established method of looking at the locations of Druidical temples.[20] He added to this increasingly outdated method, however, by tracing racial movements through the study of artefact styles. In discussing funerary urns, he wrote, 'The varieties exhibited by these urns may be characteristic of peculiar races, tribes, or persons, or expressive of their cost and value, or of the art of the day'.[21] Wilde's 1857 catalogue, however, did not treat objects of metal, the material most closely identified with Celtic art. In 1861, when he published the catalogue's second volume, which dealt with animal remains and bronze, he further explored the possibilities of tracing peoples through art objects:

> Traditional notions respecting the aboriginal inhabitants of Ireland are to be found in early Irish history [...] Numerous extravagant reports are there given; but of the actual habits or arts of the primeval people of Ireland, we really know nothing, except what may be gleaned from their monuments, and those remains preserved in the Museum of our Academy, and other similar antiquarian collections [...]

Writers on the primeval arts of different nations have left unnoticed those characteristic of the Celtic Irish people, in Pagan and very early Christian times, except such as belong to the architecture, stone tracery, and shrine decoration of the latter period. The abundant supply afforded by the remains of the former epoch in the carvings on the Pagan sepulchres of New Grange, Dowth, and other similar monuments; the various decorations on cinerary urns, and the ornamentation on our earliest metal articles of either gold or bronze, have as yet been overlooked.[22]

Wilde went on to examine swords, brooches and other metal artefacts, mostly in terms of their Celtic character. In identifying a Celtic art style, he cited a seminal speech that John Kemble had delivered on the topic to the Royal Irish Academy in 1857 when preparing for another museum exhibition.[23]

The Production of Horae Ferales

John Kemble, a student of Jacob Grimm, turned to the study of antiquities from Anglo-Saxon philology while living in Hanover in the 1850s. Through his contacts with Roach Smith, Wright and Akerman, he had become interested in identifying Anglo-Saxon objects on the Continent on the principle that 'there is some reason in every ornament why it recommended itself to some particular people'.[24] Kemble's main research problem in Hanover was the politically explosive one of separating grave goods among German, Slavic and Celtic peoples.[25] At first he had difficulty in distinguishing German and Slavic designs, though he did attribute 'the wheel of the war-chariot' to Iron Age Celts.[26] In 1855, however, he wrote two important papers outlining characteristic Anglo-Saxon grave goods.[27] He soon applied this method to the question of what constituted Celtic designs.

Kemble focused on the question of Celtic antiquities as part of his preparations for the Art Treasures Exhibition in Manchester in 1857. The exhibition organisers had commissioned him to create a major display on 'Early British, Celtic and Anglo-Saxon remains' in its Ornamental Art section, finding the topic 'perhaps, the most complete and interesting portion'.[28] Kemble hoped to use his research for the exhibition as the basis for a book called *Horae Ferales; or, Studies in the Archaeology of the Northern Nations*. His plans were cut short, however, when he died from a lung infection in March 1857, while researching Celtic art in Dublin. Despite Kemble's death, the Manchester exhibition gathered a substantial quantity of 'very fine specimens of that peculiar school of Celtic Christian art, which flourished in Ireland from the 7th to the 11th century, and exercised an important influence on all northern ornamental art'.[29] The art of Ireland's early Christian period, of which the Tara Brooch was the most famous example, was gaining prominence at the time; this, rather than prehistoric art, solidified the identification of this particular art style as being Celtic.

In addition to his important work on the Manchester exhibition, Kemble left a substantial legacy in the study of Celtic art through the speech he gave, just a month before his death, to the Royal Irish Academy, where Wilde had been working on his own exhibition catalogue. In his speech, Kemble described as 'Celtic' an art style that he felt was best represented in Britain and Ireland. For Kemble, both Celtic and Saxon remains, as part of 'our national antiquities',[30] had patriotic meaning, as he argued in the first major statement on Celtic art since Samuel Birch in 1846:

> There is a peculiar development of the double spiral line, totally unknown to the Greeks, the Etruscans, and the nations of the Teutonic North, which is essentially characteristic, not only of the Scoto-Keltic, but the Britanno-Keltic populations of these islands. [...] When, as is often the case in metal, this principle of the diverging spiral line is carried out in repoussé, – when you have those singularly beautiful curves, more beautiful perhaps in the parts that are not seen than in those that meet the eye, whose beauty, revealed in shadow more than form, – you have a peculiar characteristic, a form of beauty which belongs to no nation but our own, and to no portion of our nation but the Keltic portion. There are traces of it, faint and poor, but sufficient for identification, among the Kelts of Normandy and the Keltic Helvetians. [...] Although they began early, earlier than the intercourse of Rome with these islands, they continued late; and to the last moment of real, unmixed Keltic art, this is its great and distinguishing characteristic. [...] There is nothing like it in Etruscan art; there is little like it in Gallic or Helvetian art; it is indigenous, Gentlemen, – the art of those Keltic tribes which forced their way into these islands of the Atlantic, and, somewhat isolated here, developed a peculiar, but not the less admirable system of their own.[31]

A few months after Kemble's death, Lovell Reeve, the owner of a natural history shop in London, decided to capitalise on the growing interest in Celtic art by publishing Kemble's planned *Horae Ferales*.[32] Reeve asked Franks to prepare a section on Celtic antiquities for the book. While Franks was starting to research the topic, a number of discoveries were coming to the attention of the London archaeological community. H. Syer Cuming, the secretary of the British Archaeological Association, discovered what he called 'a veritable Celtic shield' and donated it to the British Museum.[33] Later named the Battersea Shield, this artefact soon became a definitive object of Celtic art (*pl. 13*).

In 1856, Cuming had notified the British Archaeological Association of the discovery of a number of crania associated with bronze and iron objects found between December 1854 and October 1855 by workers dredging the Thames River while building a bridge at Battersea in greater London.[34] The workers tried to keep their finds secret until they could sell them. Bateman, also a member of the Association, purchased some of the cache for his private museum. When Cuming presented these objects to the Association, he adopted the craniological ethnology of Bateman and his associates, writing that:

> the long oval crania were those of the Celtae, whilst the others of less elon-gated contour, were as certainly Roman; the presence of the bronze and iron weapons affording additional and indubitable evidence of such being the fact.[35]

Having established the presence of Celts at the site through craniology, Cuming was able to attribute the stunning bronze shield found there to Celtic defenders against the Roman invasion.

In early 1858, soon after Cuming's announcement, Franks himself exhib-ited a collection 'which he considered to belong to the latest period of the Celtic population of Britain' to the Society of Antiquaries.[36] During this exhibition, Franks described his reasoning in labelling the objects as Celtic:

> The peculiar ornaments which appear on this class of antiquities do not occur it is believed on the ancient remains of Denmark or the north of Germany. They cannot, therefore, be Danish or Saxon. That they are not Roman would appear from their being found scattered over all parts of Great Britain, and from a very analogous style of work occurring in Ireland, a country which appears to have been little known to the Romans, and in which the remains of that people are rarely brought to light. The designs are moreover not classical, though some trace of their influence may be discerned on the later productions of the Roman provinces of Britain and Gaul, especially on such as are enamelled. They are not however much anterior to the Roman period in Britain, as is shown by their occurring in company with undoubted Roman remains.

For the above reasons Mr Franks was disposed to ascribe the origin of
these and similar remains to the Celtic races, and most probably to the tribes
inhabiting Britain.[37]

Franks continued to bring objects 'with a Celtic character' to the attention
of the Society throughout the year.[38] And when he reported his visit to the
Iron Age hillfort of Danebury, he argued, on the basis of artefacts 'of late
Celtic workmanship', that it was not a Roman camp, as others had
thought.[39] Franks' identification of these materials as Celtic was a departure from the earlier practice of labelling all pre-Roman remains
indiscriminately as Celtic, for, like Cuming, he based his classification both
on the material of the remains, bronze and sometimes iron, and on the
style of decoration.[40]

   In 1863, Reeve finally published *Horae Ferales*, with Kemble's name
attached as one of three contributors, the others being Franks and the linguistic ethnologist Robert Gordon Latham. The volume was a compilation
of 'rather heterogeneous materials', including Kemble's previously published work on antiquities (notably his address to the Royal Irish Academy),
Latham's editorial preface and Franks' lengthy description of the plates, later
seen as the 'only really valuable part of this book'.[41] With three authors
working within different disciplinary traditions but addressing the same
problems, *Horae Ferales* is a telling collaboration, reflecting the increasing
specialisation of self-proclaimed ethnologists.

   Before considering the content of *Horae Ferales*, it is worthwhile to
review the context of Latham's contributions, which demonstrate the continuation of linguistic ethnology after the introduction of craniology.
Latham had been involved in the Ethnological Society of London as well as
the ethnological movement within the British Association since the 1840s.
Starting in the 1850s, he used his strength in linguistics along with his readings of classical texts to compile a number of Prichardian encyclopedic
ethnological volumes.[42] For Latham, the grand questions of ethnology were
to discover: '1. The unity or non-unity of the species 2. Its antiquity 3. Its
geographical origin', the last of these questions being answerable by deduc-
ing a probable centre from later migrations.[43] He was deeply interested,
therefore, in the original peopling of the British Isles and devoted an entire
book to the subject in 1852 after his book on the peopling of Europe left
little room for an extended discussion of the British case.[44]

   Latham shared Prichard's dislike of the word 'Celtic' to describe the language group in Britain.[45] Prichard's reasoning had been that the 'Celtic'

language group was made up of peoples different from those the classical writers described as Celtic, while Latham – who, like Kemble, preferred to spell it as Keltic, perhaps because the 'K' was truer to the original Greek 'Keltoi' – constructed a more complex theory in which even the classical usage of 'Celtic' was misapplied:

> I think, that though used to denominate the tribe and nations allied to the Gauls, ['Kelt'] was, originally, no Gallic word – as little native as *Welsh* is British.
>
> I also think that even the first populations to which it was applied were other than Keltic in the modern sense of the term.
>
> I think, in short, that it was a word belonging to the Iberian language, applied, until the time of Caesar at least, to Iberic populations.[46]

In this case, Latham treated classical sources with extreme scepticism, supporting his project of showing that much of France was originally Iberic. Many of Latham's most dearly held theories about the peopling of Europe were contradicted, not only by classical sources, but by the leading linguistic models of the day. This was especially true for his notion that Indo-European languages developed in Europe, with Slavic, in a sense his favourite of the European language groups, the purest form. While these ideas limited Latham's influence, they also meant that his peculiar brand of linguistics, which rejected the law of letter change – the very basis of Indo-European philology – tended to dominate his ethnological program over other possible sources of evidence.[47*] He argued that language was the most stable racial indicator, for 'as a general rule, the blood of a given population is more mixed than its language', but his method of relating language groups was somewhat idiosyncratic.[48]

As for the peopling of Britain, Latham accepted the three-age system but rejected the craniological model of a pre-Celtic race, because he thought factors like dietary change had a greater effect than did race replacement on skull shapes and because he rejected the 'Finn hypothesis', that Finnish and related languages preceded Indo-European ones in Europe.[49] Instead, he thought, 'The British Isles were peopled from the Keltic portion of the continent originally and exclusively'.[50] And the portion of the Continent

---

*The law of letter change explains differences in related languages through a consistent pattern of letter changes. For example, where Irish Gaelic uses a 'Q' sound, Welsh tends to use a 'P'.

that he identified as the purest Celtic homeland was Switzerland, where important archaeological discoveries were soon to confirm this opinion.[51]

In *Horae Ferales*, Latham mainly confined his argument to the Germanic aspects of Kemble's contribution to Anglo-Saxon and Celtic archaeology. He outlined the 'chief questions' facing students of material remains as seeking to know:

> A. The different populations which at different times have reasonably been supposed to have occupied the surface under consideration, beginning with the oldest and ending with the newest; [and] B. The approximate dates at which they succeeded each other.[52]

While Kemble treated these issues archaeologically by using material remains, Latham treated them 'solely and exclusively as an ethnologist', by which he meant that he used linguistic evidence. When he disagreed with Kemble's notion of ancient Saxon graves and art types – arguing instead that Germans were of a recent origin and from a small homeland 'at the mouth of the Elbe' – he supported this claim with the general principle that material remains should be treated as subordinate to historical and linguistic evidence.[53]

Though Latham was the primary editor of *Horae Ferales*, his notion of the relationship between linguistic and archaeological evidence had little impact on the reception of the book. In spite of Latham's contributions, the book was seen as a major advance in applying archaeological methods to ethnological questions by means of identifying ethnic art styles.[54] And despite Kemble's primary interest in 'our direct ancestors – the Germans', it was his notion of Celtic art, expanded on by Franks in the Description of the Plates, that helped give rise to comprehensive archaeological approaches to the Celts through their art style.[55]

In *Horae Ferales*, Franks used the three-age system to organise the plates, which he hoped would help archaeologists 'to discriminate between the features that characterize the remains of whole races from those attributable to local peculiarities'.[56] For example, he noted that bronze swords are similar throughout Europe, 'as though the weapons of one race', but with regional variations.[57] Within the three ages, Franks was most interested in the later British material. He regarded northern Germany and Denmark as the home of the most beautiful artefacts of the Stone and Bronze Ages. But for the Iron Age, he felt that 'the British Isles stand unrivalled'.[58]

Illustrated in these plates were the objects Franks labelled as belonging to the 'Late Celtic' period (*pl. 14* and *15*). In calling them Celtic, he did not rely on the classical texts or even on comparisons with Continental types where the classical texts said that Celts lived. Instead, as in his presentation to the Society of Antiquaries, he argued for their Celtic character as the only option 'to fall back upon' after showing that they could not be Roman, Saxon or Danish.[59] He then clinched the argument by showing how the art style continued in Irish medieval illuminated manuscripts and how the classical texts actually described some of the objects.[60] By presenting his case in this way, Franks was arguing for the relative autonomy of an artefact-based approach to archaeology, which he felt could match objects to races without reference to crania. His analysis contained one of the first arguments that there was a prehistoric British Iron Age, preceding Rome by one or two centuries. This new model paved the way for the possibility that Celts arrived, not in the Bronze Age, as the craniologists thought, but in the Iron Age.[61] Franks' characterisation of the Iron Age as 'Late Celtic', however, left open the possibility that the Bronze Age formed part of an early Celtic period.

In the same way that Wilson had called for a national collection of crania, Franks argued that further research could only be achieved 'by bringing together as far as possible the scattered elements [of artefacts] for our study, dispersed through various public and private collections'.[62] In 1866, when he became Keeper of the newly independent Department of British and Medieval Antiquities at the British Museum, he organised the collections according to the three-age system, within which he integrated the regionally based art styles he had identified. While Franks hoped to use the British Museum as a central storehouse for British material, his archaeological interests stretched beyond the national context. Born in Switzerland and having grown up in Italy, Franks brought an international perspective to antiquarian studies. In the 1860s, he kept abreast of new developments on the Continent through correspondences and from his post as Director of the Society of Antiquaries. In placing Britain's past in its wider European context through frequent visits to the Continent, he was following a pattern set in the previous two decades by Roach Smith. An omnivorous collector, Franks was able to draw on his vast knowledge of artefacts in order to compare types found in different regions.[63]

By the time Franks had finished work on *Horae Ferales*, finds on the Continent had come to light challenging Kemble's assertion that pure Celtic art was confined to the insular context. *Horae Ferales* was published in the same year that Franks visited Hallstatt, an Austrian salt mine connected to a cemetery that provided the first strong evidence of a local Bronze-to-

Iron Age transition. Discovered in 1846, Hallstatt was one of a number of
highly significant sites then under excavation in Central Europe. Thanks to
an especially dry winter in 1853-4, a large number of sites had literally surfaced in the shallows of Swiss lakes. These sites, which were mostly from the
Stone and Bronze Ages, provided the first substantial evidence outside of
Denmark for the three-age system.[64]

Of the Iron Age sites, La Tène contained artefacts strikingly similar to
Franks' material in *Horae Ferales (pl. 16)*. When La Tène was first discovered
on the shore of Lake Neuchâtel in 1857, there had been widespread disagreement among Continental archaeologists about which remains
corresponded to the ancient Celts. The Swiss archaeologist Frédéric Troyon
regarded the Swiss Bronze Age race as being that of 'the true
"Celts"'.[65] Troyon and Adophe von Morlot, both of whom had visited the
Museum of Northern Antiquities in Copenhagen, interpreted the Swiss
material within the Scandinavian craniological approach to the three-age
system, though they tended toward a more racist and evolutionary interpretation in which less technologically advanced races had smaller crania
(pl. 17).[66] In the English translation of the first synthesis of the Swiss lake
material, the Swiss archaeologist Ferdinand Keller argued, from growing
evidence for local continuity among the three ages, that the Celts had occupied the area from the earliest times down to the Iron Age, making the La
Tène finds, like all others from the area, Celtic.[67] Franks' work in *Horae
Ferales*, however, proved decisive in creating a narrower definition of the
Celts by showing the similarities of the ornamentation of La Tène swords
with the 'Celtic art' he had identified in Great Britain and Ireland.[68] In the
second edition of Keller's synthesis, the question of whether La Tène was
Celto-Helvetic, Roman or Alemannic was mainly answered by 'Mr.
Franks', who 'very justly lays claim to these swords as products of art by the
Celtic nations, and especially by the inhabitants of the British Isles and of
Northern Gaul'.[69] This interpretation had added appeal because it was con-
firmed by Latham's claim, on the evidence of classical authors, that ancient
Helvetia had been a Celtic source point.

Franks' contribution to the identification of the Swiss material as Celtic
is filled with irony. Because of the absence of any historical reference to
there being ancient Celts in Britain and Ireland, other sources of evidence
were needed to back up this claim. Many art historians today point to the
very site of La Tène, in an area some classical authors described as Celtic, as
evidence that designs of a similar nature in an insular context should be
called 'Celtic art'. However, the logic of the Swiss archaeologists was to call

these items Celtic, not because of what the classical sources said, but because Franks noted similarities with British and Irish art he described as Celtic in *Horae Ferales*. In other words, Franks' archaeological argument is circular, but it just happens to be supported by the classical sources Latham cited in order to make a different type of argument about Celtic migrations.

Though Franks' definition of Celtic art was supported by Latham's reading of classical sources, the ethnological approaches of the two researchers had little else in common. While Latham subordinated archaeological evidence to historical and linguistic theories, Franks hardly considered historical or linguistic evidence at all. As the composite product of three disparate, but self-consciously ethnological, contributions, *Horae Ferales* signalled the inevitable fragmentation of the discipline Prichard had promoted as a synthetic framework for addressing the question of peopling. The glaring omission in *Horae Ferales* of craniology, the most popular of the ethnological methods in the 1860s, further illustrated this growing specialisation. As the disciplines which investigated the origins of the ancient Celts branched off from ethnology, the corresponding definitions of the Celts also multiplied. As linguists, craniologists, physical anthropologists, art historians and, soon, folklorists and settlement archaeologists all proceeded with their studies of the Celts and attempted to synthesise their theories, they remained united in, if nothing else, their use of the three-age system, in which the Celts were merely the latest prehistoric arrival to Britain's shores.

Celtic Culture and Civilisation

After the publication of *Horae Ferales* in 1863, the topic of Celtic art briefly faded into obscurity. The rate of discovery of spectacular new finds, such as the Tara Brooch and Battersea Shield which appeared in the 1850s, had slowed. Franks, meanwhile, was increasingly interested in other parts of the world, and even today most of the Iron Age displays in the British Museum's Celtic Europe gallery are of material unearthed before *Horae Ferales*. It was not until the late 1870s and early 1880s that another British national museum – this one in Scotland – took the lead in research into Celtic art.

By this time, ethnology as a discipline had broken down into its constituent parts, including linguistics, physical anthropology, archaeology, history and folklore studies. In this context, craniology was no longer the most prominent method of investigating Britain's sequence of peoples and periods. As researchers like Franks began to look at artefacts and styles of ornament, the methodology of C.J. Thomsen – the Danish originator of the three-age system who studied the evolution of materials and designs rather than migrations of peoples – can be said to have finally reached Britain.

Paralleled by work on the Continent by Thomsen's followers like Hans Hildebrand, Oscar Montelius and Sophus Müller, British and Irish researchers were beginning to focus on ancient material culture without the overarching concern of assigning a race to each period. John Evans was among the first archaeologists in Britain to follow Thomsen in treating archaeological objects, rather than the races behind them, as his primary subject of research. His work resulted in a trilogy of comprehensive volumes on numismatics, objects of stone and objects of bronze.[70] Though Evans did not relate the three ages to particular prehistoric peoples, he retained the belief that the suddenness of the transitions indicated the arrival of new races. Augustus Lane Fox Pitt Rivers joined Evans in centring his research on the evolution of material forms with his two seminal papers, 'Principles of Classification', and 'On the Evolution of Culture'.[71] The Scottish museum curator Joseph Anderson, in attempting to define a 'scientific basis' for archaeology, allied himself with these two when he argued, 'Archaeology proceeds by the classification of types'.[72] For archaeologists in the 1870s and 1880s, while the question of peopling remained important, a new research problem took hold, involving social evolutionism and artefact typology as key approaches to understand the 'culture and civilisation' represented by prehistoric materials. In this context, the study of Celtic art had a renewed importance.

Anderson

Joseph Anderson was for many years a curator of the Museum of the Society of Antiquaries of Scotland. In 1879, he began a series of lectures on Scottish material culture, starting with early Christian times and moving back in time to the Stone Age. Anderson gave these lectures as the second holder of the prestigious Rhind Lectureship, endowed by the Scottish antiquary Alexander Henry Rhind, who left his fortune to the funding of lectures 'on some branch of archaeology, ethnology, ethnography, or allied topic'.[73] Back in the 1860s, Anderson had received funding from the Anthropological Society to excavate and report on human remains in Scotland. By the next decade, however, he had abandoned physical anthropology and focused instead on ornament, art style and mode of interment to describe the 'culture and civilisation' and 'gradations of advancement' of each age.[74] In this new research program, 'culture' replaced 'race' as the unit of analysis in discussing past peoples like the Celts. In examining a past culture by its art style, Anderson emphasised:

> the paramount importance of form and decoration in the determination of type; and the significance of systems of ornament as affording indications of the conditions of culture by their character, and determining the sequence of these conditions by their development. The disclosure of that significance will also have shown that it may be possible to deal with the ornament of prehistoric ages as an index of culture in much the same manner as the student of culture might deal with language and literature as supplying materials for his deductions with respect to the historic period.[75]

Anderson's focus on art and ornament contributed to his choosing to start with the early Christian period, which represented for him the pinnacle of Celtic art in Scotland. He extended the Celtic label from the art of this period to the very form of Christianity that flourished during the time when this art style was dominant, characterising early Scottish Christianity as the 'Early Celtic Church', because it contained a 'school of native art' which was 'specifically Celtic' and demonstrated an achievement peculiar to the Scottish nation.[76] At the same time that Anderson was preparing his lectures, the historian William Skene was writing a three-volume study of 'Celtic Scotland', by which he meant the period between the Roman occupation and the Norman conquest.[77] Along with Skene, Anderson named as Celtic a period of Scotland's past which he conceived to be central to the nation's history, though he departed from Skene in seeing archaeology as the primary route to understanding the development of Celtic Scotland.

In discussing the Celtic aspects of the early Scottish Church, Anderson focused on the 'intense Celticism' of the interlace design in illuminated manuscripts: 'These peculiar combinations and uses of the simple elements, which are more or less common to all decorative art, are the methods by which, at this period, the genius of the Celt expressed its sense of the beautiful in art, and thus asserted its individuality'.[78] Anderson's use of the word 'genius' here is crucial to his concept of Celtic culture and civilisation. At Oxford in the 1860s, Matthew Arnold had described 'the Celtic genius' as a permanent racial characteristic of the Celtic mind.[79] For Arnold, the mental state, or genius, of a race was the key ingredient of that race's 'culture'. For Anderson, on the other hand, the Celtic genius was not a permanent racial characteristic, but the creative impulse behind a form of artistic expression, which he called Celtic, that had evolved from earlier forms.

In his second series of lectures on the early Christian period, Anderson explored Celtic art on non-ecclesiastical objects. Though in these lectures he assigned 'the cradle of the art' to Ireland, he called Scotland's Celtic culture 'indigenous' and presented it as evidence of 'a civilisation possessing a complexity of organisation which sufficed to make culture possible'.[80] Where ethnologists had depended on migrations to explain the arrival of the Celts, Anderson, in using the term *Celtic* to refer to artistic expression, was free to explain Celtic Scotland as a local development with little foreign input.

After looking at the early Christian period, Anderson lectured on the roots of Celtic ornament, applying Franks' concept of 'late Celtic art' to the Scottish Iron Age.[81] While he agreed with Franks that Celtic art had its ultimate source on the Continent, Anderson downplayed the connection and attributed the greatest achievements of the style to artisans indigenous to Britain (*pl. 18*):

> Although remotely connected with certain developments of art that appear obscurely among the Iron Age relics of Central and Southern Europe, this special system of design received its highest development and attained its full maturity in the British Isles alone. [...] A style of art characterised by such originality of design and excellence of execution must count for something in the history of a nation's progress, must have its place to fill in the history of art itself, when once we have begun to realise the fact that art was not the exclusive privilege of classical antiquity.[82]

Anderson went on to argue that Celtic ornament, and therefore the 'culture and civilisation' in Scotland, showed a high degree of local continuity before and after the Roman occupation.[83] For Anderson, Celtic art was all but synonymous with indigenous Scottish art. He described intrusive Vikings' art as 'radically different from that of the Celtic school'.[84] He also identified a Viking region in Scotland and a border area, where Celtic ornament types mixed with Scandinavian imports.[85]

Where evidence of ornament was lacking in prehistory, Anderson turned to mode of interment, rather than to the bones themselves, some of which were 'demonstrably of Celtic character'.[86] This method was especially helpful in his analysis of the Bronze and Stone Ages, which contained little or no evidence of Celtic art and ornament. Here he examined burial evidence 'presented by the deposit itself, inclusive of the manner of burial, and all its underground accompaniments'.[87] For Scotland before the Iron Age, when burial implements contained very little ornament, Anderson not only stopped calling the local culture 'Celtic', but side-stepped the name of the people inhabiting Scotland as inessential to his project of describing the area's 'culture and civilisation'.

With his four series of Rhind Lectures on the Scottish past, Anderson removed ethnological concerns from the heart of archaeology. Spurning craniology and the question of migrations, Anderson concentrated on the development of Celtic art in Scotland as indicative of the changing 'gradations of advancement' of the region's 'culture and civilisation'.[88] His emphasis on Celtic art as representative of indigenous achievement helped make the subject a popular one for future Rhind Lecturers. He also helped establish medieval times as a definitive period in creating the Scottish 'idea of nationality'.[89] Anderson's successors, however, used his approach to understanding Scottish Celtic culture as a tool for addressing more deeply the question of peopling.

In 1892, Anderson returned to the Rhind post, this time speaking on 'The Early Christian Monuments of Scotland'. These lectures were later published in an ambitious 1,000-page volume in which Anderson and John Romilly Allen attempted to document all of Scotland's Christian monuments through photography and drawings.[90] Anderson continued to use the typological approach, which he described as the most scientific method.[91] He divided the monuments into classes, and then, after breaking down the ornament into elemental forms, attempted to build a chronological sequence, citing 'a gradual and continuous advance of artistic character traceable throughout the whole series of the monuments' (*pl. 19*).[92]

As in his earlier Rhind Lectures, Anderson's main argument was that Celtic art was essentially a Scottish phenomenon, although here he was concentrating on the Christian period. He divided Scottish monuments into three classes: 'Monuments with incised symbols only', which he attributed to late Roman times, 'Monuments with symbols and Celtic ornament carved in relief' and 'Monuments with Celtic ornament in relief, but without the symbols of the other two classes'.[93] By 'Celtic ornament', Anderson meant any combination of what he defined as the elemental forms of Celtic art: 'interlaced work, fret-work, spiral-work, with an occasional intermixture of foliageous work'.[94] Anderson argued that at the end of the Roman Christian period, represented by the first class of monuments, native artisans re-established the Celtic tradition that had flowered in prehistory: 'there was in the indigenous culture of the people a source of artistic potentiality which sufficiently accounts for the unparalleled efflorescence of their art of the Christian time'.[95] While Anderson acknowledged that Celtic art was widespread across Europe in pagan times, he argued that even then it belonged mainly to natives of Britain, where 'it was nurtured and brought to maturity'.[96]

Anderson added a geographical dimension to his chronological argument about the three classes of monuments to fortify his claim that this 'artistic culture altogether unparalleled in Europe' was a Scottish product.[97] Monuments of the first two classes, he argued, did not appear in the territory of the Dalriadic migrations from Ireland, but were to be found in areas controlled by the Picts, the natives of Scotland from Roman times. Anderson took this as proof that the Celtic art of the early Christian period had its source with the Picts who had been in Scotland since pagan times.[98] In the main section of the comprehensive publication in which Anderson's 1892 Rhind Lectures appeared, however, John Romilly Allen, who had long worked with Anderson in documenting the monuments, parted from Anderson's theory of indigenous development and put more weight on the evidence of Continental sources.[99] While Anderson's work helped define Celtic art as an important research problem for archaeologists, his work was narrowly nativistic within the Scottish context. His followers, notably Allen and Arthur Evans, internationalised Anderson's research by relating the ornament found in Scotland to discoveries from around Europe.

Allen and Evans

John Romilly Allen and Arthur Evans widened the scope of research into the origins and development of Celtic art. These dual themes of origins and development, whether applied to Celtic art or to the Celtic peoples themselves, would remain central to Iron Age archaeology for the subsequent century.

The early sources of Celtic art in pagan times were the subject of Evans' Rhind Lectures of 1895. Evans defined Celtic art as 'a distinctive national style which historically belonged to Celtic peoples' speaking Celtic languages. He traced the introduction into Britain of Celtic art to Iron Age Belgic conquerors who, in turn, had their source in the Bronze Age culture of Mycenaean Greece.[100] Evans described Mycenae as the first European site of 'Hallstatt art and crafts', an early form of Celtic art 'ultimately traceable to Egyptian and Oriental sources'.[101] He then linked Mycenae with Britain through ancient Venetian art, which he had argued previously to be closely related stylistically to artefacts from the Aylesford cemetery he had excavated. He also noted connections with art in the Illyrian Balkans, where he had travelled prior to concentrating on the archaeology of Greece.[102] After citing the Italian connection, Evans discussed forerunners of British Celtic art in Greece and Gaul.[103] Finally, he concluded his lectures with a review of 'Late Celtic Art in Britain', the place where this art 'reached its most perfect development', and, in a nod to his sponsors, 'nowhere more than Caledonia'. Evans' final emphasis on Scottish Celtic creativity complemented Anderson's theories by allowing for a unique artistic contribution of Scottish Celts (who, he said, had invaded from Belgic Gaul) after the seeds of the art style had come, through diffusion, from eastern sources: 'The elements thus brought together were of heterogeneous origin, but the genius of the Celtic race had fused them into an organic whole, and moulded them into new and beautiful forms which bore the impress of its own artistic individuality'.[104] This idea of Celtic 'genius' fitted well with Anderson's notion of Celtic 'culture and civilisation'.

Allen was also a Rhind Lecturer, holding the post in 1885. A London-born engineer from a distinguished Welsh family and deeply interested in the archaeology of Wales and Scotland, Allen had worked closely with Anderson on ancient ornament, providing the illustrations for Anderson's lectures. Allen delivered his series of Rhind Lectures on Scottish ornament from the Romano-British period through medieval times. At this stage, he followed Anderson in celebrating indigenous Scottish art for forming a national tradition 'entirely distinct from that of Greece or Rome'.[105] He also subscribed to the notion that early Scottish Christianity was part of 'the Celtic Church', which 'had an origin earlier and entirely independent of the Roman form of Christianity introduced by St. Augustine'.[106] And like Anderson, he described the art associated with this Church as a tradition of Celtic art that originated in Ireland.[107] In describing British prehistory, he was content with a simple division between Celtic and pre-Celtic periods within the context of the three ages.[108]

In 1904, Allen took a giant step out from under the shadow of Anderson's narrow focus on typology, when he produced the first book-length synthesis of Celtic art studies with the archaeological search for origins. The publication of his *Celtic Art in Pagan and Christian Times* marked the beginning of a new phase of research into the Celts, bringing together many of the trends of the late nineteenth century. Methodologically, it emphasised the importance of the large-scale excavations which were rapidly becoming the norm in archaeology (see Chapter VIII). Institutionally, it was the product of research sponsored mainly by the Rhind Lectureship, which was contributing to the growing professionalisation of archaeology. And intellectually, it

concentrated on artefact style and ornament as the defining characteristics
of past peoples (*pl.20*). This last point was crucial in that it completed the
process started by Anderson and Evans of interpreting the ancient past in
terms of cultural traditions rather than races. This represented the first alternative to the notion that the Celts were defined by their blood, as distinct
from their behaviour, since the idea of race entered studies of the ancient
Celts in the late eighteenth century.

When Allen described the subject of his book, he tried to synthesise the
various approaches to the Celts that had been diversifying during the previous half century. He defined Celtic art as 'the art of the peoples in Europe
who spoke the Celtic language', while accepting that 'although linguistically' these people were Celts, 'racially they were of mixed Celtic and Iberian
blood'.[109] In describing language, culture and race as independent variables,
all of which employed separate meanings of the word 'Celtic', he favoured
the linguistic meaning under the assumption – since shown to be inaccurate – that a one-to-one correspondence existed between speakers of Celtic
language and makers of Celtic art.[110] Allen further linked linguistic Celts
with Celtic art by attributing the coming of Goidelic Celts to Britain with
the Hallstatt period, or early Iron Age, and that of the Brythonic Celts with
the later La Tène horizon.[111] His use of the term *Celtic* for this phase of the
British past marked a victory for 'the late Sir Wollaston Franks' whose name
for this 'culture' in Britain, with roots on the Continent, was 'Late-
Celtic'.[112] Because of the confusion over the 'Late-Celtic' period being
early in relation to the Celtic Christian period, the 'Late' was soon dropped
from this designation, though Allen remained true to Franks' term.

Allen's goal in *Celtic Art* was to present facts that could help in 'forming a
theory as to the origin and development of Celtic art'.[113] Allen left little
room to form such a theory, however, concentrating instead on the facts.
His final conclusion – that the Celtic art of the Christian period was 'a local
variety of the Lombardo-Byzantine style' which was 'grafted upon the
Pagan art of the Late-Celtic period' – was hardly a controversial statement.[114] The importance of his project lay not in his conclusions, but in his
dual interest in origin and development, as well as in his conception of the
Celts, not as a race, but as a 'stage of culture', represented by a particular art
style.[115] The search for origins had been at the heart of ethnology, while
development was the overriding interest of social evolutionists. In combining
these intellectual endeavours, Allen helped set the stage for the emergence
of culture-historical investigations of past peoples, an approach that came to
define the next generation of archaeologists. In this brand of archaeology,

whose chief advocates were Montelius, Gustaf Kossinna and V. Gordon Childe, European prehistory came to be interpreted as a patchwork of ethnic groups that migrated from origin points and received new technologies mainly through diffusion.

The Politics of Celtic Art

The identification of Celtic art is generally associated with nationalism on the 'Celtic fringe'. But this chapter shows that the idea of Celtic art was born in English institutions. In the years after Queen Victoria's purchase of a copy of the Tara Brooch, John Kemble had assembled a collection of Celtic art from Ireland for the Art Treasures Exhibition in Manchester. And at the British Museum, Franks had built on Samuel Birch's preliminary work on Celtic art in order to complete Kemble's proposed *Horae Ferales*. After Franks turned his attention to other subjects, however, the base of support for Celtic art studies moved to the fringes. At the Museum of Antiquaries of Scotland and in the Rhind Lectures, Anderson's work on the topic had a profoundly pro-Scottish tone. The Rhind Lectures of Evans and Allen also emphasised Scottish contributions to Celtic art, but both scholars went much further than Anderson in viewing the Scottish material in a broader Continental perspective. In Ireland, meanwhile, though little original research was being conducted on Celtic art, the style began to flourish within the Irish Celtic Revival.

The Celts had been central to cultural revivals on the fringes before. In the literary Celtic Revival in Scotland and Wales in the mid eighteenth century, the Celts were key to notions of indigenous achievement. And in the Druidical revival led by Edward Williams in Wales at the end of the eighteenth century, the Celts were central to conceptions of Welsh intellectual and spiritual forebears. In these cases, however, as in the growth in Celtic art studies from the mid nineteenth century, there was no connection between interest in the Celts and political separatism. On the contrary, the ancient Celts had almost always been invoked during romantic revivals whose political thrust, if any, was one of increasing political unification. The Irish Celtic Revival in the late nineteenth century was the first to run against these trends.

In the decades on either side of the turn of the twentieth century, the issue of Home Rule dominated political life in Ireland, and it was also a subject of debate in Scotland. At the same time, both regions witnessed an increased interest in Celtic art, though in contrasting ways. In Scotland, which for almost a century had been identified with a distinctive Highland culture, Anderson and others tried to celebrate Scottish individuality and achievement by highlighting the art of the Celtic Christian period. While adding tremendously to knowledge of the period, these efforts did not result in any grassroots movement linking Celtic art with Scotland's regional identity. In Ireland, however, interest in Celtic art became part of the political push for independence and played a large role in a revival of traditional rural culture that was also focusing attention on Irish folklore.

The context in which Celtic art appeared in the Irish Celtic Revival was in the applied arts, including building ornamentation, furniture design and jewellery, as well as in exhibits at world's fairs. The use of Celtic art, fashioned after ancient examples, demonstrates that the art style did not just appeal to institutions like museums and world's fair committees, whose role was to display Irish culture, but it flourished within the market place. The appeal of Celtic art in Ireland went far beyond the intellectual community. The art became integrated into the symbolism of daily life and garnered widespread public support, illustrated by the popularity of commodities with Celtic themes.

Though Celtic art became associated with Irish nationalism through the applied arts, this had little to do with the intellectual movement behind the idea. Celtic art provided an alternative to the notion of a Celtic race. It implied the presence of an enduring Celtic spirit, genius, or, to use the new word of the late nineteenth century, culture. Unlike Celtic skull shapes, Celtic art was interpreted as a cultural product that did not depend on the intrusion of new people. In defining the Celts through their art, genes did not matter as much as mentalities. This was mirrored by earlier work that defined the Celts as speakers of Celtic languages, practisers of Druidism or tellers of Celtic tales. The archaeological research based away from the fringes, like that of Franks, Evans and Allen, helped to fuel the late nineteenth-century Celtic revival by adding new information, but this research was not necessarily part of the same regionalist drive that sought political independence in fringe areas.

CHAPTER VIII

THE BIRTH OF ARCHAEOLOGY

By the beginning of the twentieth century, many of the strands of research into the ancient Celts in Britain had finally coalesced into an approach – exemplified by John Romilly Allen's book on Celtic art – which we still find familiar today. Following two centuries during which each generation put forth its own definition of the Celts and introduced a new means of identifying them, the search for the ancient Celts was settling into a long period in which the basic ideas went unchallenged: the Celts were an Iron Age people, and not necessarily a race, with Bronze Age roots, characterised by their language and art. As the century turned, and continuing to the present, the discipline of archaeology served as a leading context in which researchers investigated the Celts, all the while debating how peoples such as the Celts can best be characterised.

The story of British research into the ancient Celts since the early eighteenth century coincides with the development of the disciplines that investigated the question of peopling. To some extent, the search for the Celts even helped bring about the formation of these disciplines, because it motivated thinkers to create methods of tracing this and other ancient peoples. Our story is not complete, therefore, without also looking at the origins of archaeology.

One way to locate the origins of the modern discipline of archaeology is through the people who called themselves archaeologists. Self-described archaeologists, however, are a surprisingly diverse group in the time before the name became attached to the modern discipline. Taken from Greek root words meaning the study of the distant past, archaeology has been applied to a variety of projects.

As early as 1708, Henry Rowlands defined archaeology as 'an Account of the Origin of Nations after the Universal DELUGE'. For subjects like the Celts and the peopling of Britain, where written history offered no clues, Rowlands looked to relationships among diverse languages, place names, laws and customs, coins and medals, ancient ruins and physical characteristics like skin colour.[1] The only aspect of Rowland's methods that we would recognise today as 'archaeology' is his interests in ancient coinage and ruins.

Few Celticists described themselves as archaeologists from Rowlands' time until the middle of the nineteenth century, when ethnology shifted its emphasis from language to craniology. As a discipline with its own rules of conduct, of weighing evidence, of disseminating findings and of establishing a division between professional and amateur, archaeology was the creation of the generation that established human antiquity and the three-age system in the 1850s and '60s. Discipline formation had several components, including new institutions, new theories and new ways of digging and collecting. With the addition of Celtic art as a research category, and when the notion of a Celtic race was challenged by that of a Celtic culture, Joseph Anderson provided a modern-sounding definition of archaeology, which he described as the primary means to produce 'a history of man by his works, of art by its monuments, of culture by its manifestations, and of civilisation by its developments'.[2] This chapter examines the institutional, theoretical and methodological developments behind this new meaning in light of their effects on research into the Celts.

Institutions

Before the 1840s, researchers concerned with ancient Britain tended to work either in isolation or in learned societies with generalised interests. In the early eighteenth century, William Stukeley had helped form the Society of Antiquaries of London, which was among the first of these to be more narrowly focused. Later in the century, the Society's periodical, *Archaeologia*, served as a key instrument to disseminate new ideas. In the early nineteenth century, however, the centre of gravity of such research shifted to ethnology, as articulated by James Cowles Prichard and situated in the British Association for the Advancement of Science and the Ethnological Society of London.

Thanks in part to the British Association's policy of rotating the site of its annual meeting, the new method of craniological ethnology spread in the

1840s and '50s to local antiquaries and ethnologists throughout the British Isles. At the same time that craniology was on the rise within ethnology, other new societies concerned with material remains appeared, adopting the term *archaeology* to describe their work. Of these mostly local institutions, the British Archaeological Association, founded in 1843 to encourage 'intelligent researches into British antiquities' throughout the country, and the Archaeological Institute of Great Britain and Ireland, which broke from the British Archaeological Association in the following years, provided national, rotating forums for local antiquaries to gather and tie their work into national debates.[3] Until the creation of university departments of archaeology in the twentieth century, the institutional base of the discipline remained in scientific societies.

The British Archaeological Association was founded by Charles Roach Smith, Thomas Wright, Albert Way and other fellows of the Society of Antiquaries of London looking for a fresh venue away from the 'exclusiveness and lethargy of the Antiquaries'.[4] Even before its first annual meeting, set in Canterbury in 1844, the organisers fractured over conference preparations and later over the publication of the results, with Smith and Wright on one side of the dispute and Way on the other. Way broke off, and in 1845 there were two separate meetings of the Association in Winchester. A year later, Way's group became the Archaeological Institute. Though both societies were primarily concerned with medieval and recent history, they provided an essential forum for researchers of the pre-Roman period. Membership of the two societies was not exclusive, and many members of both were also part of the Ethnological Society of London and the Society of Antiquaries.

Soon these societies became vehicles for institutional and legal reform along lines Worsaae had recommended. During his visit in 1846-7, Worsaae had urged the British to push for protective legislation in order to slow the destruction of ancient monuments and aid the formation of a national collection. The resulting movement, which brought together a number of people interested in furthering Worsaae's brand of ethnology, was led by the Scottish antiquary A. Henry Rhind, who pressed for legislative changes, hailed the three-age system as 'a total revolution in an important inquiry', and endowed the Rhind Lectureship; and by Lord James Talbot, Baron de Malahide, who used his position in Parliament to try to reform Britain's Treasure Trove law.[5] The Treasure Trove law gave the Crown the rights to seize, without compensation, many ancient objects found in the country. This resulted in what Rhind considered the 'unmitigated evil' of finds going unreported or, in the case of gold and silver objects, being melted down and sold.[6] Talbot, twice president of the Archaeological Institute and a fellow of the Society of Antiquaries, where a committee on Treasure Trove was created in 1850, submitted a new bill on Treasure Trove in 1858, though it failed. The Treasure Trove reform movement did not accomplish its immediate goal until 1871, but in the meantime it helped focus the energies of Worsaae's followers, especially those interested in the pre-Roman period. The Treasure Trove bill was followed by the 1882 Ancient Monuments Protection Act, sponsored by Lubbock and hastening the end of the unrestrained excavation activities of the barrow-diggers. By this time, the British Museum, the museum of the Society of Antiquaries of Scotland and the museum of the Royal Irish Academy represented the major collections of archaeological remains and held a growing influence on their categorisation.

As the archaeological societies were flourishing, the parent discipline of ethnology was beginning to fracture over a debate precipitated in part by the introduction of craniology. In the 1860s, linguistics was still the dominant method in ethnology. But by this time, Thurnam, Davis and other members of the burgeoning community of craniologists had entered the Ethnological Society. During the decade after Charles Darwin published *Origin of Species*, craniology became an increasingly important part of ethnological science.[7] As ethnologists integrated craniology into their study of peopling and the origins of human diversity, an emerging group of thinkers started to use the analysis of skulls as part of a polygenist and racialist program, contrasting with the monogenist disposition of the discipline under Prichard's influence. In 1863, James Hunt led a polygenist group in a break from the Ethnological Society to form the Anthropological Society of London. At the end of a lengthy and acrimonious debate between polygenist and monogenist factions, the science of ethnology, after a formal existence of only about three decades, was reformulated as anthropology. In 1871, the two societies merged as the Anthropological Institute of Great Britain and Ireland, with archaeology and physical anthropology at the forefront of the organisation's activities.

Both during the controversy and under the discipline's new name, the Celts remained an important subject of craniological inquiry. Whether as part of physical anthropological research into racial differences or of archaeological research into Britain's racial history, Celtic craniology had a stable institutional home in anthropology. The replacement of ethnology with anthropology, however, marked the disintegration of the synthesis of the various approaches to peopling under a single discipline. With this process, archaeology began to form a discipline in its own right.

These developments in Great Britain and Ireland did not happen in isolation, and the formation of archaeology as its own discipline, as distinct now from anthropology, received a boost from the international scene. By 1865, encouraged by the success of the three-age system and the establishment of human antiquity, a Europe-wide group of self-styled prehistoric archaeologists began to create an institutional base for their nascent discipline. In addition to providing a forum where methodology could be debated and professional standards set, the prehistorians offered an international perspective on a prehistoric past whose inhabitants were best understood by tracing their geographical as well as chronological extent. In contrast to ethnology, which focused primarily on peopling, prehistoric archaeology considered the additional problem of development within an emerging social evolutionist framework.

The principal figures behind the international prehistoric movement were Continental and a number of key British researchers, notably Augustus Franks, John Lubbock and John Evans, had made repeated trips to the Continent to examine Pleistocene finds in France and important excavations such as the Hallstatt cemetery in Austria. Back in Britain, Lubbock and Evans worked to institute professional archaeological standards in methodology by marginalising the activities of local barrow-diggers through protective legislation, and in the field's intellectual content by forwarding the interpretation, partially inspired by Franks' work in Celtic art, that the Celts flourished in the Iron Age and that megaliths pre-dated the Celtic Druids within the three-age sequence.

In 1865, Gabriel de Mortillet, a French Palaeolithicist newly returned to France after more than a decade of political exile in Switzerland, saw the need to institute a yearly international meeting of archaeologists so that researchers throughout Europe could keep informed about the many new finds and techniques. He made this proposal at a meeting of the Italian Society of Natural Sciences, where it was well received. The first annual meeting of the resulting International Congress of Anthropology and Prehistoric Archaeology took place in Neuchâtel, near the site of La Tène, in 1866. The next year, Mortillet used the Universal Exhibition in Paris to hold the congress' second meeting and to present the latest findings.[7] Though the archaeological exhibition in Paris was mainly dedicated to the Palaeolithic, other periods were also well represented. Within these other periods, the Celts had taken on a renewed patriotic importance for the

French, thanks to Napoleon III's sponsorship of excavations and his promotion of the image of the ancient Celts as an early example of defenders of France against imperialist aggressors. Based on recent finds like the swords of La Tène, images of Celtic warriors, including a monumental statue of Vercingetorix with the face of Napoleon III, began to appear across France and were displayed at the Universal Exhibition.

In 1868, the annual archaeological congress moved to England. Coinciding with the British Association meeting in Norwich, the third meeting of the congress attracted an impressive list of British leaders of the prehistoric movement. At the meeting, Lubbock, T.H. Huxley and E.B. Tylor, among many others, summarised their approaches to prehistory. Following Lubbock's social evolutionist doctrine in *Pre-Historic Times*, Tylor presented modern peoples as a model for understanding prehistoric peoples. Employing the notion of 'stages of civilisation', he argued that the Swiss lake-dwellers were 'rather barbarous than mere savages', making it plausible that the Indo-European Celtic tribes, whom he considered to be at a middle stage, occupied the area as anciently as the Neolithic.[8] Huxley, who had taken a keen interest in the work of craniologists and had begun to look at other possible skeletal indicators of race, presented a paper discussing the evolution of these racial forms within the long time-frame of human antiquity.[9] Lubbock, the president of the organising committee, urged participants to study 'Druidical monuments' before too many more were destroyed by industrial expansion, but his main contribution to the conference was to argue that there was little evidence that any ancient remains could be confidently assigned to the Druids.[10] Lubbock's desire to remove the Druids from archaeological discussions was becoming a key aspect of the process of discipline formation, not just in intellectual terms, but in terms of excluding the gentleman amateur contributors whose interests in archaeology were often confined to their interests in Druids.

Removing the Druids from the Megaliths

The practice of attributing ancient remains to the Druids first came under scrutiny as the three-age model was becoming the framework for Britain's prehistoric past. The trend Prichard started in the 1840s, when he downplayed the importance of the Druids in his model of peopling, was continued by the Scandinavian ethnologists and their followers. Both Thomsen and Worsaae believed that megaliths, the monuments most widely considered Druidical, were actually older than the time of Druid priests.[11] And when William Thoms translated Worsaae's book, he hoped that it would finally end the interpretation of stone monuments as being the sacrificial altars of the ancient Druids.[12] By the 1840s, when the tradition of research by local vicars and antiquaries on 'Druidical' monuments had outgrown the pages of *Gentleman's Magazine* and appeared from time to time in the proceedings of the British Association, many contributors were starting to question the Druidical connection.[13] Daniel Wilson followed this lead, calling Druidical attributions 'fancy' in light of the new three-age framework, and Thomas Bateman demonstrated that excavation could show how so-called Druidical altars were actually tombs pre-dating the Druids.[14]

The new perspective of seeing Druids as coming later than the megaliths contributed to the trend, in Celtic art studies, of associating the Celts with the Iron Age. Archaeological work on megaliths pointed to their construction in the Bronze Age, if not earlier. As Joseph Anderson argued, dismissing his predecessors' connection between Scottish standing stones and the Druids: 'In point of fact, there is nothing which is of the nature of evidence by which the stone circles of Scotland can be assigned to any race or historic order of men. Taking them at their own testimony, the only evidence they yield amounts to this, that they are the funeral marks of our Pagan predecessors of the Age of Bronze'.[15]

Not all of the early proponents of the three-age system, however, associated it with a non-Druidical interpretation of megaliths. In his museum catalogue, William Wilde continued to attribute 'circular, oblong, square and irregular-shaped enclosures', which were found '[s]cattered over the plains of central and north-west Europe', to 'the mysteries of Druidism'.[16] John Thurnam likewise thought of Stonehenge and Avebury as Druidical in *Crania Britannica*.[17] By the mid 1860s, however, Druidical attributions were seen by many as an interpretation that separated practitioners of the new field of prehistoric archaeology from a class of antiquaries of amateur status.

In *The Coins of the Ancient Britons*, Evans attempted to institute a new level of professionalism in numismatics and prove the existence of pre-Roman coins in Britain, ending a lengthy debate. He characterised Druidical attributions as unprofessional:

> Unfortunately, while Druidic speculations appear to have possessed a fatal attraction for archaeologists, the valuable though fragmentary evidence of Roman historians would seem to have been only partially examined, while that of the coins themselves has been almost entirely neglected.[18]

In *Pre-Historic Times*, Lubbock argued that megaliths were 'generally, but hastily, ascribed to the Druids', and put forth his theory, based mainly on Cunnington's excavations of tumuli near Stonehenge, that it and other similar monuments dated to the Bronze Age, before the historical existence of the Druids.[19]

During this process of intellectual professionalisation, dissenting voices failed to win much support. In the same year that *Pre-Historic Times* was published, Samuel Lysons, an antiquary whose uncle had been an important Romanist, tried to synthesise the implications of the three-age system with the Druid-based interpretive model that preceded it. The result of this effort, *Our British Ancestors: Who And What Were They?*, followed the work of Godfrey Higgins by highlighting written sources more than ancient remains. As a result, it did not hold the attention of adherents of the three-age system and Lubbock's synthesis predominated, in which Druids played virtually no role. By the 1880s, when the institutional separation between archaeologists and antiquaries was well under way, Lubbock's and Evans' books came to form 'the text-books on the subject', and the Druidical theories were seen not to 'meet the requirements of modern science'.[20]

Unsurprisingly, the issue of the meaning of Britain's many megalithic monuments focused on Stonehenge, its most prominent example. As the earlier attribution of Stonehenge as a Druid temple was overthrown, the only two remaining options were that it was older than the Druids, as in Lubbock's Bronze Age argument, or younger, dating to the little-known period in Britain's past between the departure of the Romans and the arrival of northern tribes. In the ensuing debate, Lubbock's argument was countered by James Fergusson, a prolific historian of architecture who spent the first half of his career working in India.

Fergusson shared Lubbock's scepticism towards the Druid theory and frustration from its persistence:

> The notion may safely be left to die a natural death; but the Druidical theory of Dr. Stukeley has become a part of our stock-belief, and "Druidical remains" is the generic name applied to all the rude stone monuments in every part of the country.[21]

Fergusson, however, sought to reunite Stonehenge with Celtic builders by assigning it:

> to that great Arthurian period to which we owe all that we know of the poetry and of the mythology of the Celtic race, and which seems to have

been their culminating point in the early form of their civilization.[22]

Fergusson seems to have reached this conclusion primarily through his notion of permanent religious characteristics within different races, about which he gained a broad perspective during his time in India. Stonehenge thus became incorporated into his wider argument that the Celtic influence on Christianity, manifest in Irish Catholicism, was corrupt:

> It must be already clear that the Reformation in the sixteenth century was nothing more than a rebellion of the Arian races of Europe against the Buddhism which the Celtic races had superinduced upon the Christianity of the Bible.[23]

It is ironic how Fergusson dismissed Stukeley's Druid theory but replaced it with one that derived equally from modern religious tensions.

Fergusson first set out his views on Stonehenge in 1860 and refined them in the years leading to his 1872 book, *Rude Stone Monuments*. By 1870, he moved away from his original theory that megaliths were Celtic, though he retained his belief that they were post-Roman.[24] In interpreting prehistory with a racial determinist outlook, he started to see megalith-builders as a widespread, homogenous and undeveloped people, 'certainly one of the least progressive races of mankind'.[25] Part of his shift away from Celts might have been the growing picture of them as an accomplished Iron Age race, too far up the social evolutionist scale for them to have made such 'rude' monuments, which he attributed to the direct descendants of 'cave men'.[26] Despite the thoroughness of Fergusson's survey of megaliths in *Rude Stone Monuments*, his idiosyncratic theory of their origins isolated him from the growing international network of prehistorians.

For British prehistorians, the Norwich setting of the third International Congress of Prehistoric Archaeology in 1868 provided the perfect forum for establishing standards for their discipline, and the question of the megaliths figured prominently in the proceedings. Alfred Lionel Lewis, a long-time researcher of megalithic monuments, argued with Lubbock over whether these monuments, still popularly termed 'Druidic', were actually related to the ancient Druids. In a paper 'On Certain Druidic Monuments in Berkshire', Lewis presented his case ostensibly from a neutral position, admitting that 'objections are raised to the use of the word "Druidic"; but I employ it here as a short, convenient, and universally understood term'.[27] After expressing misgivings about broaching the topic for fear of arousing controversy, he eventually stated his belief that 'the term Druidic is not only convenient but *correct*; and that these monuments must be attributed to the Celtic nations'.[28] In the discussion after the paper, Lubbock argued that 'the Druids had nothing whatever to do with the erection of those stones', which, as in his argument in *Pre-Historic Times*, he placed along with Stonehenge in the Bronze Age.[29]

When Lewis held fast to his Druid theory in Norwich, he represented a declining minority. Just before his paper, the Scottish antiquary John Stuart repeated an argument he had made more than a decade earlier to the British Association that the theory of the Druidical origins of megaliths came from the outdated ideas of Aubrey and Stukeley and that it had no basis in ancient writings or on 'authority of facts, observation, or analogy'.[30] Yet at a meeting of the Anthropological Institute in 1871, Lewis presented another paper espousing the Druidical origins of megaliths.[31] In order to show that he had stayed abreast of new developments in the field, Lewis proposed a model of British races based on physical anthropology carried out by John Beddoe. In the discussion that followed, Luke Burke argued that for Lewis' theory to be valid it needed to be based more on geological than on historical data. W. Boyd Dawkins also disputed the claim, saying that the connection between ancient monuments and racial types had not yet been worked out with enough certainty to assign megaliths to Druids. In spite of these arguments, Lewis persisted in his Druid theory, demonstrating the ability of druidophiles to revise their reasoning rather than their conclusions in the face of criticism.

The appeal of the connection between Druids and megaliths provided a motivation for a number of researchers, like Lewis, to study the monuments and present their findings at archaeological meetings. Before the twentieth century, core members of the prehistoric movement rarely studied these monuments in detail themselves, leaving the field open to researchers enamoured with the Druid theory or to fringe theorists like Fergusson. At Stonehenge, for example, a popular guidebook of the 1850s identified the site as Druidical, and it was not until 1901 that the Society of Antiquaries sponsored an excavation there, confirming the site's pre–Druidical status.[32]

Another way for megalith enthusiasts to adapt to the new standards of the prehistorians was to present simple observations of the monuments without discussing the question of the builders. This approach was taken by two generations of the Lukis family. Frederick Corben Lukis had surveyed megaliths since the 1840s, describing them in his earlier writing as 'Druidical remains', but, unlike Lewis, he quickly changed his descriptions to accommodate the new theory that they dated to the Bronze Age or earlier.[33] In the 1870s and '80s, Lukis' son William Collings Lukis continued his father's interest in the topic, focusing more on survey and minimising discussion of the monuments' origins. By publicly castigating unorthodox theorists like Fergusson and Lewis, Lubbock and his colleagues effectively forced gentlemen antiquaries like the Lukises to refrain from theorising about the origins of the monuments they observed, thereby establishing a divide between amateur observers and a professional class of theorists.

The Decline of Barrow-Digging

Just as surveyors of megaliths started to defer to the prehistorians for the interpretations of their finds, barrow-diggers likewise concentrated their efforts on descriptions of their excavations and left ethnological discussions of chronology and racial sequences to specialists. In contrast to previous generations of barrow-diggers, who had given a strong voice to the Druid theory, the diggers of the late nineteenth century downplayed the Druids, either ignoring them or citing theories that denied their relevance to the barrows. In this sense, the barrow-digging tradition in this period is transitional between the unrestrained Druidical attributions of their predecessors and the developments around the turn of the twentieth century that brought an end to the enterprise of regional-scale excavations of large numbers of burials.

Many of the barrow-diggers of the late nineteenth century were close friends, if not relatives, leading to a uniformity in their approach. Their research is generally categorisable by county, the research unit within which most of them worked. In Dorset, Charles Warne initially classified remains by the traditional set of peoples – Celtic, Roman, Saxon, Danish – defining as Celtic anything before the arrival of the Romans and tracing Celts in other countries simply by the appearance of barrows.[34] In his largest and final book on the topic, however, he confined his contribution to describing his finds and included a wide-ranging ethnological chapter by T. William Wake Smart.[35] Similarly, in Yorkshire, William Greenwell collected skulls in order to assign skull types to various ages, but he turned to George Rolleston, who was trying to establish the study of anthropology at Oxford, to analyse the skulls in detail. Rolleston confirmed Thurnam's theory that long barrows corresponded with long skulls and round barrows with round skulls; but he did not use the term *Celtic* to describe the latter because he wanted to avoid confusion with linguistics, and he was unsure if the round skulls really belonged to the Celts.[36]

Other barrow-diggers simply chose to ignore ethnological concerns. Thurnam continued to excavate Wiltshire barrows, but curtailed his earlier ethnological interests, concentrating mainly on describing his finds and only referring briefly to his long/long, round/round theory.[37] In Cornwall, William Copeland Borlase, a descendant of the eighteenth-century Borlase, wrote his own book on ancient local burial customs, but refused to consider a Druidical component to the same monuments that his ancestor had seen as part of this ancient priesthood.[38] Rooke Pennington, J.C. Atkinson and William Turner compiled findings from Derbyshire, Cleveland and Buxton respectively, but had little to say about the peoples they uncovered.[39] Finally, J.R. Mortimer brought the age of barrow-digging to a close in 1905 with his massive descriptive tome on Yorkshire.[40]

Though the barrow-diggers hoped that their work would be relevant to ethnology, they contributed little to ethnological theory. The wealth of new evidence they produced never challenged craniological orthodoxy and acted instead as a sort of benign confirmation of it. By the end of the century, their activity was abating, not only because of new protectionist legislation, but because the information potential of the graves seemed to be exhausted. In the meantime, the national institutional base for prehistoric archaeology in the late nineteenth century remained rooted in the tradition of physical anthropology in which it was born. Along with the British Association, the Anthropological Institute, which represented the reunion of the Ethnological Society and the breakaway Anthropological Society, formed the centre of gravity for British archaeology, and in this context the field continued to be heavily influenced by the craniologists.

While craniology remained at the centre of British archaeology, Wilson's model, in which a pre-Celtic Neolithic race was followed by a series of Celtic invasions in the Bronze Age, was rarely questioned. Huxley tried to combine historical, linguistic and skeletal evidence to study Celtic migrations, but could only remark, rather banally, that 'the language spoken' by both the tall/blond and short/dark physical types 'of people in Britain, at or before the Roman conquest, was exclusively Celtic'.[41] In the 1880s, Dawkins put together a major synthesis of recent archaeological and geological finds, basing his sequence largely on 'osteological enquiry', combined with 'ethnology, history, and geography'.[42] Dawkins' primary interest was the Palaeolithic, however, and his racial sequence for later pre-history was almost identical to Wilson's. As Wilson's racial sequence became part of the received wisdom of archaeology, there seemed little point in continuing to research skulls in detail. Meanwhile, more fertile grounds for researching the peopling of Britain were beginning to appear elsewhere, in the archaeology of large-scale sites as well as in other disciplinary traditions within anthropology.

Large-Scale Excavations

As archaeologists like Joseph Anderson developed the study of art and ornament, new kinds of archaeological sites were replacing the barrow as the most fertile source of new evidence. As the late nineteenth century witnessed the final phase of an almost 200-year tradition of barrow-digging, a new phase was beginning in which settlement sites and large-scale cemeteries figured prominently in new research goals. In intellectual terms, by offering a wider behavioural context and range of evidence, these sites enabled archaeologists to study past ways of life on a larger scale than was allowed by examining individual barrow burials. The sites also provided archaeologists with fresh evidence that could be used to weigh the possibility that cultural change was the product of diffusion instead of the migrations or invasions which had figured large in the models proposed by craniologists, linguists and folklorists. Intensive single-site excavations also aided in the establishment of new professional standards; far more complex an undertaking than the opening of barrows, they required a coordinated team of diggers and a level of financing beyond the reach of many of the independent gentlemen archaeologists who comprised the barrow-digging tradition.

Munro

Archaeologists in Britain turned their attention to settlements in the decades after the famous Swiss lakeside excavations of the 1850s. The Scottish antiquary Robert Munro surveyed similar sites in Scotland before delivering the Rhind Lectures of 1888 as an attempted synthesis of lakeside archaeology in Europe.[43] The wealth of material unearthed from Swiss lakes and related sites had been synthesised in 1866 and 1878 by Ferdinand Keller, and Munro conceived of his lectures as the next in this series on lakeside material. Continuing the ethnological tradition, Munro retained a strong interest in the migrations of peoples, but without basing his ideas on craniology. In place of skulls, Munro turned to artefact style as a more reliable indicator of racial affiliation, and he placed particular emphasis on the art of the Celts, which he defined by what Continental archaeologists had come

to call La Tène art and artefacts, after the type-site for the second half of the
Iron Age:

> So important are these antiquities considered by archaeologists that the
> name La Tène has now become a generic expression, and represents a spe-
> cial group which in both form and style of ornamentation, cannot be
> confounded with any other, either Greek, Roman, Etruscan or Phoenician.
> Who were these new comers into Switzerland who suddenly intruded
> themselves on the peaceful lake-dwellers? To this question there is no
> response from the skulls and other portions of human skeletons found at La
> Tène. Out of ten skulls submitted to Professor Virchow he found that five
> were brachycephalic and two dolichocephalic, while the other three had
> intermediate cranial indices. We must therefore fall back on the character of
> the antiquities; and for this purpose I place before you some typical exam-
> ples of this remarkable group culled from various sources for the purpose of
> showing their complete identity with those from the oppidum La Tène.
> Having satisfied ourselves on this point I proceed to glance rapidly over the
> geographical area in which such objects are found, with the view of show-
> ing to what people they belonged.[44]

After surveying European sites with La Tène attributes, Munro argued
against Keller's 'preconceived notion that the lake-dwellings of the Stone
and Bronze Ages were due to the Celts' and recalled the connection Franks
had drawn between the La Tène 'style of ornamentation' and 'the customs of
the ancient Celtic races'.[45] Franks, however, had called this art style 'late
Celtic', leaving open the question, not just of the character of the early
Celtic peoples, but of the origin of the Celts. Ironically, Franks himself had
revised his usage of the term *Celtic* since the publication of *Horae Ferales*,
and now, like Anderson and Allen, used it only in the context of the British
Isles:

> The term Late Celtic is better suited to this country than to France, where
> the word Celtic has been much abused. There the corresponding term
> would be Gaulish, an origin now adopted by most French archaeologists for
> relics of this character.[46]

Nevertheless, Munro sought a Continental origin of the Iron Age Celts who,
he argued, could not have descended from local Bronze Age people on
account of the long-noticed difference in grip size of bronze and iron swords:

The few indications derived from the data supplied by lake-dwelling research suggest the idea that the evolution of the Celts in Europe coincides with the substitution of iron for bronze in the manufacture of the most important cutting implements and weapons, and that the earlier stages of this transition are to be found considerably to the east of the Rhine districts – as, for example, at Hallstadt.[47]

Under Munro's archaeological approach, the Celts had an autochthonous origin point in east-central Europe and then spread westward, leaving evidence of their existence in the form of language, La Tène artefacts and lake-dwellings.[48] In spurning craniology as having little practical value, Munro abandoned the craniological model in which the Celts were Bronze Age invaders. As carriers of Celtic art, the Celts for Munro invaded in the Iron Age.

Glastonbury, Aylesford and Cranborne Chase

In the years before the turn of the twentieth century, the two most significant of the large-scale sites in Britain that had an impact on ideas about the Celts were the Aylesford urn-field, examined by members of the Evans family in 1886, and the Glastonbury lake village, discovered by Arthur Bulleid in 1892. Meanwhile, the leading proponent of large-scale site excavations was Augustus Henry Lane Fox who, after taking the name Pitt Rivers as a condition of inheriting a sizeable and archaeology-rich estate on Cranborne Chase in southern England, argued, 'the everyday life of the people is, beyond all comparison, of more interest than their mortuary customs'.[49]

Though Pitt Rivers documented the skeletons he excavated, he did not seek out racial types but instead focused his attention on reconstructing the expansive sites he spent his career uncovering. Aside from being a methodological shift, this concentration on settlement sites reflected a wider change in emphasis – in which Pitt Rivers played an important role – from the ethnological question of which races came to Britain at which times to the evolutionary question of how society in Britain progressed from simple forms deep in prehistory to its modern complexity.

As the owner of many of the sites he investigated and financier of his own excavations, Pitt Rivers could impose his own research agenda, which tended to exclude ethnological concerns. This was not a pattern easily replicated elsewhere. The excavation of the Glastonbury lake village, 'the most important archaeological investigation' of its time in the British Isles, was run by a committee of notables with varying research goals (pl. 21).[50]

By 1894, two years after its discovery by Bulleid, a local antiquary interested both in 'determining who the inhabitants were' by examining 'human remains' and in looking into 'the kind of life they led', the British Association assembled a team, including Munro, Dawkins, Pitt Rivers and Evans, to work towards these differing objectives.[51] Within this committee, however, the study of human remains was becoming increasingly marginalised as Pitt Rivers' approach to settlement sites came to dominate.

Though Pitt Rivers' influence was evident in the setting of a research agenda for Glastonbury, the archaeologist most actively involved was Munro, who had taken a leadership position on the committee. Like Pitt Rivers, Munro was interested in fleshing out the daily life of the site's inhabitants 'from the stand-point of the archaeological materials they have left behind them in the form of stray, broken and worn out objects of their domestic, social and military life', or what he called evidence of 'the culture and civilization of the village occupiers', echoing Anderson's favoured phrase. [52] Unlike Pitt Rivers, however, Munro had long used archaeological evidence to address ethnological issues. In his Rhind Lectures of 1888, for example, he equated the spread of Celtic art with the migrations of the Celtic race. In the second annual site report, Munro drew attention to five unearthed skulls, but cited instead the designs on artefacts 'highly ornamented with devices which unmistakably show "late Celtic" art' when he considered the affiliations of the villagers.[53]

By the publication of the final Glastonbury site report in 1911, Munro separated the problem of migration from that of the diffusion of Celtic art: 'The precise way in which the primary elements of Late-Celtic art were introduced into Britain is a matter of conjecture'.[54] The growing disciplinary separation between physical anthropologists and archaeologists gave Munro the opportunity to remove the difficult problem of migration from his studies of artefacts and to refer the issue to the craniologists. In the report, Munro did not personally address the ethnological question of the race and origins of the inhabitants, but was content to cite the ideas of Dawkins, who outlined the results of his craniological investigations in three short chapters affixed to the end of the report's second volume. Dawkins' argument, that the inhabitants had been racially 'Iberic' but spoke a Celtic language of the Brythonic variety, was of declining relevance to Munro's growing interest in cultural diffusion.[55]

When Arthur Evans presented evidence of the Aylesford cemetery to the Society of Antiquaries, the question of diffusion versus migration was chief among his concerns. Evans cited evidence of what 'Mr. Franks has given the name of "late Celtic"' in determining the affiliations of the urn-field, whose cremation burials precluded analysis by craniologists (*pl. 22*).[56] After examining the burial customs represented at the site, Evans considered diffusion, rather than simple migration, as a possible element of cultural change. Just as Pitt Rivers had shown how the persistence of older types of pottery in newer cultural horizons indicated that earlier inhabitants were not necessarily replaced by new arrivals, Evans noted:

> on the outskirts of the area occupied by graves of this class there occurred some relics and interments of an earlier character, and tending to show that, side by side with the later Celtic invaders from beyond the Channel, this site was still partially inhabited by representatives of the race that inhabited Britain before the arrival of the Gaulish intruders who introduced the new sepulchral forms.[57]

For Evans, therefore, Celtic artefacts in Britain did not necessarily indicate the presence of Celtic invaders. In the same way that Munro argued that Celtic art might represent the diffusion of the art style instead of the simple spread of a people, Evans argued that these types of '"urn-fields" containing cremation interments' throughout Europe represented 'the diffusion of the Early Iron Age culture, and the final triumph of iron over bronze', but he left open the possibility that particular sites might be the product of foreign invaders.[58]

Before taking on the issue of whether Aylesford represented cultural diffusion or invasion, Evans looked to the Continent for earlier examples of cremation and of Late Celtic art in order to find the roots of this Early Iron Age culture. Using work done by Mortillet, he found such an area in northern Italy, in the 'Illyro-Italic province' on one of 'the main avenues of commerce between the Adriatic ports and the Central European regions'.[59] Without the benefit of absolute dating techniques, Evans pinpointed this area on the basis of its geographic position. Art of the 'La Tène Period' could be found in 'North Germany and Scandinavia' and 'Belgic Gaul' as well as northern Italy, leading Evans to search for a 'common centre of radiation'.[60] After comparing the Aylesford artefacts and examples of cremation with those in Italy and in Britain from earlier times, Evans argued, 'This sudden break with pre-existing sepulchral usages and the traditional indigenous forms of pottery points to the progress of a conquering race'.[61] Rather than name this race as Celtic, he described it as being part of the La Tène horizon, comprising a mixture of Celtic and Illyro-Italic traditions, though he called the Aylesford cemetery 'the first beginnings of Late-Celtic art in Britain'.[62]

Despite opening up the possibility of diffusion, and in contrast to Munro's hesi-
tancy to comment on the issue, Evans concluded his Aylesford study with a new
version of the old Celtic migrations story. Nevertheless, in conjunction with Pitt
Rivers, Munro and Anderson, Evans helped put forward a new model of the
Celts, not as a race of people, but as participants in a cultural tradition that included cremations and, more importantly, a particular style of art.

While the site reports produced by Pitt Rivers, Munro and Evans signalled a major methodological shift in archaeology, it was John Romilly
Allen's work on Celtic art that digested these developments and set the
agenda for archaeology in the twentieth century. Allen's book was instrumental in bringing about the end of the predominance of the racial
interpretation of the Celts; he proposed further settlement-site research as
the best source of new information: 'until the large number of inhabited
and fortified sites belonging to this period are systematically investigated
our knowledge must necessarily remain incomplete'.[63] Of such settlement
sites, the one 'which bids fair to rival all others in the varied nature of the
relics obtained in it, and the light they help to throw on the arts and indus-
tries of the Early Iron Age in Great Britain' – in a sense, the model site – was
the Glastonbury lake village.[64]

Allen's call for more such research was answered over the following
decades, which witnessed major excavations at the Meare lake village,
Hengistbury Head, Wookey Hole, All Cannings Cross and a series of camps
in Wiltshire.[65] In the meantime, he worked with existing evidence, mainly
from chance finds and burial sites. As the twentieth century progressed,
these new digs resulted in new kinds of evidence, like subsistence patterns,
which challenged the ascendancy of ancient art and ornament.
Nevertheless, Allen's contribution set a new standard for research into the
ancient Celts and was the first of a continuing string of books about Celtic
art modelled on his example.

The Collapse of the Anthropological Synthesis

Despite the major developments in the late nineteenth century that both
redirected research priorities and created new professional standards as a part
of discipline formation, archaeology was still intellectually and institutionally
a branch of anthropology. This parent-discipline was also home to linguistics, physical anthropology and folklore. As the nineteenth century drew to
a close, however, it was increasingly clear that these constituent branches

were moving in different directions, precluding the possibility of a single anthropological interpretation of the Celts and leading the way for them to become disciplines in their own right.

Celtic Folklore

Though the word was not coined until 1846, folklore had arisen as a category of evidence within both the general antiquarian collecting tradition and the ethnological tradition of tracing the origins of various races. The study of folklore started to become established as its own disciplinary tradition in the 1860s, when members of the Ethnological Society treated folklore as a distinct source of ethnological evidence and when a number of books dealing primarily with folklore started to appear. In this emerging field, the tracing of racial movements had a diminished importance as folklore became a route to understanding so-called savage and barbarian peoples within a growing evolutionist framework. Folklore quickly took on political significance insofar as it achieved the status held by language and physiology as a reliable indicator of racial affiliation. People in the British Isles who possessed remnants of what was being identified as Celtic folklore appeared to many not just to have descended from ancient Celts but to be Celts themselves. The study of Celtic folklore and its political implications both reached a turning point in 1867, the year the Breton poet Charles de Gaulle organised the first Pan Celtic Conference, intended as a step toward Celtic political unification, and the year of publication of Matthew Arnold's definition of Celtic literature, launching the discipline of Celtic Studies in the British Isles.[66]

Borrowing the greater part of his theories from the Frenchman Ernest Renan's 'La Poésie des Races Celtiques', Arnold lectured to an Oxford audience in 1865 and 1866 to the effect that the word 'sentimental' captured the essence of 'the Celtic genius', as manifest in Celtic writings.[67] His notion of an unchanging Celtic genius conflated what classical texts said about Celts, evidence from early Welsh and Irish sources and folklore on the modern 'Celtic fringe' into a single racial character.[68] Arnold's analysis had a tremendous impact, despite his surprising unfamiliarity with the sources. His lectures had the effect of promoting the study of Celtic literature and of setting the tone for such studies. His insistence 'on the benefit we may all derive from knowing the Celt and things Celtic more thoroughly', and his call to set up a chair of Celtic at Oxford, helped Celtic Studies to gain momentum and provided a new academic role for the expanding collections of stories, both oral and written, from Celtic regions.[69] At the same

time, his image of Celtic literature – as sentimentalist, feminine and nostal-
gically anti-modern – perfectly mirrored the social evolutionist image of
folklore itself as the spiritual and non-scientific knowledge system of primitive societies. As Celtic folklorists joined in Arnold's call for further study of
Celtic literature, they followed his lead in attributing to the Celts a primitive level of civilisation that contrasted with the scientific progress of
Anglo-Saxon England.

By the late 1870s and '80s, when a number of chairs of Celtic Studies
appeared across the British Isles, the study of folklore took a step towards
disciplinary independence in the founding of the Folk-Lore Society. The
Society was dominated by prehistorians interested in using folklore to
reconstruct the early stages of cultural evolution. Alfred Nutt, a leading
member of the Society, mined Celtic folklore in order to discover which
elements descended from the earliest days of Celtic migrations to Britain.
Nutt's work, in turn, inspired a fast-growing community of scholars to collect folk-tales from Ireland, Scotland, and Wales.

For the most part, collectors of Celtic folklore were little interested in
the implications of their work on the question of peopling, except for a few
scholars who debated the possible Aryan and pre-Aryan elements in the
stories. Chief among these was John Rhys, who occupied the newly inau-
gurated Jesus Professorship of Celtic at Oxford. Thanks to his interest in
peopling, Rhys was appointed Rhind Lecturer, like Joseph Anderson and
John Romilly Allen before him. Starting in 1888, four Rhind Lecturers in
five years offered surveys of the peopling of Britain on the basis of evidence
from different disciplinary traditions, indicating how anthropology's constituent branches were still considered to be working in harmony to address
the same questions. Robert Munro was the Rhind Lecturer in 1888, speaking on European lake settlement sites. Then in 1889 Rhys offered a different
interpretation of Celtic origins and migrations. In 1891 John Beddoe spoke
on physical anthropology, and in 1892 Joseph Anderson surveyed Celtic art.

Rhys took as his task the analysis of Celtic texts, in terms both of their
content and of the languages themselves, which were increasingly seen as
holding information about the Celtic character.[70] The focus of Rhys'
research was not the origin point of the Celts, but what the evidence of the
various Celtic dialects indicated about the sequence of migrations and the
affiliations of the different groups within the Celtic family. Though he
favoured the Baltic area as the source of Celtic migrations, he did not dwell
on the matter, writing, 'Our business here, however, is to try to understand
what is meant by Celtic, and how the Celtic nations of the present day stand

in respect of one another'.[71] Rhys oriented his analysis around the long-noticed linguistic difference between Q Celtic (Irish Gaelic, Scottish Gaelic and Manx) and P Celtic (Welsh, Cornish and Breton), arguing that Q Celts arrived in the British Isles first and were pushed westward by the later arrival of the P Celts. While these ideas were fairly orthodox, Rhys put forward the unconventional theory that the Q Celts were part of the greater Aryan language family, while the P Celts represented a mixture of Aryans with other groups. He supported this idea, not just with linguistic arguments, but with an analysis of folklore in an attempt to isolate Aryan and non-Aryan elements.[72]*

Rhys understood the limitations of his literary approach to Celtic origins and supplemented his analysis with the results of other disciplinary traditions, especially those that covered early prehistory. He cited craniologists in attributing a pre-Celtic, possibly Iberian race to the British Neolithic; and he added to this picture by arguing from manuscript sources that the Picts were descended from these early inhabitants of Britain.[73] In his book-length study of Britain's racial history, he even argued for the superiority of craniology over his own approach, indicating how little Munro's lectures had influenced him:

> Skulls are harder than consonants, and races lurk behind when languages slink away. The lineal descendants of the neolithic aborigines are ever among us, possibly even those of a still earlier race.[74]

Nevertheless, he felt that the evidence of languages and early writings had much to offer in fleshing out the ethnological history of Britain.

While Rhys brought Celtic folklore into more general debates about the peopling of Britain, the most significant effect of folklore studies was to help popularise the notion that the Celts represented a primitive culture that had modern representatives on the fringes of Britain. This notion was reinforced by physical anthropologists, led by Beddoe, who argued that past racial movements left a measurable residue in living populations. The growing idea of modern Celts became highly politicised with the submission of the first Home Rule Bill for Ireland in 1886. Though Pan Celticism had been maturing as a political and cultural movement for about two decades, the Home Rule Bill, which came under consideration at the beginning of

---

*For linguists and folklorists, 'Aryan' was a synonym for Indo-European and did not yet have the connotations bestowed by the Nazis.

what became known as the Celtic Revival in Ireland, was the first political manifestation of the aspirations of self-defined modern Celts in the British Isles for self-governance. Many opponents of Home Rule seized upon the racist argument that the Celtic blood of the Irish made them unsuitable for self-government. Proponents of Home Rule, meanwhile, celebrated their Celtic ancestry in a revival reminiscent of the Scottish and Welsh romantic regionalists of earlier revivals, but with nationalist overtones.

In Ireland, the late nineteenth-century Celtic Revival was characterised by a proliferation of societies, mainly literary and athletic, meant to preserve indigenous traditions. While revivalists often used the term Gaelic to describe these traditions, as in the Gaelic Athletic Association and in the crafts-oriented Gaelic League, the term *Celtic* was also given prominence, for example when Pro-Home Rule Irish Catholics in Glasgow founded the Celtic football club in 1888. Though athletics and crafts were key components of the Celtic Revival, the movement was primarily literary. Just as romantic regionalists like Evan Evans, James Macpherson and Edward Williams defined their Celtic heritage in terms of a literary tradition, Irish nationalists celebrated poetry, folklore and the language that was being rapidly replaced by English. W.B. Yeats' collection of folklore from western Ireland, culminating in his 1893 publication of *The Celtic Twilight*, was instrumental in describing a native Irish Celtic voice, which could then be emulated in new poetry. With the work of Yeats and his followers, Celtic folklore became closely allied with the Irish Home Rule movement. In contrast, the anthropological study of the Celts proved unhelpful for the Irish Celtic Revival, because leading anthropologists like Lubbock, Beddoe and Huxley considered both Ireland and Britain to be mixed, with evidence of Celtic blood everywhere.[75]

Beddoe

The physical anthropologist John Beddoe used the post of Rhind Lecturer in 1891 to offer a completely different approach to the same questions that Rhys had addressed. Since the 1850s, Beddoe had studied living people's hair and eye colours, which he thought were passed from generation to generation 'irrespectively of the climatic and other agencies which may be at work upon them', and so could be used as a reliable indicator of race.[76] He had also worked extensively with Davis, mainly relating ancient skull types with measurements drawn from modern Britons, and had succeeded Hunt as president of Anthropological Society. The topic of Beddoe's lectures, 'The Anthropological History of Europe', covered more territory than Rhys' discussion of the British Isles, but was equally oriented around the question of Aryan migrations. Because Beddoe's main evidence was physical characteristics, however, he structured his lectures around the additional question of the 'degree of permanence of types'.[77]

Beddoe's lectures offered a somewhat encyclopedic review of Europe's races based chiefly on skull types. He addressed the question of the Celts in the second lecture, when he discussed the confusion among what historical sources said about them, what the archaeological record seemed to indicate about their skulls and what the evidence of place names and linguistics contributed to the picture. All he could really conclude – in sharp contrast to Munro's optimism – was that little was known for certain from these different lines of evidence about Celtic origins and migrations.[78] At the end of his series, Beddoe left the increasingly controversial question of Aryan migrations without a firm conclusion, but argued that skull types remained consistent within races and that 'certain qualities do adhere to certain races', though he rejected the notion that any race is superior to any other.[79] For future research, Beddoe thought that skulls would hold the answer to the peopling of Europe and he hoped to reverse the existing situation in which 'the craniological record of prehistoric ages is very insufficient'.[80]

More than 20 years before his Rhind Lectures, Beddoe had won the Welsh National Eisteddfod essay contest with a paper on the ethnology of Britain oriented around his measurements of living populations. He expanded this to book form in 1885, as *The Races of Britain*. Here he reviewed craniological evidence supporting the racial divisions surrounding the three ages, but became hesitant in employing the word Celtic 'for several reasons', including the fact that Paul Broca, the French physical anthropologist whose work was followed by many in the British anthropological community, was limiting it to refer only to a people with 'short, thick-set figures and large, broad heads and faces' that he had identified in Gaul, where Roman writers placed the Celts.[81] To help resolve the mixed and somewhat confused racial picture of Britain's past, Beddoe invented what he called the 'index of nigrescence', which combined hair and eye colour measurements taken from around Britain. By assigning a single number to each British and Irish county, Beddoe created a map that showed a gradient of nigrescence running from light tones in the east to darker tones in the west (especially in Wales, Ireland and the Scottish Highlands), with a light region in the north of Scotland, where there was a strong Scandinavian influence (*pl. 23*).[82] Though he restricted his use of the term *Celtic*, the clear implication of the map was that the darker patches were associated with areas generally considered Celtic. In his conclusions, Beddoe affirmed the index of nigrescence as the best method of sorting out the mixture of races living in Britain.

Despite Beddoe's faith in the index of nigrescence and in the results of craniology, he followed Rhys in thinking that ethnological questions were only 'capable of solution' with 'the cooperation of anthropologists with antiquarians and philologists'.[83] After three Rhind Lecturers, Munro, Rhys and Beddoe, presented complementary approaches to the question of the peopling of Britain, it was becoming clear that progress would require a combined project, incorporating the often conflicting results of these diverse disciplinary traditions. In the decade that followed, the Rhind Lectureship returned to its earlier emphasis on history, surveys of Scottish monuments and, as its sole contribution to the question of peopling, further studies of Celtic art and ornament. In the wider research community, however, an attempt at an anthropological synthesis was under way.

The British Association Survey

Many of the rival approaches to defining and researching the Celts in the late nineteenth century came together in the course of an ambitious ethnographic survey conducted by the British Association in conjunction with local societies and more specialised national societies. Set against the backdrop of 'Celticist' agitation for Home Rule in Ireland, most of the prehistorians and leaders of anthropology, many of whom were Unionists, took it for granted that the British Isles were racially mixed.[85] The survey's goals were to understand how this mixture might be differently manifest in different regions and what the mixture might reveal about the peopling of the islands. The five departments of the survey each represented a different approach:

(1) Physical types of the inhabitants; (2) Current traditions and beliefs; (3) Peculiarities of dialect; (4) Monuments and other remains of ancient culture; and (5) Historical evidence as to continuity of race.[85]

The survey was organised by leading members of each of these fields, with a committee including Francis Galton, A.C. Haddon, Anderson, Allen, Dawkins, Pitt Rivers and Rhys. Haddon, who had interests in physical anthropology and folklore, was the leading figure behind the creation of the survey in 1892.

In his analysis of the problems of this wide-sweeping survey, the historian James Urry argued that it quickly failed to produce the desired ethnological results, not because the committee thought of its methodology and assumptions as flawed, but because the sought-after data was hard to collect and even harder to synthesise. As the survey ended, its constituent fields, including archaeology, dispersed and became entrenched as specialised and mostly independent disciplinary traditions which would never again have equal status as potential contributors to the issue of peopling.[86] The survey's data collection problems in physical anthropology heralded the decline of a disciplinary tradition that had never reached its stated goals of identifying racial types and had for too long been sustained by the belief that all would become clearer with more evidence. Physical anthropological surveys generally had begun to produce an unmanageable amount of data that was increasingly difficult to resolve into racial patterns. Though Beddoe's work had been widely influential, his followers, like Haddon and Galton, ran into difficulty in confirming or expanding on his results. Craniometry had fallen under increasing attack as disagreement remained as to which skull types belonged to which races and as new craniometric evidence often contradicted existing models. For a time, physical anthropologists attempted to formulate increasingly intricate schemes, like Beddoe's index of nigrescence, to distill racial types from a combination of factors. The American anthropologist William Ripley, for example, combined six independently variable categories in arguing for the existence of three basic races in Europe.[87] Eventually, the continued inability of any new schemes to reach consensus about Europe's racial history led to stagnation and opened the door for rival methods to address the question of peopling.

As physical anthropology started to lose its position as the foremost source of ethnological evidence, the linguistic and folklore-related disciplinary traditions from the survey began to shed their ethnological aspects. From its inception, folklore studies had never been home to much ethnological research, with the exception of Rhys' contributions. And despite Rhys' continuing faith in physical anthropology and the discipline's wide support in universities and scientific societies, physical anthropology was becoming less relevant to researchers actively looking at the question of peopling. As the survey was disbanded in 1899, the peopling of Britain nevertheless remained an attractive topic of research. It remained a focal question within prehistoric archaeology, the only one of the branch disciplines of ethnology to enter the twentieth century with continuing confidence that its methods were equal to the task of tracing the movements of peoples from their origins to their current diversity.

Even though the greatest quantity of research into the ancient Celts has taken place in the twentieth century, it is actually the least dynamic period since the early eighteenth century in terms of fundamental changes in the meaning of the term *Celtic* and in the creation of new methods of describing them. In many ways, Allen's *Celtic Art* was a blueprint, widely followed and, after all these years, still available in bookshops. His definition of the Celts remains familiar, as does his use of archaeological methods, including settlement-site excavation and comparison of styles of ornament. Of course many of the details changed as more material subsequently came to light, as new methods of analysis were invented and as frameworks of interpretation continually shifted. Indeed, the development of Iron Age archaeology in the twentieth century would make an interesting subject in its own right. But changes in interpretation that have been of great importance within the discipline have had little relevance to public perceptions of this ancient people. Allen's Celts are not very different from our Celts, while they are distinct from, say, the Celts as understood by Daniel Wilson or Evan Evans or Edward Lhuyd.

As the twentieth century unfolded, a version of the Celts as first described by late nineteenth-century archaeologists appeared repeatedly in lists of the great peoples of the ancient world. In 1914, the French archaeologist Henri Hubert completed a two-volume study of the Celts in which he presented a seamless picture of a culture that had risen to become 'torch bearers in the ancient world'.[88] This was published in English in 1934 as part of a series called *The History of Civilization*. Since then, the British Celts in both their pre- and post-Roman guises have appeared in similar series, notably in the Ancient Peoples and Places books edited by Glyn Daniel (T.G.E. Powell's *The Celts* in 1958 and Nora Chadwick's *Celtic Britain* in 1964). Books like these continue to appear regularly, rarely questioning whether the Celts should in fact be taken to represent a single, integrated cultural unit and showing little awareness of how recently this idea developed.

From the perspective of the twenty-first century, it seems that archaeology is coming full circle. As the discipline further deepens our understanding of pre-Roman Britain, the notion that it was in some way Celtic is falling out of favour. Archaeologists today have re-articulated a simple question: If there were Celts in ancient Britain, how and when did they arrive? Greek and Roman writers offered conflicting accounts of the Celts but never described them as being in the British Isles, and the connections between the Iron Age inhabitants of these islands and the Continental Celts are less straightforward than had been imagined previously. To label all Iron Age central and western European peoples as *Celtic*, in distinction to, say, the Greeks and Romans in the south and the Germans in the north, is to impose a collectivity on an unbounded socio-political system whose own conceptual units were probably smaller than what we think of as the Celtic world. It is now the turn of the present generation to provide its own definition of the Celts, but it is far from clear whether this will continue to include ancient Britain.

EPILOGUE

Archaeologists are now debating whether it is useful to say that the Celts in fact came to Britain. To put this debate in perspective, it is instructive to review how it came to pass that most people assume that they did. There are a host of factors behind the sudden application of the term *Celtic* to the British Isles in the early eighteenth century and many more behind the subsequent changes, as the term gradually took on a meaning that we recognise. Over the centuries, each generation produced its own meaning and its own methods of tracing the Celts. Because the process of redefining the term lasted so long and involved so many different disciplines, it is not easy to explain succinctly how the Celts came to Britain.

The ultimate source for the name *Celt* is the ancient texts which employed the word in a variety of ways – some contradictory, most of them unspecific and none of them directly relevant to the British Isles. In 1703, Paul-Yves Pezron initiated the sequence of events that brought the Celts to Britain when he tried to link Brittany to biblical history and came up with a novel definition of the Celtic language as being the parent tongue of all of Europe. His contemporary Thomas Brown drew a connection between the eastern origins of these Celts with the supposed eastern origins of Druidism. William Stukeley then applied these ideas to British material remains and became the first to describe them as Celtic. It took another generation, however, before Evan Evans argued that the Celts were distinct from Goths and other European peoples, rather than ancestral to them.

After this, James Douglas, William Cunnington and Richard Colt Hoare excavated burials in a new kind of search for the Celts, though they did little to change the picture that had arisen in linguistics. James Cowles Prichard, in *The Eastern Origin of the Celtic Nations*, fixed the modern definition of the Celtic languages when he used linguistic evidence to draw connections among the Cornish, Welsh, Breton, Irish, Highland Scottish and Manx. Ironically, as the leading Celtic linguist and ethnologist of his day, Prichard soon became the first to apply Scandinavian-style craniology to the British past, launching a half-century of physical anthropology in a fruitless quest to quantify a Celtic race. After Prichard, the evidence of Celtic material remains – be they skulls, art or settlement patterns – replaced linguistic evidence as the most dynamic source of new definitions of the Celts.

In the 1840s, William Wilde and Daniel Wilson drew on cranial evidence to argue for the first time that the Celts were not the original inhabitants of the British Isles but arrived in the Bronze Age. Following this, a series of museum curators including Samuel Birch, John Kemble, Augustus Wollaston Franks and Joseph Anderson constructed a picture of Celtic art that identified the Celts as living in the Iron Age. Added to Matthew Arnold's notion of a Celtic spirit identifiable in poetry, the study of Celtic ornament helped establish Celtic culture as an alternative object of research to a Celtic race. Finally, archaeologists like Robert Munro, Arthur Evans and John Romilly Allen promoted the excavation of large-scale sites as a way to gain a clearer picture of ancient Celtic ways of life. From late nineteenth-century archaeology arose the outline of the modern, popular understanding of the Celts as an Iron Age culture that arrived in Britain with a new style of art, way of life and beliefs and which spoke a certain type of language.

In short, our notion of the ancient Celts has come about through an unlikely combination of factors and derived from a variety of individual motivations. It is a long way from the Greek and Roman sources, which never used the words 'Celtic' or 'Gallic' to describe the inhabitants of ancient Britain, to Allen's *Celtic Art in Pagan and Christian Times*. If research into pre-Roman Britain were to start again from scratch, it is hard to imagine that the term *Celtic* would play a significant role. It is no wonder, then, that many archaeologists would like to do away with the term and move out from under the shadow of previous researchers. Almost 200 years ago, Prichard bemoaned the fact that he felt stuck with a usage of the term *Celtic* that was inappropriate. It remains to be seen if today's archaeologists can undo what Prichard could not and change popular conceptions.

In contemporary archaeology, the history of Celtic scholarship has begun to receive scrutiny within the controversy about the use of the Celtic label for ancient Britain. Having reviewed that history here, what can we now offer to this debate?

The sceptics who triggered the re-evaluation of the Celtic label have offered two central arguments: 1) that the label is misleading because it contradicts our understanding of Iron Age Europe as a more diverse place than is implied by the collective name of the Celts, and 2) that the term introduces biases into interpretations because of its political connotations. On the other side of the debate, researchers maintain that *Celtic* describes a real cultural phenomenon in antiquity, that this Celtic culture was present in the British Isles and that it does not necessarily matter whether the culture exactly matches classical descriptions of the ancient Celts. In addition to being an argument over which definitions of the Celts should take priority, this debate is about how peoples can be categorised.

Since Pezron, the term *Celtic* has had many different meanings, supporting a range of approaches to understanding pre-Roman Britain. New theories about ancient Britain have arisen alongside new uses of the word. For many of today's archaeologists there is a tendency to avoid cultural labels while treating the question of prehistoric affiliations as a research problem rather than a simple matter of categorising finds. But for art historians who have identified an Iron Age tradition of ornament and for linguists looking at the history of languages such as Gaelic and Welsh, the term *Celtic* fulfils an essential function of describing a broad cultural phenomenon through the use of a widely recognised word. Celtic art, Celtic languages and the historical Celtic tribes, however, do not match up with each other in a straightforward way. Yet the common use of the term Celtic for these phenomena implies that they do. This situation has led to a widening gulf between the continuing popular understanding that there were Celts in ancient Britain as part of a wider grouping with Continental Celts, and the growing view in archaeology that this is a mischaracterisation of prehistory.

The archaeologist Simon James has made the most spirited attempt to bridge this divide between archaeologists and the public by putting forth the case that dearly-held notions about the Celts are mistaken. Arguing that the ancient inhabitants of Britain 'did not use this name for themselves' and that the term *Celtic* 'has accumulated so much baggage, so many confusing meanings and associations, that it is too compromised' to be applied to the Iron Age, James concluded that the ancient Celts 'must be rejected as an ethnic label for the populations of the islands during the Iron Age'.[1] James' standard for calling the Iron Age inhabitants by the name of Celtic is not just that they would have had to have recognised this term for themselves (they probably would not have, though there is no way for us to know) but that they would have to have been an *ethnicity*.

Like *Celtic* itself, *ethnicity* is a contested term with no widely accepted meaning within the academic world. Let us look at James' definition of an ethnic group: 'Any group of people who set themselves apart from others, on the basis of their perceptions of cultural difference and/or common descent'.[2] It seems that, for James, what distinguishes an ethnic group from any other collection of people, like a race or culture, is that it is self-defined and constructed from the group's own perceptions, rather than from genes or inherited customs. But to what extent is this category useful for an archaeologist working on Iron Age Europe? Defining a prehistoric people's self-perceptions is far from straightforward. Some have proposed Celtic art or beliefs as a window into the prehistoric mind, but there is not always a clear correlation between self-perceptions and material culture. All groups of people are heterogeneous, making it impossible to establish a firm boundary on an ethnic group. Where do we draw the circle? Are ethnic groups generally large or small? There is a burgeoning interest in the archaeology of prehistoric ethnicities, and this is not the place to become deeply involved with the issue other than to say that a single, widely agreed definition of ancient ethnicities is unlikely to emerge.

By setting ethnicity as his standard for calling Britain Celtic, James has effectively disengaged from the work of previous researchers. Even today, archaeologists who continue to use *Celtic* as a broad category do not argue that it represents a single ethnic group.[3] From Pezron in 1703 through Allen in 1904, no writer discussed the ancient Celts as an 'ethnicity'. The word itself, if not the concept, is modern, having not been widely used before the end of the Second World War, when the horrors of Nazism precluded further scientific discussion of race. In the eighteenth and nineteenth centuries, the many writers who discussed the ancient Celts had different ideas about what constituted a people. For historians like Pezron, steeped in biblical-historical sources, a people was a named group like a tribe, held together through political unity. Even Pezron recognised that there are often differences between what a group calls itself and the name by which it is widely known. Others defined Celts by their spoken language or by their religion. Around the turn of the nineteenth century, the word 'race' became applied to both ancient and modern peoples. A race was variously defined by its language, customs or physical characteristics. With the growth of physical anthropology towards the end of the century, race became firmly linked to the blood of its constituents. At that time writers like Arnold and Anderson started to articulate the culture concept, which defined a people not by its biology but by its beliefs, customs and language. These writers were not concerned about what the ancient Celts thought themselves to be.

While James targeted public conceptions with his deconstructionist book on British Celts, John Collis addressed the archaeological evidence used to describe any ancient peoples – whether in Britain or on the Continent – as Celtic. In *The Celts: Origins, Myths and Inventions*, Collis drew upon the history of Celtic scholarship, the historical evidence for the Celts in the ancient texts and the archaeology of Iron Age Europe in order to make three key arguments: 1) that the term *Celtic* has been misapplied to material culture, 2) that there were multiple origins to what other archaeologists refer to as the Iron Age Celtic culture (which therefore cannot be explained through an origin-and-spread model), and 3) that this culture was so internally variable that it is questionable whether it can be grouped together as one entity that is distinct from its neighbours. In short, for Collis, the so-called 'Celtic culture' should not really be called 'Celtic', and, in any case, was not a unified or bounded group.

Collis, James and what James terms other 'post-Celticist' archaeologists have made important arguments about the ancient Celts not having been homogeneous throughout Europe, not having had a single origin point from which they spread, and not having conceived of themselves as part of a single entity.[4] But this point of view is not so different from the theories of Prichard, Wilson, Anderson and others, who did not see the Celts as a unified race that simply migrated to Britain and did not imagine that the Celts called themselves Celts. Do the 'post-Celticists' put forth sufficient reasons to abandon the term *Celtic* to describe the world of the British and Irish Iron Age? And if they do, then how can the abandonment of the term be achieved?

Certainly the arguments of the sceptics signal the need for caution in casually describing the insular past as Celtic. Researchers must at least be clear about what kind of group they think the Celts were. They were not a race, as race is not just a distasteful categorisation, but in fact has no scientific basis. Despite all the measurements and surveys, first in the nineteenth century and continuing into the twentieth and even twenty-first, and with the introduction of new DNA technologies, there is no way to describe a people through its blood alone. The Celts were not an ethnicity, because, as

James argued, it is debatable whether the Celts would have thought of themselves as such. And, as Collis argued, whether or not the Celts represent a unified archaeological culture depends on how one reads the historical evidence and on one's tolerance for internal diversity and local continuity under the collective name of 'Celtic'. What remains is a broad term that is historically inaccurate and contains a great deal of ambiguity, but is nevertheless widely recognised and understood as a rough synonym for the peoples of Iron Age western Europe.

The real battle that the sceptics face is not over the use or abandonment of the term *Celtic*, for it inevitably will be used, under whatever meaning, as it has been since the early eighteenth century. Rather, the battle is over what definition the word has. If *Celtic* is understood to carry no certain racial, ethnic or archaeological meaning, then the sceptics will have won the argument. If *Celtic* is to have a meaning more specific than an abbreviation for Iron Age western Europe, then it is the task of Celtic scholars to create a definition that enters into common usage. Currently, neither side seems to be winning the debate, because public ideas about the ancient Celts tend to derive from outdated notions of race or ethnicity and reflect neither the sceptical viewpoint nor the work of contemporary archaeologists.

The popularity of outdated ideas is the motivation for the other main argument that the sceptics have put forth against *Celtic*: that the term has become so politically loaded as to be a distraction. Archaeologists including James and Nick Merriman have argued that the mere use of the term *Celtic* brings unwanted political motivations into the archaeology of the Iron Age.[5] They say that researchers cannot be objective when talking about the ancient Celts while so-called Celtic regions of the British Isles are associated with particular political goals and may identify with the Iron Age past. Is there a way to shed our own political biases and reach objectivity? Does dropping the term *Celtic* move us closer to this goal or does it merely represent an alternative political expression?

Some commentators suggest self-knowledge as a way to avoid bias. Michael Dietler outlined this position in relation to the archaeology of the Celts of Iron Age France: 'Clearly, archaeologists must continually strive to be self-critical in evaluating the social and political contexts of their interpretive perspectives and their epistemological tools'.[6] James took this idea a step further. After reiterating the position that all archaeologists should be 'self-critical, not only regarding their political and cultural prejudices, but also their emotional responses', he provided, in some detail, an account of his own ethnic background and political orientation for readers to take into

account while evaluating his ideas.[7] Collis also addressed his personal background and politics, but only to refute particular accusations of bias put
forward by his rivals.[8] It is a contradiction, and perhaps a little arrogant, to
interpret the history of the social sciences as the product of socio-political
biases while, at the same time, maintaining that we can control our own
biases simply by examining ourselves. This notion of the corrective power
of self-knowledge in the face of bias has inspired a growing interest in the
history of archaeology, especially among archaeologists hoping to use their
knowledge of the past to improve the discipline.

Though the mitigation of socio-political bias is the stated goal of many
histories of archaeology, the history of changes in ideas about the Celts
indicates that politics and notions of identity are simply inherent to research
into the ancient past. It also shows that, self-knowledge or not, the history
of archaeology cannot be attributed to simplistic socio-political motivations. Sometimes political influence is confined to the setting out of
questions and the defining of methodology. Other times the politics of particular researchers can in fact lead to clearly biased conclusions. The
relationship between politics and disciplinary practice is often more subtle
than is generally appreciated, and in any case politics cannot be avoided
through the exclusion of a name. The history of definitions of the Celts, far
from enabling us to mitigate political biases, has now become part of the
centuries-old argument over what constitutes a people and how a people
can be studied in the past. But peoples do not come in discrete packages.
The Celts are, and always were, a creation of the human mind.

APPENDIX

SELECTED RESEARCHERS WHO 'BROUGHT' THE CELTS TO BRITAIN

John Aubrey (1626-97)

1663, Work begins on *Monumenta Britannica*
King Charles II asked Aubrey to write a description of the megalithic monument of Avebury. In *Monumenta Britannica* (unpublished until 1980), Aubrey argued that it was a temple of the Druids. Though influential in connecting megalithic monuments with the Druids, Aubrey never mentioned the Celts in relation to ancient Britain.

Thomas Brown (1663-1704)

1702, *A Short Dissertation about the Mona of Caesar and Tacitus*
Having heard of Pezron's theories about the eastern origins of the Celts, Brown argued that the ancient Druids also originated in the east. The linking of the Druids to Pezron's conception of the Celts was an essential step in the labelling of ancient monuments as Celtic.

Paul-Yves Pezron (1639-1706)

1703, *L'Antiquité de la Nation*
Pezron finally published his theory, already in circulation for about a decade, that the Celts originated in the east and were the ancestors of all Europeans. He made this argument using a combination of linguistic and biblical-historical sources. Pezron's definition of the Celts was dominant for most of the eighteenth century.

Edward Lhuyd (1660-1709)

1707, *Archaeologia Britannica*
Having rejected Pezron's conception of the ancient Celts, Lhuyd relied on the classical sources that described them as a tribe in Gaul. Lhuyd was the first to argue persuasively that the

Gaelic language is part of the language family that includes Welsh and Breton.

Henry Rowlands (1655-1723)

1708, *Mona Antiqua Restaurata*

Following Pezron's conception of the Celts as the first peoples of Europe, equally ancestral to all modern Europeans, Rowlands argued that his native Anglesey contained their purest remnants. He based this argument on 'Druidical' monuments he identified and the survival of the Welsh language. For Rowlands, the Druids preserved knowledge of God from the Old Testament patriarchs, and he thought of Welsh as closely related to Hebrew. This manuscript was not published until Rowland's death in 1723.

John Toland (1670-1722)

1718, *The History of the Druids, Containing an Account of the Antient Celtic Religion and Learning*

A friend of Aubrey, Lhuyd and Stukeley, Toland described Druidism as the religion of the Celts and thought of Celts and Druids as inseparable. His native language, Irish Gaelic, he took to be the purest descendant of the Celtic tongue. He surveyed megalithic monuments, which he described as Druidical, and argued that these provided evidence of Celtic occupation. His book was never finished, and the evidence of his work comes in the form of a detailed funding proposal, published after his death.

William Stukeley (1687-1765)

1721, at Avebury, sketched 'View of the Cell of the Celtic Temple'

Influenced by Toland's connection between the ancient Celtic language and 'Druidical' monuments, Stukeley was the first to describe British material remains as Celtic. His conception of Celtic monuments joined Pezron's notion of Celtic languages as the dominant interpretation of the ancient Celts in the eighteenth century.

William Borlase (1695-1772)

1754, *Observations on the Antiquities Historical and Monumental, of the County of Cornwall*

Writing about his native Cornwall, Borlase followed Stukeley in combining observations of 'Druidical' monuments with Pezron ideas about the ancient Celts.

Lewis Morris (1700-65)

1757, *Celtic Remains*

Morris put together a collection of ancient Welsh manuscripts which he called *Celtic Remains* and which was published mor than a century later in *Archaeologia Cambrensis*. Though he concentrated on Welsh, Gaelic and Breton sources in describing the Celts, Morris followed Pezron in treating all modern Europeans as descendants of them.

Evan Evans (1731-88)
& Bishop Thomas Percy (1729-1811)

1761, Correspondence

In a series of letters, Evans and Percy concluded that the Celts were the ancestors of the Welsh, Irish, Scottish and Breton, but not of any other Europeans. This argument was based not on linguistics, but on the history of Druidism, which they traced through bardic literature. This definition of the Celts, contrasting with Pezron's, began to take hold towards the end of the eighteenth century.

James Douglas (1753-1819)

1786-93, *Nenia Britannica*

Publication proceeded in series on Douglas' work on burials, which he excavated in order to identify to which peoples (Celts, Britons, Romans, Saxons or Danes) the artefacts belonged. This was the first time an attempt had been made to categorise material remains in this way and led to a more limited view of Celtic remains than the more generalised one forwarded by Stukeley.

William Jones (1746-94)

1786, 'On the Hindus'

In addition to linking Sanscrit to the family of European languages, Jones created a multi-source methodology of tracing the peopling of the world back to a point of origin from its current diversity. This was part of the development of the field of ethnology.

Edward Williams (1747-1826)

1803, *A Vindication of the Celts, from Ancient Authorities*

Using the bardic name Iolo Morganwg, Williams distributed manuscripts he had forged in an attempt to show that the Druids and their practices had survived in Wales. His work helped to popularise the idea that Wales is Celtic.

Edward Davies (1756-1831)

1804, *Celtic Researches, on the Origin, Traditions and Language, of the Ancient Britons*

Davies added to Williams' work in arguing that Druidical rituals survived in Wales. Yet he followed Pezron's conception of the Celts as an Old Testament people once spread widely throughout Europe. For Davies, Wales was not unique in its Celtic heritage, but was the place where Celtic tradition was best preserved.

William Cunnington (1754-1810)

1809, Letter to Thomas Leman

Like Douglas, Cunnington excavated burials, which he thought provided better evidence than written records for the past peoples of Britain. In general, he assigned most of his finds to the Celts.

Richard Colt Hoare (1758-1838)

1810-21, *The Ancient History of Wiltshire*

As Cunnington's ultimate sponsor, Colt Hoare published the results of his years of excavations in series over two volumes. Instead of merely adopting Stukeley's argument that the Celts were the first inhabitants of Britain, Colt Hoare drew this conclusion on the basis of the artefacts Cunnington had uncovered. Colt Hoare also confirmed Stukeley's argument that Stonehenge was Celtic in origin.

James Cowles Prichard (1786-1848)

1813, *Researches into the Physical History of Man*

1831, *The Eastern Origin of the Celtic Nation*

Prichard was the driving force behind the creation of ethnology as a discipline that used many sources of evidence to trace the peopling of the world. His studies of linguistics firmly established that the language sub-family that included Gaelic, Welsh, Breton, Cornish and Manx, was a member of the Indo-European language family. Though unhappy with the term *Celtic* for this sub-family, he used the word in deference to tradition. Towards the end of his career, he helped introduce craniology into what was then an ethnological discipline dominated by linguistics. Prichard argued that the Celts were the first inhabitants of Britain, but thought that other peoples had reached Continental Europe before the Celts.

Christian Jürgensen Thomsen (1788-1865)

1836, *Ledetraad til Nordisk Oldkyndighed*

A Danish museum curator and numismatist, Thomsen created the three-age system, dividing European prehistory into successive ages of stone, bronze and iron. Using this system, British ethnologists soon placed the Celts in the Bronze Age and argued that a pre-Celtic race populated Britain in the Stone Age.

William Wilde (1815-76)

1844, 'The Ethnology of the Ancient Irish'

A Dublin physician better known for being the father of Oscar Wilde, William Wilde was the first person in the British Isles to use the three-age system to argue, on the basis of skull measurements, that the Celts were not the first inhabitants of these islands, but arrived in the Bronze Age.

Jens Jacob Asmussen Worsaae (1821-86)

1846, Visit to Great Britain and Ireland

A student of Thomsen, Worsaae toured the British Isles promoting craniology and the three-age system as essential to ethnology.

Samuel Birch (1813-85)

1846, 'On the Torc of the Celts'

A curator in the British Museum, Birch was the first person to use the phrase 'Celtic art' in reference to curvilinear motifs dating from the Iron Age to early Christian times in Britain and Ireland.

Daniel Wilson (1816-92)

1850, 'Inquiry into the Evidence of the Existence of Primitive Races in Scotland prior to the Celtae'

Working in the Society of Antiquaries of Scotland, Wilson became the second person (after Wilde) to argue on the basis of skull measurements that the Celts were not the first inhabitants of Britain. Wilson was influential in making craniology an essential part of ethnology, or what he was starting to refer to as archaeology.

John Kemble (1807-57)

1857, 'Address to the President and Members of the Royal Irish Academy'

In the course of preparing material for exhibition in Manchester, Kemble visited Dublin where, in a speech, he was the first to provide an elaborate definition of Celtic art. This was published in *Horae Ferales* in 1863. A student of Anglo-Saxon philology, Kemble turned to archaeology while living in Hanover. His work on distinguishing Saxon and Slavic designs while there helped him to think of ornament as characteristic of a people.

Thomas Bateman (1821-61)

1861, *Ten Years' Digging in Celtic and Saxon Grave Hills*

Joseph Barnard Davis (1801-81)

1856-65, *Crania Britannica*

& John Thurnam (1810-73)

These three were the most prominent of the barrow-diggers who put their faith in collecting skulls in order to identify Britain's racial sequence within the three-age framework. Despite decades of collecting and analysing prehistoric skulls, they could not reach a consensus on which shape was typically Celtic.

Augustus Wollaston Franks (1826-97)

1863, *Horae Ferales*

Upon Kemble's death, Franks, a curator at the British Museum, assumed responsibility for publishing Kemble's work. Franks used the term 'Late-Celtic art' to describe British and Irish Iron Age ornament, and this term was widely used for the subsequent half century. Franks also drew comparisons between domestic material and recent finds from Switzerland.

John Lubbock (1834-1913)

1865, *Pre-Historic Times*

Later Lord Avebury, Lubbock was a major figure in the establishment of archaeology as an independent discipline in the late nineteenth century. His book *Pre-Historic Times* integrated Scandinavian craniology and the three-age system into British archaeology and helped affirm the notion that the Celts arrived in the Bronze Age.

Matthew Arnold (1822-88)

1865, *The Study of Celtic Literature*

Arnold argued, on the basis of literature and folklore, that the essence of Celts can be reduced to the notion of sentimentality. He helped establish Celtic Studies as a discipline.

Joseph Anderson (1832-1916)

1879-82, Rhind Lectures

A curator at the Museum of the Society of Antiquaries of Scotland, Anderson studied Celtic art, not as a simple ethnological index of racial affiliation, but as a way to understand the 'culture and civilisation' of Britain's past peoples. He conducted extensive surveys and constructed an elaborate typology of Celtic art.

Robert Munro (1835-1920)

1882, *Ancient Scottish Lake-Dwellings*

Inspired by the great lakeside settlement digs in Switzerland, Munro conducted similar excavations in Scotland. In synthesising the results of such sites from around Europe, Munro argued that the Celts had an origin point in east-central Europe and then spread westward. He traced this spread, not through Celtic bones, but through Celtic art and settlement patterns.

John Beddoe (1826-1911)

1885, *The Races of Britain*

In the context of growing disillusionment with the prospects of craniology for identifying the Celts in prehistory, Beddoe constructed increasingly complex schemes for measuring contemporary peoples in order to find traces of the Celts. His 'index of nigrescence' implied that Celts had a darker mixture of eye, hair and skin colour than later peoples.

John Rhys (1840-1915)

1889, Rhind Lectures

A prominent scholar of Celtic folklore, Rhys used the evidence of language and literature to argue for waves of Celtic migration into Britain and Ireland.

Arthur Evans (1851-1941)

1895, Rhind Lectures

Through a combination of large-scale excavations and travels abroad, Evans used evidence of Celtic art to construct a model in which the Celts spread to Britain from southern Europe. In this model, he proposed both diffusion and migration as means by which the Celts came to Britain.

John Romilly Allen (1847-1907)

1904, *Celtic Art in Pagan and Christian Times*

Allen had worked with Anderson on Celtic art. In *Celtic Art in Pagan and Christian Times* Allen brought together many of the trends in late nineteenth-century British archaeology, including large-scale excavations, declining interest in craniology and reliance on art and ornament to define past peoples.

SECONDARY SOURCES

There is an ever-increasing supply of secondary sources on the topics covered in this book. In general, I have used endnotes only for primary sources. Below, I have given a list of the secondary sources that were useful to me in putting together the history of Celtic scholarship. In many cases I have indicated particular pages that are especially relevant.

Chapter I: Introduction

Eighteenth-century ideas about the Celts
Piggott, Stuart. *Ancient Britons and the Antiquarian Imagination*. New York: Thames and Hudson, 1989, 129
 – *Ruins in a Landscape: Essays in Antiquarianism*. Edinburgh: Edinburgh University Press, 1976
 – *William Stukeley: An Eighteenth-Century Antiquary*, 2nd edition. New York: Thames and Hudson, 1985, 65-67

Questioning the Celtic label and images of the Celts
Brown, Terence (ed.). *Celticism*. Amsterdam and Atlanta: Rodopi, 1996
Champion, Timothy. 'The Power of the Picture: The Image of the Ancient Gaul', in *The Cultural Life of Images: Visual Representation in Archaeology*, Brian Leigh Molyneaux (ed.). London and New York: Routledge, 1997, 213-229
Chapman, Malcolm. *The Celts: The Construction of a Myth*. New York: St Martin's Press, 1992
Collis, John. *The Celts: Origins, Myths and Inventions*. Stroud: Tempus, 2003
Dietler, Michael. '"Our Ancestors the Gauls": Archaeology, Ethnic Nationalism, and the Manipulation of Celtic Identity in Modern Europe', *American Anthropologist* 96 (1994), 584-605
Graves-Brown, Paul, Jones, Siân and Gamble, Clive (eds). *Cultural Identity and Archaeology: The Construction of European Communities*. London and New York: Routledge, 1996

Hale, Amy and Payton, Philip (eds). *New Directions in Celtic Studies*. Exeter: University of Exeter Press, 2000

James, Simon. *The Atlantic Celts: Ancient People or Modern Invention?* London: British Museum Press, 1999

Morse, Michael A. 'What's in a Name? The "Celts" in Presentations of Prehistory in Ireland, Scotland, and Wales', *Journal of European Archaeology* 4 (1996), 305-328

Piccini, Angela. 'Filming through the Mists of Time: Celtic Constructions and the Documentary', *Current Anthropology* 37 Supplement (February, 1996), S87-98, S111

Williams, J.H.C. *Beyond the Rubicon: Romans and Gauls in Republican Italy*. Oxford: Oxford University Press, 2001, 6-14

The peopling of the British Isles before 1703

Evans, Joan. *A History of the Society of Antiquaries*. Oxford: The Society of Antiquaries, 1956, 8-13

Kendrick, T.D. *British Antiquity*. London: Methuen and Co., 1950

Annius of Viterbo

Allen, Don Cameron. *The Legend of Noah: Renaissance Rationalism in Art, Science, and Letters*. Urbana: University of Illinois Press, 1949, 113-117

Grafton, Anthony. *Defenders of the Text: The Traditions of Scholarship in an Age of Science, 1450-1800*. Cambridge, Mass., and London: Harvard University Press, 1991, 76-103

George Buchanan

Collis, John. 'George Buchanan and the Celts in Britain', in *Celtic Connections*. R. Black, W. Gilles and R. Ó Maolalaigh (eds). Proceedings of the Tenth International Congress of Celtic Studies 1, 1999, 91-107

Trevor-Roper, H.R. 'George Buchanan and the Ancient Scottish Constitution', *The English Historical Review* Supplement 3 (1966), 19, 35

Camden's Britannia

Mendyk, Stan A.E. *'Speculum Britanniae': Regional Study, Antiquarianism, and Science in Britain to 1700*. Toronto: University of Toronto Press, 1989, 6

Piggott. *Ruins in a Landscape* 33-53

Van Norden, Linda. 'Celtic Antiquarianism in the "Curious Discourses"', In *Essays Critical and Historical Dedicated to Lily B. Campbell*. Berkeley and Los Angeles: University of California Press, 1950, 65

Images of ancient Britons and Saxons

Hodgen, Margaret T. *Early Anthropology in the Sixteenth and Seventeenth Centuries*. Philadelphia: University of Pennsylvania Press, 1964, 145, 214

MacDougall, Hugh A. *Racial Myth in English History*. Montreal: Harvest House, 1982, 2

Smiles, Sam. *The Image of Antiquity: Ancient Britain and the Antiquarian Imagination*. New Haven and London: Yale University Press, 1994, 129-131

Chapter II: From Noah's Ark to Europe

The emergence of the idea of the Celtic language family
Bonfante, G. 'A Contribution to the History of Celtology', *Celtica* 3 (1956), 17-34
 – 'Some Renaissance Texts on the Celtic Languages and Their Kinship', *Études Celtiques* 7 (1955-6), 414-427
Chapman. *The Celts.*, 207
James, Simon. 'Celts, Politics and Motivation in Archaeology', *Antiquity* 72 (1998), 205-206
Mallory, J.P. *In Search of the Indo-Europeans*. London: Thames and Hudson, 1989, 9-12

Pezron and the debate over France's Celtic versus Frankish origins
McDonald, Maryon. *'We Are Not French!': Language, Culture, and Identity in Brittany*. London and New York: Routledge, 1989, 100
Morgan, P.T.J. 'The Abbé Pezron and the Celts', *The Transactions of the Honourable Society of Cymmrodorion* 1965,, 286-295
Poliakov, Léon. *The Aryan Myth*. Translated by Edmund Howard. London: Sussex University Press, 1974, 23
Schnapp, Alain. *The Discovery of the Past*. London: British Museum Press, 1996, 132

Edward Lhuyd
Emery, Frank. *Edward Lhuyd F.R.S. 1660-1709*. Caerdydd, Wales: Gwasg Prifysgol Cymru, 1971
Ovenell, R.F. *The Ashmolean Museum 1683-1894*. Oxford: Clarendon Press, 1986, 31-40, 49
Piggott. *Ancient Britons*, 22-26

Antiquarianism and romanticism
Colley, Linda. *Britons: Forging the Nation 1707-1837*. London: Pimlico, 1992, 172
Piggott, *Ancient Britons*, 124-125.
 – 'Prehistory and the Romantic Movement', *Antiquity* 11 (1937), 31

Chapter III: Romancing the Druids

Early scholarship on the Druids
Kendrick, T.D. *The Druids*. London: Methuen and Co., 1927
Owen, A.L. *The Famous Druids: A Survey of Three Centuries of English Literature on the Druids*. Oxford: Clarendon Press, 1962
Piggott, Stuart. *The Druids*. London: Thames and Hudson, 1968
Early antiquarianism
Chippindale, Christopher. *Stonehenge Complete*, 2nd edition. New York and London: Thames and Hudson, 1994
Hunter, Michael. *John Aubrey and the Realm of Learning*. London: Duckworth, 1975
 – 'The Royal Society and the Origins of British Archaeology', *Antiquity* 45 (1971), 113-121, 187-192

Mendyk. *'Speculum Britanniae'*

Michell, John. *Megalithomania: Artists, Antiquarians and Archaeologists at the Old Stone Monuments.* Ithaca: Cornell University Press, 1982

Ó Raifeartaigh, T. (ed.). *The Royal Irish Academy: A Bicentennial History 1785-1985.* Dublin: The Royal Irish Academy, 1985

The Celtic Revival

Chapman, Malcolm. *The Gaelic Vision in Scottish Culture.* London: Croom Helm; Montreal: McGill-Queen's University Press, 1978

Morgan, P.T.J. *The Eighteenth Century Renaissance.* Llandybïe, Dyfed, Wales: Christopher Davies, 1981

Snyder, Edward D. *The Celtic Revival In English Literature 1760-1800.* Gloucester, Mass.: Peter Smith, 1965[1923]

Chapter IV: The Growth of Ethnology

The discovery of the Indo-European language family

Aarsleff, Hans. *The Study of Language in England, 1780-1860.* Minneapolis: University of Minnesota Press, 1983, 3-5, 13-14

Cannon, Garland. *The Life and Mind of Oriental Jones, the Father of Modern Linguistics.* Cambridge: Cambridge University Press, 1990, 242-244

Mallory. *In Search of the Indo-Europeans*, 9-12

The Welsh and Scottish cultural revivals

Morgan, P.T.J. 'From Death to a View: The Hunt for the Welsh Past in the Romantic Period', In *The Invention of Tradition*, Eric Hobsbawm and Terence Ranger (eds). Cambridge: Cambridge University Press, 1983, 43-100

Trevor-Roper, Hugh. 'The Invention of Tradition: The Highland Tradition of Scotland', in *The Invention of Tradition*, Eric Hobsbawm and Terence Ranger (eds). Cambridge: Cambridge University Press, 1983, 15-41

Williams, Gwyn A. *Madoc: The Making of a Myth.* London: Eyre Methuen, 1979

The history of ethnology

Morrell, Jack and Thackray, Arnold. *Gentlemen of Science.* Oxford: Clarendon Press, 1981, 11, 25, 224, 283-286

Stocking, George W., Jr. 'From Chronology to Ethnology: James Cowles Prichard and British Anthropology, 1800-1850', in James Cowles Prichard, *Researches into the Physical History of Man*, George W. Stocking Jr. (ed.). Chicago and London: The University of Chicago Press, 1973, ix-cx

– *Victorian Anthropology.* New York: The Free Press, 1987, 47-53, 243-245

Vermeulen, Han F. 'Origins and Institutionalization of Ethnography and Ethnology in Europe and the USA, 1771-1845', in *Fieldwork and Footnotes: Studies in the History of European Anthropology*, Han F. Vermeulen and Arturo Alvarez Roldán (eds). London and New York: Routledge, 1995, 39-59

Chapter V: Celtic Monuments

Stukeley, Stonehenge and the Society of Antiquaries

Chippindale. *Stonehenge Complete*, 71

Evans. *A History of the Society of Antiquaries*, 50-54

Lynch, Barbara D. and Lynch, Thomas. 'The Beginnings of a Scientific Approach to Prehistoric
    Archaeology in 17th and 18th Century Britain', *Southwestern Journal of Anthropology* 24, no. 1 (1968): 33-
    65

Piggott. *William Stukeley*

– *Ruins in a Landscape*, 114

Smiles. *The Image of Antiquity*, 194-214

Trigger, Bruce G. *A History of Archaeological Thought*. Cambridge: Cambridge University Press, 1989, 65-66

Douglas and early excavation

Daniel, Glyn. *The Idea of Prehistory*. Cleveland and New York: The World Publishing Company, 1962

Jessup, Ronald. *Man of Many Talents: An Informal Biography of James Douglas 1753-1819*. London and
    Chichester: Phillimore and Co., 1975

Marsden, Barry M. *The Early Barrow-Diggers*. London: Book Club Associates, 1974

– *Pioneers of Prehistory: Leaders and Landmarks in English Archaeology (1500-1900)*. Lancashire: G.W. and A.
    Hesketh, Ormskirk and Northridge, 1983

Rhodes, Michael. 'Faussett Rediscovered: Charles Roach Smith, Joseph Mayer, and the Publication of
    Inventorium Sepulchrale', in *Anglo-Saxon Cemeteries: A Reappraisal*, Edmund Southworth (ed.). Phoenix
    Mill, Gloucestershire: Alan Sutton, 1990, 25-64

Colt Hoare, Cunnington and Ancient Wiltshire

Chippindale, Christopher. 'John Britton's 'Celtic Cabinet' in Devizes Museum and Its Context', *The*
    Antiquaries Journal 65 (1985), 121-138

– *Stonehenge Complete*, 113-125

Cunnington, Robert H. *From Antiquary to Archaeologist: A Biography of William Cunnington 1754-1810*, James
    Dyer (ed.). Aylesbury, Buckinghamshire: Shire Publications, 1975

Piggott. *Ancient Britons*, 152-157

Woodbridge, Kenneth. *Landscape and Antiquity: Aspects of English Culture at Stourhead 1718-1838*. Oxford:
    Clarendon Press, 1970

Chapter VI: Celtic Skulls

The three-age system and its spread

Ash, Marinell. '"A fine, genial, hearty band": David Laing, Daniel Wilson and Scottish Archaeology', in *The*
    Scottish Antiquarian Tradition: Essays to Mark the Bicentenary of the Society of Antiquaries of Scotland and Its

Museum, 1780-1980, A.S. Bell (ed.). Edinburgh: John Donald, 1981, 86-113

Daniel, Glyn. *The Three Ages: An Essay on Archaeological Method*. Cambridge: Cambridge University Press, 1943

Gräslund, Bo. 'The Background to C.J. Thomsen's Three Age System', in *Towards a History of Archaeology*, Glyn Daniel (ed.). London: Thames and Hudson, 1981, 45-50

 – *The Birth of Prehistoric Chronology: Dating Methods and Dating Systems in Nineteenth-Century Scandinavian Archaeology*. Cambridge: Cambridge University Press, 1987

Klindt-Jensen, Ole. *A History of Scandinavian Archaeology*. London: Thames and Hudson, 1975

Morse, Michael A. 'Craniology and the Adoption of the Three-Age System in Britain', *Proceedings of the Prehistoric Society* 65 (1999), 1-16

Rodden, Judith. 'The Development of the Three Age System: Archaeology's First Paradigm', in *Towards a History of Archaeology*, Glyn Daniel (ed.). London: Thames and Hudson, 1981, 51-68

Wilkins, Judith. 'Worsaae and British Antiquities', *Antiquity* 35 (1961), 214-220

From ethnology to anthropology

Cooter, Roger. *Phrenology in the British Isles*. Metuchen, N.J., and London: The Scarecrow Press, Inc., 1989

Stepan, Nancy. *The Idea of Race in Science: Great Britain 1800-1960*. London and Basingstoke: The Macmillan Press, 1982

Stocking. *Victorian Anthropology*

Biographies

Trigger, Bruce G. 'Sir Daniel Wilson: Canada's First Anthropologist', *Anthropologica* 8, no. 1 (1966), 3-28

Wilson, T.G. *Victorian Doctor: Being the Life of Sir William Wilde*. London: Metheun and Co., 1942

Chapter VII: Celtic Art

Display in the British Museum

Kendrick, T.D. 'The British Museum and British Antiquities', *Antiquity* 28 (1954), 132-142

Wilson, David M. *The Forgotten Collector: Augustus Wollaston Franks of the British Museum*. London: Thames and Hudson, 1984

John Kemble and identifying Anglo-Saxons and Celts

Rhodes. 'Faussett Rediscovered'

Sklenár, Karel. *Archaeology in Central Europe: The First 500 Years*. Translated by Iris Lewitová. Leicester: Leicester University Press, 1983, 91-101

Ireland and the politics of Celtic art

Camille, Michael. 'Domesticating the Dragon: The Rediscovery, Reproduction, and Re-Invention of Early Irish Metalwork', in *Imagining an Irish Past: The Celtic Revival 1840-1940*, T.J. Edelstein (ed.). Chicago: The David and Alfred Smart Museum of Art, the University of Chicago, 1992, 1-21

Curtis. L.P., Jr. *Anglo-Saxons and Celts: A Study of Anti-Irish Prejudice in Victorian England*. Bridgeport, Conn.:

Conference on British Studies, University of Bridgeport, 1968, 98–116

Harris, Neil. 'Selling National Culture: Ireland at the World's Columbian Exposition', in *Imagining an Irish Past: The Celtic Revival 1840-1940*, T.J. Edelstein (ed.). Chicago: The David and Alfred Smart Museum of Art, the University of Chicago, 1992, 82–105

Hutchinson, John. *The Dynamics of Cultural Nationalism: The Gaelic Revival and the Creation of the Irish Nation State*. London: Allen and Unwin, 1987

Ó Raifeartaigh (ed.). *The Royal Irish Academy*

Sheehy, Jeanne. *The Rediscovery of Ireland's Past: The Celtic Revival 1830-1930*. London: Thames and Hudson, 1980

From 'race' to 'culture'

Stocking, George W., Jr. *Race, Culture, and Evolution: Essays in the History of Anthropology*. Second edition. Chicago and London: University of Chicago Press, 1982

Celtic art

Jacobsthal, Paul. *Early Celtic Art*, 2 vols. Oxford: Clarendon Press, 1944

Megaw, Ruth, and Megaw, Vincent. *Celtic Art: From Its Beginnings to the Book of Kells*. London and New York: Thames and Hudson, 1989

Chapter VIII: The Birth of Archaeology

The history of anthropology

Stocking. *Victorian Anthropology*

Urry, James. 'Englishmen, Celts, and Iberians: The Ethnographic Survey of the United Kingdom, 1892–1899', In *Functionalism Historicized: Essays on British Social Anthropology*, George W. Stocking Jr. (ed.). Madison: University of Wisconsin Press, 1984, 83–105

'Celtic' folklore

Chapman. *The Gaelic Vision in Scottish Culture*. 81–116.

Dorson, Richard M. *The British Folklorists: A History*. Chicago: University of Chicago Press, 1968

Hale, Amy. 'Rethinking Celtic Cornwall: An Ethnographic Approach', in *Cornish Studies: Five*, Philip Payton (ed.). Exeter: University of Exeter Press, 1997, 85–99

Sims-Williams, Patrick. 'The Invention of Celtic Nature Poetry', in *Celticism*, Terence Brown (ed.). Amsterdam and Atlanta: Rodopi, 1996, 97–124

The history of archaeology

Bibby, Geoffrey. *The Testimony of the Spade*. New York: Alfred A. Knopf, 1956

Bowden, Mark. *Pitt Rivers: The Life and Archaeological Work of Lieutenant-General Augustus Henry Lane Fox Pitt Rivers, DCL, FRS, FSA*. Cambridge: Cambridge University Press, 1991

Chapman, William. 'The Organizational Context in the History of Archaeology: Pitt Rivers and Other

British Archaeologists of the 1860s', *The Antiquaries Journal* 69 (1989): 23-42

Daniel, Glyn. *A Hundred Years of Archaeology*. London: Gerald Duckworth and Co., 1950

Levine, Philippa. *The Amateur and the Professional: Antiquarians, Historians and Archaeologists in Victorian England, 1836-1886*. Cambridge: Cambridge University Press, 1986

Marsden. *Pioneers of Prehistory*, 56-77

Trigger. *A History of Archaeological Thought*

Van Riper, A. Bowdoin. *Men among the Mammoths: Victorian Science and the Discovery of Human Prehistory*. Chicago and London: The University of Chicago Press, 1993

General interest surveys on the Celts

Cunliffe, Barry. *The Ancient Celts*. Oxford: Oxford University Press, 1997

James, Simon. *The World of the Celts*. London: Thames and Hudson, 1993

Powell, T.G.E. *The Celts*. London: Thames and Hudson, 1958

Epilogue

The archaeology of ethnicities

Chapman, Malcolm. 'Social and Biological Aspects of Ethnicity' in *Social and Biological Aspects of Ethnicity*, Malcolm Chapman (ed.). Oxford: Oxford University Press, 1993, 1-46

Jones, Siân. *The Archaeology of Ethnicity: Constructing Identities in the Past and Present*. London: Routledge, 1997

Renfrew, Colin. *The Roots of Ethnicity: Archaeology, Genetics and the Origins of Europe*. Rome: Unione Internazionale degli Instituti di Archeologia Storia e Storia dell'Arte, 1993

Shennan, Stephen. 'Introduction: Archaeological Approaches to Cultural Identity', in *Archaeological Approaches to Cultural Identity*. Stephen Shennan (ed.). London: Unwin Hyman, 1989, 6-11

How the history of archaeology might improve the discipline

Daniel, Glyn. 'Introduction: The Necessity for an Historical Approach to Archaeology', In *Towards a History of Archaeology*, Glyn Daniel (ed.). London: Thames and Hudson, 1981, 10

Pinsky, Valerie. 'Commentary: A Critical Role for the History of Archaeology', in *Critical Traditions in Contemporary Archaeology: Essays in the Philosophy, History and Socio-Politics of Archaeology*, Valery Pinsky and Alison Wylie (eds). Cambridge: Cambridge University Press, 1989, 90

Trigger, Bruce G. 'Writing the History of Archaeology: A Survey of Trends', in *Objects and Others: Essays in Museums and Material Culture*, George W. Stocking Jr., Madison: University of Wisconsin Press, 1985, 232

NOTES

Chapter I: Introduction

1   Malcolm Chapman, *The Celts: The Construction of a Myth*. New York: St. Martin's Press, 1992, 201-208

2   Simon James, *The Atlantic Celts: Ancient People or Modern Invention?* London: British Museum Press, 1999, 43-66

3   Stuart Piggott, *Ruins in a Landscape: Essays in Antiquarianism*. Edinburgh: Edinburgh University Press, 1976, 63

4   John Collis, *The Celts: Origins, Myths and Inventions*. Stroud: Tempus, 2003, 34-92

5   Ruth and Vincent Megaw, 'Ancient Celts and Modern Ethnicity', *Antiquity* 70 (1996) 180; Collis, 'Celtic Myths', *Antiquity* 71 (1997): 195, 199

6   In his account of this story, Piggott, *Ruins in a Landscape*, 58, confused Richard White (1539-1611) with the illustrator John White, whose artwork appears in Plate 2

7   George Buchanan, *The History of Scotland*. London: Edward Jones, 1690, 58

8   *Ibid.*, 59

9   William Camden, *Britain*, trans. Philémon Holland. London: Georgii Bishop and Ioannis Norton, 1610, 16

10 *Ibid.*, 26

11 Aylett Sammes, 'Preface to the Reader', *Britannia Antiqua Illustrata: Or, the Antiquities of Ancient Britain, Derived from the Phoenicians*. London, 1676, 147-152

Part One: Languages

1   Edward Lhuyd, 'The Preface', *Archaeologia Britannica, Giving Some Account Additional to What Has Been Hitherto Publish'd, of the Languages, Histories and Customs of the Original Inhabitants of Great Britain*, vol. 1, Glossography, Oxford, 1707, 1

2   James Cowles Prichard, *Eastern Origin of the Celtic Nations Proved by a Comparison of Their Dialects with the Sanscrit, Greek, Latin, and Teutonic Languages*. London: J. and A. Arch, 1831, 24

Chapter II: From Noah's Ark to Europe

1   Henry Rowlands, *Mona Antiqua Restaurata: An Archaeological Discourse on the Antiquities, Natural and Historical, of the Isle of Anglesey, the Antient Seat of the British Druids*. Dublin: Robert Owen, 1723, 317

2   Paul-Yves Pezron, *The Antiquities of Nations; More Particularly of the Celtae or Gauls, Taken to be Originally the Same People as Our Ancient Britains*, trans. David Jones. Little Britain: S. Ballard; Cornhill: R. Burrough, 1706 [1703]

3   Paolo Emilio, *De Antiquitate Gallicarum*. Lyons, 1485

4   Cosmo A. Gordon (ed.), *Professor James Garden's Letters to John Aubrey 1692-1695*. The Miscellany of the Third Spalding Club 3. Aberdeen: The Third Spalding Club, 1960, 35

5   *Ibid.*, 36; Dionysius Vossius, *R. Mosis Maimonidae, De Idololatria Liber, cum interpreta-*

tione Latina & Notis. Amsterdam, 1641, 7

6   'A Letter from Mr. Monroe to Dr. Sloane giv-
     ing an Account of the Acts of Some Learned
     Men at Paris', 29 October 1700, *Royal Society
     Early Letters* EL/M2/16

7   Pezron, *The Antiquities of Nations,* v

8   *Ibid.,* xii

9   R.T. Gunther (ed.), *Life and Letters of Edward
     Lhwyd,* Early Science in Oxford 14. Oxford,
     1945, 134

10   Lhuyd, 'A Letter from the Late Mr. Edward
     Lhwyd, Keeper of the Ashmolean Museum in
     Oxford, to Dr. Tancred Robinson, F.R.S.
     Giving a Farther Account of What He Met
     with Remarkable in Natural History and
     Antiquities, in His Travels thro' Wales',
     Philosophical Transactions 27, no. 335 (1712), 502

11   Gunther (ed.), *Life and Letters of Edward Lhwyd,*
     379

12   *Ibid.,* 379

13   *Ibid.,* 400

14   *Ibid.,* 436

15   *Ibid.,* 412, 441, 489

16   *Ibid.,* 489

17   Lhuyd, 'The Preface', *Archaeologia Britannica,* 1

18   Lhuyd, *Archaeologia Britannica,* 267

19   Lhuyd, 'The Preface', *Archaeologia Britannica,* 1

20   *Ibid.,* 1

21   *Ibid.,* 1

22   Lhuyd, 'A Translation of the Welsh Preface to
     the Glossography', *Archaeologia Britannica,* 8

23   *Ibid.,* 4, 8

24   Lhuyd, 'The Preface', *Archaeologia Britannica,* 2

25   Lhuyd, 'A Translation of the Welsh Preface to
     the Glossography', *Archaeologia Britannica,* 9

26   Thomas Innes, *A Critical Essay on the Ancient
     Inhabitants of the Northern Parts of Britain, or
     Scotland,* vol. 1. London: William Innys, 1729, 73

27   David Malcolme, *A Collection of Letters, in
     Which the Imperfection of Learning, Even among
     Christians, and a Remedy for It, Are Hinted,* no.
     1. Edinburgh, 1739, 1-3. Malcolme's main
     attempt to tie together disparate languages
     appears in his 1738 *Essay on the Antiquities of
     Great Britain and Ireland*

28   John Toland, *A Collection of Several Pieces of Mr.
     John Toland,* vol. 1. London: J. Peele, 1726, 7,
     204-228

29   John Clerk, 'To My Good Friend Roger Gale,
     Esq.: An Enquiry into the Ancient Languages
     of Great Britain, Being a Copy of a Paper
     Intended for the Philosophical Society at

     Edenborough', The Family Memoirs of the
     Rev. William Stukeley, M.D. and the
     Antiquarian and Other Correspondence of
     William Stukeley, Roger & Samuel Gale, etc.,
     The Publications of the Surtees Society 73 (1882
     for 1880), 340, 350

30   Francis Wise, *A Letter to Dr. Mead Concerning
     Some Antiquities in Berkshire.* Oxford: Thomas
     Wood, 1738

31   Wise, *Some Enquiries Concerning the First
     Inhabitants, Language, Religion, Learning, and
     Letters of Europe.* Oxford: J. Fletcher, S. Parker
     and D. Prince, 1758, 15, 31

32   Rowland Jones, *The Circles of Gomer.* London,
     1771, 47

33   Jones, *The Origin of Language and Nations,
     Hieroglyfically, Etymologically, and Topographically
     Defined and Fixed, after the Method of an
     English, Celtic, Greek and Latin English Lexicon.*
     London, 1764, Preface

34   John Cleland, *The Way to Things by Words, and
     to Words by Things; Being a Sketch of an Attempt
     at the Retrieval of the Antient Celtic, or, Primitive
     Language of Europe.* London: L. Davis and C.
     Reymers, 1766, ii

35   James Parsons, *Remains of Japhet: Being
     Historical Enquiries into the Affinity and Origin of
     the European Languages.* London, 1767, x, 37

36   *Ibid.,* 39-49

37   *Ibid.,* xvii

38   e.g., Ruth Megaw and Vincent Megaw, *Celtic
     Art: From Its Beginning to the Book of Kells.*
     London and New York: Thames and Hudson,
     1989, 12; T.G.E. Powell, *The Celts.* London:
     Thames and Hudson, 1958, 18; Simon James,
     The World of the Celts. London: Thames and
     Hudson, 1993, 8-9

39   Malcolm Chapman, *The Gaelic Vision in Scottish
     Culture.* London: Croom Helm; Montreal:
     McGill-Queen's University Press, 1978, 37

40   P.T.J. Morgan, 'From Death to a View: The
     Hunt for the Welsh Past in the Romantic
     Period', *The Invention of Tradition,* ed. Eric
     Hobsbawm and Terence Ranger. Cambridge:
     Cambridge University Press, 1983, 67

Chapter III: Romancing the Druids

1   Hector Boece, *Scotorium Historiae a Prima
     Gentis Origine.* Paris, 1526

2   John Aubrey, *Monumenta Britannica,* 2 vols.
     Sherborne, Dorset: The Dorset Publishing
     Co., 1980, 1982

3   Edmund Gibson (ed.), *Camden's Britannia, Newly Translated into English: With Large Additions and Improvements*. London: A. Swalle, A. and J. Churchil, 1695, 108-109, 673, 683-684

4   William Sacheverell, *An Account of the Isle of Man*. London: J. Hartley, R. Gibson, Tho. Hodgson, 1702, 18, 23

5   Gunther (ed.), *Life and Letters of Edward Lhwyd*, 442; Lhuyd, 'Translation of the Welsh Preface to the Glossography', *Archaeologia Britannica*, 1

6   Martin Martin, *A Description of the Western Islands of Scotland*. London: Andrew Bell, 1703, vi. The title page of this book lists the year erroneously as 1673

7   A.L. Owen, *The Famous Druids: A Survey of Three Centuries of English Literature on the Druids*. Oxford: Clarendon Press, 1962, 109-113

8   Martin, *A Description of the Western Islands of Scotland*, 9

9   *Ibid.*, 105

10 *Ibid.*, 87, 358.

11 Thomas Brown, 'A Short Dissertation about the Mona of Caesar and Tacitus, the Several Names of Man, & c'., William Sacheverell, *An Account of the Isle of Man*, 152; Sacheverell, *An Account of Isle of Man*, Introduction

12 Brown, 'A Short Dissertation', 155

13 *Ibid.*, 166

14 Rowlands, *Mona Antiqua Restaurata*, Preface.

15 *Ibid.*, 203

16 *Ibid.*, 205-206

17 *Ibid.*, 22, 33, 308

18 *Ibid.*, 35

19 *Ibid.*, 45

20 *Ibid.*, 87

21 Rowlands, *Mona Antiqua Restaurata*, 2nd edition. London: J. Knox, 1766

22 D. Silvan Evans, 'Preface', in Lewis Morris, *Celtic Remains*, ed. D. Silvan Evans, *Archaeologia Cambrensis*, 4th series, 9 (1878), 3-4

23 Morris, *Celtic Remains*, xviii-xix

24 *Ibid.*, xxiii

25 *Ibid.*, xxiii

26 Evan Evans (ed.), *Some Specimens of the Poetry of the Antient Welsh Bards*. London: J. Dodsley, 1764; Thomas Percy (ed.), *Reliques of Ancient English Poetry*, 3 vols. London: J. Dodsley, 1765

27 Aneirin Lewis, 'Introduction', *The Percy Letters: The Correspondence of Thomas Percy and Evan Evans*, ed. Aneirin Lewis, vol. 5. Louisiana State University Press, 1957, v; Owen, *The Famous Druids*, 194-5

28 Lewis (ed.), *The Percy Letters*, 62

29 *Ibid.*, 63-68

30 *Ibid.*, 53-54

31 *Ibid.*, 66

32 *Ibid.*, 82

33 *Ibid.*, 88. The footnote is Percy's

34 *Ibid.*, 91

35 Percy, 'Proofs that the Teutonic and Celtic Nations Were *ab origine* Two Distinct People', in Paul Henry Mallet, *Northern Antiquities: Or, A Description of the Manners, Customs, Religion and Laws of the Ancient Danes, And Other Northern Nations; Including Those of Our Own Saxon Ancestors*, trans. Thomas Percy, vol. 1. London: T. Carnan and Co., 1770, ii

36 *Ibid.*, iii

37 *Ibid.*, vi

38 *Ibid.*, vi-vii

39 *Ibid.*, xiii, xxiv-xxv

40 Chapman, *The Gaelic Vision in Scottish Culture*, 48-52

41 Edward D. Snyder, *The Celtic Revival in English Literature 1760-1800*. Gloucester, Mass.: Peter Smith 1965[1923], 83

42 James Macpherson, *An Introduction to the History of Great Britain and Ireland*. London: T. Becket and P.A. De Hondt, 1771, 18-20

43 *Ibid.*, 35

44 John Whitaker, *The Genuine History of the Britons Asserted Against Mr. Macpherson*, 2nd edition. London: J. Murray, 1773, is among the most vicious point-by-point refutations

45 e.g. John Williams, *An Account of Some Remarkable Ancient Ruins, Lately Discovered in the Highlands, and Northern Parts of Scotland*. Edinburgh: William Creech, 1777

46 Charles O'Conor, *Dissertations on the History of Ireland*. Dublin, 1753; *Dissertations on the History of Ireland*, 2nd edition. Dublin, 1766

47 *Ibid.*, 29

48 *Ibid.*, 10

49 Sylvester O'Halloran, *An Introduction to the Study of the History and Antiquities of Ireland*. London: J. Murray, 1772, i

50 *Ibid.*, 3

51 *Ibid.*, 55

52 Charles Vallancey, *A Grammar of the Iberno-Celtic, or Irish Language*. Dublin: G. Faulkner, T. Ewing and R. Moncrieffe, 1773; *An Essay*

Towards Illustrating the Ancient History of the Britannic Isles. London: John Nichols, 1786

53   T.D. Kendrick, *The Druids.* London: Methuen and Co., 1927, 26

54   Lhuyd, 'The Preface', *Archaeologia Britannica,* 3

55   Piggott, *Ruins in a Landscape,* 114

Chapter IV: The Growth of Ethnology

1   Jacob Bryant, *A New System, Or, An Analysis of Ancient Mythology,* vol. 3. London: T. Payne, 1776, 134

2   *Ibid.,* 533

3   William Jones, *The Works of Sir William Jones,* vol. 1. London: G. G. and J. Robinson and R.H. Evans, 1799

4   Jones, *Works of William Jones,* 2nd edition, vol. 3. 1807; reprint, London: Routledge/Thoemmes Press, 1993, 25

5   *Ibid.,* 32

6   *Ibid.,* 34

7   Roy Harris, 'Introduction', to William Jones, *Works of William Jones.* 2nd edition, vi

8   Jones, *Works of William Jones,* 2nd edition, 36-45

9   *Ibid.,* 48, 52, 78, 102

10   *Ibid.,* 134-135

11   *Ibid.,* 185-186

12   Max Müller, *Lectures on the Science of Language,* vol. 1. London: Longman, Green, Longman, and Roberts, 1861, 150-151, 158-160

13   Jones, *Works of William Jones,* 2nd edition, 139

14   William Webb, *An Analysis of the History and Antiquities of Ireland, prior to the Fifth Century. To Which is Subjoined, a Review of the General History of the Celtic Nations.* Dublin: W. Jones, 1791, 1

15   *Ibid.,* 22

16   William Betham, *The Gael and Cymbri.* Dublin: William Curry, Jun. and Co., 1834

17   George Petrie, *A Letter to Sir William R. Hamilton.* Dublin, 1840

18   Webb, *An Analysis of the History and Antiquities of Ireland,* 22-24

19   *Ibid.,* iv

20   *Ibid.,* 56

21   *Ibid.,* 66

22   *Ibid.,* 80-3

23   O. Jones, E. Williams and W. Owen (eds), *The Myvyrian Archaiology of Wales, Collected out of Ancient Manuscripts,* 3 vols. London, 1801-7; E. Williams, *A Vindication of the Celts, from Ancient Authorities.* London: E. Williams, 1803

24   Edward Davies, *Celtic Researches, on the Origin, Traditions and Language, of the Ancient Britons.* London, 1804, 547

25   *Ibid.,* 118-119

26   *Ibid.,* 4-18

27   *Ibid.,* 122-130

28   e.g., various articles in *The Cambrian Journal,* which started in 1854

29   John Pinkerton, *Enquiry into the History of Scotland Preceding the Reign of Malcolm III. Or the Year 1056.,* vol. 1. London: George Nicol, 1789, 14

30   Pinkerton, *A Dissertation on the Origin and Progress of the Scythians or Goths.* London: George Nicol, 1787, iii, vi-vii; *Enquiry into the History of Scotland,* vol. 1, 13, 17

31   John Ritson, *Memoirs of the Celts or Gauls.* London: Payne and Foss, 1827, which was published long after Riston's death in 1803, is an example of a book from this period oriented against Pinkerton's theories

32   George Chalmers, *Caledonia,* vol. 1. London: T. Cadell and W. Davies; Edinburgh: A. Constable and Co., 1807, 7

33   *Ibid.,* 27

34   *Ibid.,* 69-72

35   James Cowles Prichard, *Researches into the Physical History of Man,* 1st edition. London: John and Arthur Arch, 1813, iii

36   Thomas Hodgkin, 'Obituary of Dr. Prichard', *Journal of the Ethnological Society of London* 2 (1850), 185-186

37   Prichard, *Researches,* 1st edition, 526-527

38   *Ibid.,* 528

39   *Ibid.,* 535

40   *Ibid.,* 534

41   *Ibid.,* 557-558

42   Prichard, *Researches into the Physical History of Mankind,* 2nd edition, vol. 2. London: John and Arthur Arch, 1826, 111

43   *Ibid.,* 116

44   *Ibid.,* 133

45   *Ibid.,* 117

46   *Ibid.,* 137

47   Prichard, 'Remarks on the Application of Philological and Physical Researches to the History of the Human Species', *Report of the First and Second Meetings of the British Association for the Advancement of Science* [henceforth BAAS Report, with the year referring to the year of the meeting] 1832, 529

48   *Ibid.,* 535

49 Prichard, *The Eastern Origin of the Celtic Nations Proved by a Comparison of Their Dialects with the Sanscrit, Greek, Latin, and Teutonic Languages.* London: J. and A. Arch, 1831, 3

50 *Ibid.*, 4

51 *Ibid.*, 8

52 *Ibid.*, 9-10, 13

53 *Ibid.*, 14

54 *Ibid.*, 16-17

55 *Ibid.*, 19

56 R.G. Latham, 'Supplementary Chapter', to Prichard, *The Eastern Origin of the Celtic Nations Proved by a Comparison of Their Dialects with the Sanscrit, Greek, Latin, and Teutonic Languages*, ed. R.G. Latham, 2nd edition. London: Howlston and Wright, and Bernard Quaritch, 1857, 375

57 Prichard, *Researches into the Physical History of Mankind*, 3rd edition, vol. 3. London: Sherwood, Gilbert, and Piper, 1841, 108-109

58 Prichard, *Eastern Origin of the Celtic Nations*, 24

Chapter V: Celtic Monuments

1 Letter to Bryan Faussett quoted in Ronald Jessup, *Man of Many Talents: An Informal Biography of James Douglas 1753-1819.* London and Chichester: Phillimore and Co., 1975, 111-112, 265

2 William Stukeley, *Itinerarium Curiosum, Or, An Account of the Antiquitys and Remarkable Curiositys in Nature or Art, Observ'd in Travels thro' Great Brittan.* London, 1724, 102, 109

3 *Ibid.*, Preface

4 *Ibid.*, 45

5 *Ibid.*, 40

6 *Ibid.*, 5

7 *Ibid.*, 5

8 *Ibid.*, 48

9 *Ibid.*, 48, 54, 56

10 Isaac Newton, *The Chronology of Ancient Kingdoms Amended.* London: J. Tonson, J. Osborn and T. Longman, 1728

11 J.G. Keysler, *Antiqvitates Selectae Septentrionales et Celticae.* Hanover: Nicolai Foersteri, 1720. As the title suggests, Keysler considered that the megaliths might be Celtic, but rejected the idea

12 e.g., William Baxter, *Glossarium Antiquitatum Britannicarum.* London, 1719; William Musgrave, *Belgium Britannicum.* London: William Taylor and John Sprint, 1719

13 Stukeley, *An Account of a Roman Temple, and Other Antiquities near Graham's Dike in Scotland.* London, 1720, 23-24

14 Martin, *A Description of the Western Islands of Scotland*, 365

15 Stukeley, *Abury: A Temple of the British Druids, with Some Others Described wherein Is a More Particular Account of the First and Patriarchal Religion; and of the Peopling of the British Isles*, vol. 2. London, 1743, 28

16 John Toland, *A Collection of Several Pieces of Mr. John Toland*, vol. 1. London: J. Peele, 1726, 1, 4

17 *Ibid.*, 7, 204-228

18 *Ibid.*, 45

19 *Ibid.*, 62-64

20 *Ibid.*, 98

21 M.I. Guenebault, *Le Réveil de l'Antique Tombeau de Chyndonax, prince des Vacies, Druides, Celtiques, Dijonnois.* Dijon, 1623

22 Stukeley, *Itinerarium Curiosum*, 97

23 *Ibid.*, 98

24 *Ibid.*, 71, 73, 74, 91, 95

25 *Ibid.*, 102

26 *Ibid.*, 109

27 Stukeley, *Itinerarium Curiosum*, 2nd edition, vol. 2. London: Baker and Leigh, 1776, 169

28 Stukeley, *The History of the Temples of the Antient Celts*, Bodleian MS. Eng.misc.c.323, 71-72

29 Stuart Piggott, *William Stukeley: An Eighteenth Century Antiquary*, 2nd edition. London: Thames and Hudson, 1989, 65, 88

30 Stukeley, *The History of the Temples of the Antient Celts*, 21

31 *Ibid.*, 77-79

32 *Ibid.*, 81

33 Piggott, *William Stukeley*, 108

34 *Ibid.*, 77

35 Quoted in Piggott, *William Stukeley*, 97

36 Stukeley, *Stonehenge: A Temple Restor'd to the British Druids.* London: W. Innys and R. Manby, 1740, Preface

37 *Ibid.*

38 Stukeley, *Abury*, i

39 *Ibid.*, 78; *Stonehenge*, 55-56

40 Stukeley, *Abury*, ii, 4

41 Toland, *A Collection of Several Pieces of Mr. John Toland*, 40, 121-129

42 Stukeley, *Stonehenge*, 8

43 Stukeley, *Palaeographica Britannica: Or, Discourses on Antiquities in Britain*, no. 1. London: R. Manby, 1743; no. 2. Stamford, 1746; no. 3. London: C. Corbet, 1752

44   William Borlase, *Observations on the Antiquities Historical and Monumental, of the County of Cornwall*. Oxford, 1754, v

45   *Ibid.*, 5, 14-16, 22

46   *Ibid.*, 14, 76

47   *Ibid.*, v

48   *Ibid.*, vi, 152

49   *Ibid.*, 2

50   e.g.,Haviland, 'On the First Peopling of This Island', *Archaeologia* 1 (1770): 49-55; John Pettingal, 'A Dissertation on the *Gule of August*, as Mentioned in our Statute Laws', *Archaeologia* 2 (1773): 60-67; John Walker, 'On the Antient *Camelon*, and the *Picts*', *Archaeologia* 1 (1770): 230-237

51   Samuel Johnson, *A Journey to the Western Islands of Scotland*, vol. 1. Dublin: A. Leathley, J. Exshaw, H. Saunders, D. Chamberlain, W. Sleater, J. Potts, T. Ewing, W. Wilson, R. Mancrieffe and C. Jenkin, 1775, 95

52   George Birkbeck Hill (ed.), *Boswell's Life of Johnson*, revised and enlarged by L.F. Powell, vol. 3. Oxford: Clarendon Press, 1934, 333

53   Francis Grose, *The Antiquities of England and Wales*, vol. 4. London: S. Hooper, 1776

54   Grose, *The Antiquities of Ireland*, vol. 1. London: S. Hooper, 1791, ii

55   Camden, *Britannia: Or, A Chorographical Description of the Flourishing Kingdoms of England, Scotland, and Ireland, and the Islands Adjacent; From the Earliest Antiquity*, trans. and enlarged by Richard Gough, vol. 1. London: T. Payne and Son, and G.G.J. and J. Robinson, 1789, iii

56   Alexander Gordon, *Itinerarium Septentrionale: Or, A Journey thro' Most of the Counties of Scotland, and Those in the North of England*. London, 1726, 177

57   Thomas Pownall, 'A Description of the Sepulchral Monument at New Grange, near Drogheda, in the County of Meath, in Ireland', *Archaeologia* 2 (1773): 241

58   Bryan Faussett, *Inventorium Sepulchrale*, ed. Charles Roach Smith. London, 1856, 37.

59   John Hutchins, *The History and Antiquities of the County of Dorset*, vol. 1. London, 1774, ix, xx

60   Letter to Faussett quoted in Jessup, *Man of Many Talents*, 92, 186-88

61   Letter to Faussett quoted in *Ibid.*, 111-112, 265

62   James Douglas, *Nenia Britannica: Or, A Sepulchral History of Great Britain; From the*

63   Earliest Period to Its General Conversion to Christianity. London: Benjamin and John White, 1793, 78

63   *Ibid.*, vi

64   Douglas, *A Dissertation on the Antiquity of the Earth*. London, 1785, 22-24

65   Douglas, *Nenia Britannica*, 131

66   *Ibid.*, 185

67   *Ibid.*, 122-131

68   *Ibid.*, v

69   *Ibid.*, 190

70   *Ibid.*, 78; Pinkerton, *Enquiry into the History of Scotland*, vol. 1, 17

71   Douglas, *Nenia Britannica*, 156, 191; letter to Major Hayman Rooke, 16 Nov., 1774, quoted in Jessup, *Man of Many Talents*, 238

72   Douglas, *Nenia Britannica*, 191

73   *Ibid.*, 191

74   *Ibid.*, 150

75   John Milner, 'Barrows in Dorsetshire', *The Gentleman's Magazine Library: Archaeology part 1*, ed. George Lawrence Gomme. London: Elliot Stock, 1886, 102-103

76   Samuel Greathead, 'Inquiries Respecting the Origin of the Inhabitants of the British Islands', *Archaeologia* 16 (1812): 96

77   D.D.A. Simpson, 'Introduction: Ancient Wiltshire', to Sir Richard Colt Hoare, *The Ancient History of Wiltshire*. East Ardsley, West Yorkshire: E.P. Publishing, 1975, 11-12

78   Richard Colt Hoare, *The Ancient History of Wiltshire*, vol. 1. London: William Miller, 1812, 7

79   *Ibid.*, 7

80   *Ibid.*, 18, 28

81   Giraldus De Barri, *The Itinerary of Archbishop Baldwin through Wales, A.D. MCLXXXVIII*, trans. and annotated by Richard Colt Hoare, 2 vols. London: William Miller, 1806

82   Colt Hoare, *Journal of a Tour in Ireland, AD 1806*, London: W. Miller, 1807, xxiv, 273-278

83   Colt Hoare, *The Ancient History of Wiltshire*, vol. 1, 2

84   *Ibid.*, 7-9

85   *Ibid.*, 12

86   *Ibid.*, 17

87   *Ibid.*, 23-26

88   *Ibid.*, 27

89   *Ibid.*, 30

90   Letter from William Cunnington to Thomas Leman, Heytesbury 1809, quoted in Kenneth Woodbridge, *Landscape and Antiquity: Aspects of*

English Culture at Stourhead 1718-1838.
Oxford: Clarendon Press, 1970, 276. The footnotes are Cunnington's

91   Quoted in Robert H. Cunnington, *From
      Antiquary to Archaeologist: A Biography of
      William Cunnington 1754-1810*, ed. James
      Dyer. Aylesbury, Buckinghamshire: Shire
      Publications, 1975, 76

92   Colt Hoare, *The Ancient History of Wiltshire*,
      vol. 2. London: Lackington, Hughes, Harding,
      Mavor and Lepard, 1821, 118-122

93   e.g.,Edward Daniel Clarke, 'Observations upon
      Some Celtic Remains', *Archaeologia* 18 (1817):
      340-343; 'An Account of Some Antiquities
      Found at Fulbourn in Cambridgeshire',
      Archaeologia 19 (1821): 56-61; Cf. John Collis,
      'The Origin and Spread of the Celts', *Studia
      Celtica* 30 (1996), 22

94   e.g., various papers in Gomme (ed.), *The
      Gentleman's Magazine Library: Archaeology part
      1*, 81-297; *Archaeology part 2*, 1-167

95   William Augustus Miles, *A Description of the
      Deverel Barrow, Opened A.D. 1825*. London:
      Nichols and Son, 1826, 10-11

96   Alexander Blair and Francis Ronalds, *Sketches
      at Carnac (Brittany) in 1834*. London: Richard
      Taylor, 1836; Godfrey Higgins, *The Celtic
      Druids*. London: R. Hunter, 1827; Samuel
      Rush Meyrick and Charles Hamilton Smith,
      *The Costume of the Original Inhabitants of the
      British Islands*. London: R. Havell, 1815, 44-50

Chapter VI: Celtic Skulls

1   Thomas Hodgkin, 'On Inquiries into the
      Races of Man', BAAS *Report* 1841: 54

2   Royal Society of Northern Antiquaries of
      Copenhagen, *Guide to Northern Archaeology*, ed.
      and trans. Earl of Ellesmere. London: James
      Bain, 1848, 65-66

3   *Ibid.*, 69

4   Sven Nilsson, *The Primitive Inhabitants of
      Scandinavia: An Essay on Comparative
      Ethnography, and a Contribution to the History of
      the Development of Mankind*, ed. and trans. John
      Lubbock, 3rd edition. London: Longmans,
      Green, and Co., 1868, 107

5   Royal Society of Northern Antiquaries, *Guide
      to Northern Archaeology*, xvi; *Report Addressed by
      the Royal Society of Northern Antiquaries to Its
      British and American Members*. Copenhagen,
      1836, 18

6   Richard King, 'Address to the Ethnological

Society of London', *Journal of the Ethnological
Society of London* 2 (1850), 20

7   Prichard, *Researches*, 3rd edition, vol. 3, xviii

8   Prichard, *Researches*, 1st edition, 46; 2nd edi-
      tion, 158. The quotation is from the 1st edi-
      tion

9   Prichard, *Researches*, 3rd edition, vol. 3, 200

10   *Ibid.*, xxi

11   Hodgkin, 'Obituary of Dr. Prichard', 204

12   Prichard, *The Natural History of Man:
      Comprising Inquiries into the Modifying Influence
      of Physical and Moral Agencies on the Different
      Tribes of the Human Family*. London: H.
      Baillicrc, 1843, 191

13   *Ibid.*, 192

14   *Ibid.*, 188-197

15   Prichard, 'On the Relations of Ethnology to
      Other Branches of Knowledge', *The New
      Edinburgh Journal* 43, no. 76. October. (1847),
      321

16   Nilsson, 'On the Primitive Inhabitants of
      Scandinavia', trans. Norton Shaw, BAAS
      Report 1847: 32; *The Primitive Inhabitants of
      Scandinavia*, xlviii

17   Anders Retzius, 'On Certain American, Celtic,
      Cimbric, Roman and Ancient British Skulls',
      BAAS *Report* 1849, 86. Prichard later sent
      skulls to Retzius for racial identification, as
      documented in Retzius' 1856 article on eth-
      nology, translated in 1860 as 'Present State of
      Ethnology in Relation to the Form of the
      Human Skull', trans. C. A. Alexander, *Annual
      Report of the Board of Regents of the Smithsonian
      Institution*. Washington, 1860, 253

18   Prichard, *Researches*, 3rd edition, vol. 3, 8

19   Prichard, 'On the *Crania* of the Laplanders and
      Finlanders', *Proceedings of the Zoological Society
      of London* 12 (1844), 129-135

20   Prichard, *Researches*, 3rd edition, vol. 3, xx

21   *Ibid.*, 167

22   Retzius, 'On the Ethnographical Distribution
      of Round and Elongated Crania', BAAS
      Report 1846, 116

23   Nilsson, 'On the Primitive Inhabitants of
      Scandinavia,' 31-32

24   Joseph Barnard Davis and John Thurnam,
      *Crania Britannica: Deliniations and Descriptions of
      the Skulls of the Aboriginal and Early Inhabitants
      of the British Islands*, vol. 1. London, 1865, 13-
      33

25   Prichard, *The Natural History of Man*, 186, 192-
      193; *Researches*, 3rd edition, vol. 3, xxi

26 R. Williams, 'On Local Hereditary Difference of Complexion in Great Britain, with Some Incidental Notice of the Cimbri', BAAS *Report* 1845, 81-82

27 Samuel George Morton, *Crania Americana: A Comparative View of the Skulls of Various Aboriginal Nations*. Philadelphia: J. Dobson; London: Simpkin, Marshall, and Co., 1839, 15-18

28 William R. Wilde, *Narrative of a Voyage to Madeira, Teneriffe, and along the Shores of the Mediterranean*, vol. 1. Dublin: William Curry, Jun. and Co., 1840, 345-357

29 Wilde, 'The Ethnology of the Ancient Irish', *The Dublin Literary Journal* 2, 1844, 247

30 *Ibid.*, 232

31 Wilde, *The Beauties of the Boyne, and Its Tributary, the Blackwater*. Dublin: James McGlashan, 1849, 218-220; 'The Ethnology of the Ancient Irish', 233

32 Wilde, *The Beauties of the Boyne*, 221-222, 231, 238; 'The Ethnology of the Ancient Irish', 233

33 J.J.A. Worsaae, *The Primeval Antiquities of Denmark*, trans. and enlarged William J. Thoms. London: John Henry Parker, 1849, 121

34 William Thoms, '*Danemark's Vorzeit Durch Altherthumer und Grabhugel Beleuchtet* von J.J.A. Worsaae 1844', *Archaeological Journal* 2 1846, 291-292

35 Worsaae, 'An Account of the Formation of the Museum at Copenhagen, and General Remarks on the Classification of Antiquities Found in the North and West of Europe', *Proceedings of the Royal Irish Academy* 3. 1847, 311

36 *Ibid.*, 328

37 *Ibid.*, 329

38 Worsaae, *Primeval Antiquities*, 131-133

39 Worsaae, 'An Account of the Formation of the Museum', 331; *Primeval Antiquities*, 140

40 *Ibid.*, 134

41 *Ibid.*, vi; Royal Society of Northern Antiquaries, *Guide to Northern Archaeology*, 64

42 Worsaae, *Primeval Antiquities*, 131-132

43 *Ibid.*, 142-143

44 'Review of *An Account of the Danes and Norwegians in England, Scotland, and Ireland*,' *The Athenaeum*, 1265, Jan. 24 (1852), 106

45 Worsaae, *An Account of the Danes and Norwegians in England, Scotland, and Ireland*. London: John Murray, 1852, 357

46 Worsaae, 'An Account of the Formation of the Museum', 343

47 Worsaae, *An Account of the Danes and Norwegians*, 297

48 *Ibid.*, 3-4

49 Worsaae, *Primeval Antiquities*, 1

50 Wilde, *The Beauties of the Boyne*, v

51 *Ibid.*, ix

52 *Ibid.*, xii

53 Prichard, 'On the Various Methods of Research Which Contribute to the Advancement of Ethnology, and of the Relations of that Science to Other Branches of Knowledge', BAAS *Report* 1847, 237

54 *Ibid.*, 246

55 Daniel Wilson, *Synopsis of the Museum of the Society of Antiquaries of Scotland*. Edinburgh: Society of Antiquaries of Scotland, 1849, 1

56 Wilson, 'Inquiry into the Evidence of the Existence of Primitive Races in Scotland prior to the Celtae', BAAS *Report* 1850, 142

57 '"Inquiry into the Evidence of the Existence of Primitive Races in Scotland prior to the Celtae" by Mr. D. Wilson', *The Athenaeum* 1191, Aug. 24 (1850), 908

58 Nilsson, 'On the Primitive Inhabitants of Scandinavia', 31-32

59 Wilson, 'Inquiry into the Evidence of the Existence of Primitive Races', 143; *Prehistoric Annals of Scotland*, 2nd edition, vol. 1. London and Cambridge: Macmillan and Co., 1863, 236

60 Wilson, 'Inquiry into the Evidence of the Existence of Primitive Races', 143

61 *Ibid.*, 144

62 Wilson, *The Archaeology and Prehistoric Annals of Scotland*, 1st edition. Edinburgh: Sutherland and Knox; London: Simpkin, Marshal and Co. and J. H. Parker, 1851, xii-xiv, 1-5, 43

63 *Ibid.*, 5

64 *Ibid.*, xii-xiii

65 *Ibid.*, xiii

66 *Ibid.*, 12

67 Prichard, 'On the Various Methods of Research', 237; *Researches*, 3rd edition, vol. 3, xxi; Wilson, *Archaeology and Prehistoric Annals*, 10

68 *Ibid.*, xiv-xv

69 *Ibid.*, xvi

70 *Ibid.*, 182

71 Prichard, *Researches*, 3rd edition, vol. 5, 554; Wilson, *Archaeology and Prehistoric Annals*, 218,

1, 19

72   *Ibid.*, 10

73   *Ibid.*, 161–162, 343

74   *Ibid.*, 183

75   *Ibid.*, 343

76   *Ibid.*, 350

77   *Ibid.*, 229–232

78   *Ibid.*, xiv

79   *Ibid.*, 173

80   Thomas Bateman, *Vestiges of the Antiquities of Derbyshire and the Sepulchral Usages of Its Inhabitants from the Most Remote Ages to the Reformation.* London: John Russell Smith, 1848, 1

81   Bateman, *Ten Years' Diggings in Celtic and Saxon Grave Hills, in the Counties of Derby, Stafford, and York, from 1848 to 1858.* London: J.R. Smith, 1861, Preface: v, Introduction: ii–iii; Joan Evans, *A History of the Society of Antiquaries.* Oxford. The Society of Antiquaries, 1956, 286, misattributes this quotation to Bateman's *Vestiges of the Antiquities of Derbyshire*

82   Bateman, *A Descriptive Catalogue of the Antiquities and Miscellaneous Objects Preserved in the Museum of Thomas Bateman at Lamberdale House, Derbyshire.* Bakewell, 1855

83   Davis and Thurnam, *Crania Britannica*, Preface

84   T. Price, *An Essay on the Physiognomy and Physiology of the Present Inhabitants of Britain; with Reference to Their Origin, as Goths and Celts.* London: J. Rodwell, 1829

85   George Combe, *A System of Phrenology*, 5th edition, vol. 2. Edinburgh: MacLachlan, Stewart and Co., 1843, 334, 356–371

86   A list of skull collections open to the public at the time is provided in D.G. Goyder (ed.), *The Phrenological Almanac and Psychological Annual*, vol. 1. Glasgow: J. and G. Goyder, 1845, 60–61

87   Thurnam, 'On Danish Tumuli, and Importance of Preserving Crania Found in Tumuli', *The Archaeological Journal* 7 (1850): 34–35

88   Davis, 'On the Forms of the Crania of the Ancient Britons', BAAS *Report* 1854: 127; 'On Some of the Bearings of Ethnology upon Archaeological Science', *The Archaeological Journal* 13 (1856), 316

89   Davis, 'On the Forms of the Crania', 128

90   *Ibid.*, 128

91   Davis and Thurnam, *Crania Britannica*, Plates 1–5

92   *Ibid.*, Preface

93   *Ibid.*, 2

94   *Ibid.*, 198

95   *Ibid.*, 229

96   *Ibid.*, 230, Plate 59, 6; Thurnam, 'On the Two Principal Forms of Ancient British and Gaulish Skulls', *Memoirs Read before the Anthropological Society of London* 1 (1865): 120–168, 459–519

97   Davis and Thurnam, *Crania Britannica*, 155

98   *Ibid.*, 156

99   Thomas Wright, *The Celt, the Roman, and the Saxon: A History of the Early Inhabitants of Britain, Down to the Conversion of the Anglo-Saxons to Christianity.* London: Arthur Hall, Virtue, and Co., 1852, vii

100   *Ibid.*, viii

101   e.g., Wright, 'On the Early Ethnology of Britain', BAAS *Report* 1854, 130

102   Wilson, *Archaeology and Prehistoric Annals*, 183; Wright, *The Celt, the Roman, and the Saxon*, 4

103   Thomas Burgon, 'On a Mode of Ascertaining the Places to which Ancient British Coins Belong', *The Numismatic Chronicle* 1 (1839), 38

104   J.Y. Akerman, 'Further Observations on the Coinage of the Ancient Britons', *The Numismatic Chronicle* 1 (1839), 73–90

105   John Evans, 'On the Date of British Coins', *The Numismatic Chronicle* 13 (1850): 128; *The Coins of the Ancient Britons.* London: J. Russell Smith, 1864; Edward Hawkins, 'Observations upon British Coins', *The Numismatic Chronicle* 1 (1839): 13–26; C.J. Thomsen, 'Remarks on the Ancient British and Anglo-Saxon Coinage', *The Numismatic Chronicle* 3 (1841), 116–122

106   James Hunt, 'Knox on the Celtic Race', *Anthropological Review* 6 (1868): 175–191; Robert Knox, *The Races of Men: A Philosophical Enquiry into the Influence of Race over the Destinies of Nations.* London, 1850, 324

107   e.g. John Collingwood Bruce, *The Roman Wall.* London: John Russell Smith, 1851, 33–34; J. M'Elheran, *Celt and Saxon: Address to the British Association, on the Ethnology of England.* Belfast: R. & D. Read, 1852

108   Thurnam, 'The Two Principal Forms of Crania amongst the Early Britons', *The Anthropological Review* 2 (1864), ccxxxii–ccxxxiii

109   Wilson, 'Inquiry into the Physical Characteristics of the Ancient and Modern Celt of Gaul and Britain', *The Anthropological Review* 3 (1865), 52–84

110   *Ibid.*, 58, 63

111 Wilson, *Prehistoric Annals*, 2nd edition, vol. 1,
     236, 280, 282
112 Wilson, 'Inquiry into the Physical
     Characteristics of the Ancient and Modern
     Celt', 53
113 Wilson, *Prehistoric Annals of Scotland*, 2nd edi-
     tion, vol. 1, 236
114 Wilson, 'Inquiry into the Physical
     Characteristics of the Ancient and Modern
     Celt', 57
115 Wilson, 'Ethnical Forms and Undesigned
     Artificial Distortions of the Human Cranium',
     The Canadian Journal of Industry, Science, and Art
     7, no. 41 (1862), 399-446; 'Illustrations of the
     Significance of Certain Ancient British Skull
     Forms', *The Canadian Journal of Industry,
     Science, and Art* 8, no. 44 (1863), 127-157
116 Wilson, 'Inquiry into the Physical
     Characteristics of the Ancient and Modern
     Celt', 72-84
117 John Beddoe, 'On the Ancient and Modern
     Ethnography of Scotland', *Proceedings of the
     Society of Antiquaries of Scotland* 1 (1855), 243-
     257
118 Joseph Prestwich, 'On the Occurrence of
     Flint-Implements, Associated with the
     Remains of Extinct Mammalia, in
     Undisturbed Beds of a Late Geological
     Period', *Proceedings of the Royal Society of
     London* 10 (1860), 58-59
119 e.g., Wilson, *Prehistoric Annals of Scotland*, 2nd
     edition, vol. 1, 287
120 John Lubbock, *Pre-Historic Times, as Illustrated
     by Ancient Remains, and the Manners and
     Customs of Modern Savages*. London and
     Edinburgh: Williams and Norgate, 1865, 91
121 *Ibid.*, 3-4
122 *Ibid.*, 19
123 *Ibid.*, 49
124 *Ibid.*, 60
125 *Ibid.*, 98
126 *Ibid.*, 116-117

Chapter VII: Celtic Art
1   'Proceedings of the Central Committee of the
     British Archaeological Association', *The
     Archaeological Journal* 2 (1846), 186
2   Samuel Birch, 'On the Torc of the Celts',
     Archaeological Journal 2 (1846), 368; Part 2 of
     the paper appears in *Archaeological Journal* 3
     (1846), 27-38

3   Augustus Wollaston Franks, *A Book of
     Ornamental Glazing Quarries, Collected and
     Arranged from Ancient Examples*. London: John
     Henry Parker, 1849
4   Akerman, *An Archaeological Index to Remains of
     Antiquity of the Celtic, Romano-British, and
     Anglo-Saxon Periods*. London: John Russell
     Smith, 1847, 11
5   Franks, *Catalogue of Works of Antient and
     Mediaeval Art Exhibited at the House of the
     Society of Arts*. London, 1850, 5
6   Franks, 'The Collection of British Antiquities
     in the British Museum', *The Archaeological
     Journal* 9 (1852), 7, 9
7   Franks, 'On the Additions to the Collection of
     National Antiquities in the British Museum',
     The Archaeological Journal 11 (1854), 23, 25
8   Franks, 'Notes on Bronze Weapons Found on
     Arreton Down, Isle of Wight', *Archaeologia* 36
     (1855), 331
9   *Ibid.*, 331
10   Akerman, 'On Some of the Weapons of the
     Celtic and Teutonic Races,' *Archaeologia* 34
     (1852), 172
11   Birch, 'On the Torc of the Celts'
12   *Descriptive Catalogue of the Collection of
     Antiquities, and Other Objects, Illustrative of Irish
     History, Exhibited on the Occasion of the Twenty-
     Second Meeting of the British Association for the
     Advancement of Science, September, 1852*. Belfast:
     Archer and Sons, 1852
13   Papers in BAAS *Report* 1852 and 1857
14   *Descriptive Catalogue*, Preface, Appendix
15   *Ibid.*, 3
16   Quoted in R.B. McDowell, 'The Main
     Narrative', *The Royal Irish Academy: A
     Bicentennial History 1785-1985*, ed. T. Ó
     Raifeartaigh. Dublin: The Royal Irish
     Academy, 1985, 37, 39
17   Martin Haverty, *The Aran Isles: Or, A Report of
     the Excursion of the Ethnological Section of The
     British Association from Dublin to the Western
     Islands of Aran, in September, 1857*. Dublin: At
     the University Press, 1859, 3, 21, 28, 29
18   Wilde, *A Descriptive Catalogue of the Antiquities
     of Animal Materials and Bronze in the Museum of
     the Royal Irish Academy*. Dublin: Hodges,
     Smith, and Co., 1861, 252
19   *Ibid.*, 350, 353
20   Wilde, *A Descriptive Catalogue of the Antiquities
     of Stone, Earthen, and Vegetable Materials, in the*

21 *Ibid.*, 170

22 Wilde, *A Descriptive Catalogue of the Antiquities of Animal Materials and Bronze*, 351, 387

23 *Ibid.*, 638

24 John Kemble, 'Address to the President and Members of the Royal Irish Academy', *Horae Ferales: Or, Studies in the Archaeology of the Northern Nations*, ed. R.G. Latham and A.W. Franks. London: Lowell Reeve and Co., 1863, 81

25 Kemble, 'Lecture at the Opening of the Hanoverian Museum', *Horae Ferales*, 61

26 *Ibid.*, 61

27 Kemble, 'Burial and Cremation', *Archaeological Journal* 12 (1855), 309–337; 'On Mortuary Urns Found at Stade-on-the-Elbe, and Other Parts of North Germany, Now in the Museum of the Historical Society of Hanover,' *Archaeologia* 36 (1855), 270–283

28 *Catalogue of the Art Treasures of the United Kingdom Collected at Manchester in 1857.* London, 1857, 163

29 *Ibid.*, 163

30 'Proceedings at the Meetings of the Archaeological Institute', *The Archaeological Journal* 13 (1856), 92

31 Kemble, 'Address to the President and Members of the Royal Irish Academy', 79–80

32 'Archaeological Intelligence', *The Archaeological Journal* 14 (1857), 295

33 H. Syer Cuming, 'On Further Discoveries of Celtic and Roman Remains in the Thames, off Battersea', *The Journal of the British Archaeological Association* 14 (1858), 330

34 Cuming, 'On the Discovery of Celtic Crania in the Vicinity of London', *The Journal of the British Archaeological Association* 13 (1857), 237–240

35 *Ibid.*, 238

36 *Proceedings of the Society of Antiquaries of London* 4 (1858), 144–145

37 *Ibid.*, 145

38 *Ibid.*, 165–167

39 *Ibid.*, 241–242. Letter to Edward Hawkins, December 11, 1858, *British Museum Trust Papers* 61 (1858), 257

40 e.g., *Proceedings of the Society of Antiquaries of London*, 2nd series 1 (1860), 161–163

41 'Review of *Horae Ferales*', *The Athenaeum* 1900, March 26 (1864), 432–433

42 Latham, *Descriptive Ethnology*, 2 vols. London: John Van Voorst, 1859; *The Natural History of the Varieties of Man.* London: John Van Voorst, 1850

43 Latham, *Man and His Migrations.* London: John Van Voorst, 1851, 49, 101, 156

44 Latham, *The Ethnology of the British Islands.* London: John Van Voorst, 1852; *The Ethnology of Europe.* London: John Van Voorst, 1852

45 Prichard, *Eastern Origin of the Celtic Nations*, 2nd edition, 59

46 Latham, *The Ethnology of Europe*, 35–36

47 Latham, 'Supplementary Chapter', to Prichard, *Eastern Origin of the Celtic Nations*, 377

48 Latham (ed.), *Eastern Origin of the Celtic Nations*, 2nd edition, 32

49 *Ibid.*, 48–52 (fn. 7); *The Ethnology of the British Islands*, 27, 220

50 *Ibid.*, 220

51 Latham (ed.), *The Eastern Origin of the Celtic Nations*, 2nd edition, 85

52 Latham, 'Editor's Introduction', *Horae Ferales*, 1

53 Kemble, 'Burial and Cremation', *Horae Ferales*, 85; 'Lecture at the Opening of the Hanoverian Museum', 36, 63; Latham, 'Editor's Introduction', 12, 13, 17, 19

54 'Review of *Horae Ferales*', 433

55 Kemble, 'Lecture at the Opening of the Hanoverian Museum', 63

56 Franks, 'Description of the Plates', *Horae Ferales*, 127

57 *Ibid.*, 159

58 *Ibid.*, 172

59 *Ibid.*, 184

60 *Ibid.*, 185

61 *Ibid.*, 189

62 *Ibid.*, 189

63 e.g., *Proceedings of the Society of Antiquaries of London*, 2nd series 1 (1860): 233

64 Robert Munro, *The Lake-Dwellings of Europe.* London, Paris, and Melbourne: Cassell and Co., 1890

65 Lubbock, *Pre-Historic Times*, 161

66 A. Morlot, 'General Views on Archaeology', trans. Philip Harry, *Annual Report of the Board of Regents of the Smithsonian Institution.* Washington, 1861, 310–312

67 Ferdinand Keller, *The Lake Dwellings of Switzerland and Other Parts of Europe*, trans. John Edward Lee. London: Longmans, Green, and Co., 1866, 313–314

68 Franks, 'Description of the Plates', 188

69 Keller, *The Lake Dwellings of Switzerland and Other Parts of Europe*, trans. John Edward Lee, 2nd edition, vol. 1. London: Longmans, Green, and Co., 1878, 410, 425

70 Evans, *The Coins of the Ancient Britons; The Ancient Stone Implements, Weapons, and Ornaments, of Great Britain*. London: Longmans, Green, Reader, and Dyer, 1872; *The Ancient Bronze Implements, Weapons, and Ornaments, of Great Britain and Ireland*. London: Longmans, Green and Co., 1881

71 Augustus Lane Fox Pitt Rivers, *The Evolution of Culture and Other Essays*, ed. J.L. Myres. Oxford: Clarendon Press, 1906, 1-44

72 Joseph Anderson. *Scotland in Early Christian Times: The Rhind Lectures in Archaeology – 1879*. Edinburgh: David Douglas, 1881, 1, 123

73 14 December, 1874, *Proceedings of the Society of Antiquaries of Scotland* 11 (1876): 14

74 Anderson, *Scotland in Early Christian Times*, 6; *Scotland in Pagan Times: The Bronze and Stone Ages*. Edinburgh: David Douglas, 1886, 1, 385

75 *Ibid.*, 386-387

76 Anderson, *Scotland in Early Christian Times*, 23-26

77 William F. Skene, *Celtic Scotland: A History of Ancient Alban*, vol. 1, History and Ethnology. Edinburgh: Edmonston and Douglas, 1876; vol. 2, Church and Culture. Edinburgh: David Douglas, 1877; vol. 3, Land and People. Edinburgh: David Douglas, 1880

78 Anderson, *Scotland in Early Christian Times*, 157-158

79 Matthew Arnold, *The Study of Celtic Literature*. Long Acre: David Nutt, 1910, 25, 61

80 Anderson, *Scotland in Early Christian Times (Second Series): The Rhind Lectures in Archaeology for 1880*. Edinburgh: David Douglas, 1881, vi, 48, 109

81 Anderson, *Scotland in Pagan Times: The Iron Age*. Edinburgh: David Douglas, 1883, 112

82 *Ibid.*, 172-173

83 *Ibid.*, 307

84 *Ibid.*, 25, 31

85 *Ibid.*, 66

86 *Ibid.*, 31

87 Anderson, *Scotland in Pagan Times: The Bronze and Stone Ages*, 97

88 *Ibid.*, 1, 385

89 Anderson, *Scotland in Early Christian Times*, 13

90 Anderson, 'The Early Christian Monuments of Scotland, Being (in Substance) The Rhind Lectures for 1892', in J. Romilly Allen, *The Early Christian Monuments of Scotland: A Classified, Illustrated, Descriptive List of the Monuments, with an Analysis of Their Symbolism and Ornamentations*. Edinburgh: Society of Antiquaries of Scotland, 1903, iii-cxxii

91 *Ibid.*, iii

92 *Ibid.*, xi-xii, lviii, lxvii

93 *Ibid.*, xi, lxviii

94 *Ibid.*, lviii

95 *Ibid.*, lxix

96 *Ibid.*, xcix

97 *Ibid.*, ci

98 *Ibid.*, cix-cxii

99 Allen, *The Early Christian Monuments of Scotland*, 369-371

100 Arthur Evans, 'The Rhind Lectures', *The Scotsman*, 11 December 1895, 10

101 Evans, 'The Rhind Lectures', *The Scotsman*, 12 December 1895, 7

102 Evans, 'The Rhind Lectures', *The Scotsman*, 14 December 1895, 7

103 Evans, 'The Rhind Lectures', *The Scotsman*, 17 December 1895, 7; 'The Rhind Lectures', *The Scotsman*, 19 December 1895, 6

104 Evans, 'The Rhind Lectures', *The Scotsman*, 21 December 1895, 7

105 Allen, *Early Christian Symbolism in Great Britain and Ireland before the Thirteenth Century: The Rhind Lectures in Archaeology for 1885*. London: Whiting and Co., 1887, vi

106 *Ibid.*, 78

107 *Ibid.*, 85

108 *Ibid.*, 241

109 Allen, *Celtic Art in Pagan and Christian Times*. London: Methuen and Co., 1904, xv

110 *Ibid.*, 1

111 *Ibid.*, 6-14, 17

112 *Ibid.*, xvi

113 *Ibid.*, xv

114 *Ibid.*, 303

115 *Ibid.*, 22

Chapter VIII: The Birth of Archaeology

1 Rowlands, *Mona Antiqua Restaurata*, Preface

2 Anderson, *Scotland in Early Christian Times*, 1

3 Albert Way, 'Introduction', *The Archaeological Journal* 1 (1845), 1

4 Quoted in Evans, *A History of the Society of*

Antiquaries, 227

5   A. Henry Rhind, 'On the History of the
     Systematic Classification of Primeval Relics',
     The Archaeological Journal 13 (1856), 210;
     Rhind, *The Law of Treasure-Trove: How Can It
     Be Best Adapted to Accomplish Useful Results?*
     Edinburgh: Thomas Constable and Co., 1858;
     Wilson, *Archaeology and Prehistoric Annals*, xix

6   Rhind, *British Antiquities: Their Present Treatment
     and Their Real Claims*. Edinburgh: Adam and
     Charles Black, 1855, 46

7   'Origin and Designation of the Congress',
     *International Congress of Prehistoric Archaeology:
     Transactions of the Third Session*. London:
     Longmans, Green, and Co., 1869, xiii–xiv

8   E.B. Tylor, 'The Condition of Prehistoric
     Races, as Inferred from Observations of
     Modern Tribes', *International Congress of
     Prehistoric Archaeology*, 12, 20

9   T.H. Huxley, 'Notes on the Human Remains',
     in Samuel Laing, *Pre-historic Remains of
     Caithness*. London and Edinburgh: Williams
     and Norgate, 1866, 83-148; 'On the
     Distribution of the Races of Mankind and its
     Bearing on the Antiquity of Man',
     International Congress of Prehistoric Archaeology,
     92-97

10   Lubbock, 'The President's Address',
     International Congress of Prehistoric Archaeology, 8

11   Royal Society of Northern Antiquaries, *Guide
     to Northern Archaeology*, ix-x; Worsaae, 'An
     Account of the Formation of the Museum at
     Copenhagen', 329

12   Thoms, 'Preface by the Editor of the English
     Edition', in Worsaae, *Primeval Antiquities*, xi

13   e.g., T. Rankin, 'On the Ancient Tumuli in the
     Yorkshire Wolds', BAAS *Report* 1845, 82; Blair,
     'On Some Remarkable Primitive Monuments
     Existing at or near Carnac (Brittany); and on
     the Discrimination of Races by Their Local
     and Fixed Monuments', BAAS *Report* 1849,
     82-83; Abraham Hume, 'On the Ethnology of
     the Liverpool District, with Notices of the
     Hoylake Antiquities', BAAS *Report* 1854, 129;
     John Stuart, 'On the Sculptured Stones of
     Scotland', BAAS *Report* 1859, 197-200

14   Bateman, *Ten Years' Diggings*, xi; Wilson,
     Archaeology and Prehistoric Annals, 343

15   Anderson, *Scotland in Pagan Times: The Bronze
     and Stone Ages*, 136-137

16   Wilde, *A Descriptive Catalogue of the Antiquities
     of Stone, Earthen, and Vegetable Materials*, 129

17   Davis and Thurnam, *Crania Britannica*, 125

18   Evans, *The Coins of the Ancient Britons*, 17-18

19   Lubbock, *Pre-Historic Times*, 50, 56

20   Gomme, 'Introduction', *The Gentleman's
     Magazine Library: Archaeology part 1*, v, xi

21   James Fergusson, 'Stonehenge', *Quarterly
     Review* 108, no. 215 (July 1860): 204

22   *Ibid.*, 211

23   *Ibid.*, 223

24   Fergusson, 'Non-Historic Times', *Quarterly
     Review* 128, no. 256 (April 1870), 432-473

25   *Ibid.*, 472

26   Fergusson, *Rude Stone Monuments in All
     Countries: Their Age and Uses*. London: John
     Murray, 1872, 329

27   A.L. Lewis, 'On Certain Druidic Monuments
     in Berkshire', *International Congress of Prehistoric
     Archaeology*, 37

28   *Ibid.*, 42

29   *Ibid.*, 45

30   Stuart, 'On the Sculptured Stones of Scotland,'
     197; 'Stone Circles and Alignments',
     International Congress of Prehistoric Archaeology,
     32

31   Lewis, 'The Builders of the Megalithic
     Monuments of Britain', *The Journal of the
     Anthropological Institute of Great Britain and
     Ireland*, 1 (1872): 70-73

32   Documented in Christopher Chippindale,
     Stonehenge Complete, 2nd edition. New York
     and London: Thames and Hudson, 1994, 150,
     167-172

33   F.C. Lukis, 'Observations on the Primeval
     Antiquities of the Channel Islands', *The
     Archaeological Journal* 1 (1845): 142-151, 222-
     232; 'On the Sepulchral Character of
     Cromlechs in the Channel Islands', *The
     Journal of the British Archaeological Association* 4
     (1849), 323-337

34   Charles Warne, *Dorsetshire: It's Celtic, Roman,
     Saxon and Danish Vestiges*. London: D.
     Sydenham, 1865; *The Celtic Tumuli of Dorset:
     An Account of Personal and Other Researches into
     the Sepulchral Mounds of the Durotriges*. London:
     John Russell Smith, 1866, Preface, 19

35   Warne, *Ancient Dorset: The Celtic, Roman,
     Saxon, and Danish Antiquities of the County,
     Including the Early Coinage* 1872

36   George Rolleston, 'General Remarks upon the
     Series of Prehistoric Crania', William
     Greenwell, *British Barrows: A Record of the
     Examination of Sepulchral Mounds in Various*

Parts of England. Oxford: Clarendon Press,
1877, 627–633

37 Thurnam, 'On Ancient British Barrows,
Especially Those of Wiltshire and the
Adjoining Counties (Part I. Long Barrows)',
Archaeologia 42 (1869), 161-244; 'On Ancient
British Barrows, Especially Those of Wiltshire
and the Adjoining Counties (Part II. Round
Barrows)', Archaeologia 43 (1869), 285–552

38 William Copeland Borlase, Naenia Cornubiae:
A Descriptive Essay, Illustrative of the Sepulchres
and Funereal Customs of the Early Inhabitants of
the County of Cornwall. London: Longmans,
Green, Reader, and Dyer, 1872

39 J.C. Atkinson, Forty Years in a Moorland Parish:
Reminiscences and Researches in Danby in
Cleveland. London: Macmillan and Co., 1891;
Rooke Pennington, Notes on the Barrows and
Bone-Caves of Derbyshire London: Macmillan
and Co., 1877; William Turner (ed.), Ancient
Remains, Near Buxton. Buxton: C.F. Wardley,
1899

40 J.R. Mortimer, Forty Years' Researches in British
and Saxon Burial Mounds of East Yorkshire.
London: A. Brown and Sons, 1905

41 Huxley, 'On the Ethnology of Britain', Journal
of the Ethnological Society of London, new series,
2 (1870), 383

42 W. Boyd Dawkins, Early Man in Britain and
His Place in the Tertiary Period. London:
Macmillan and Co., 1880, 309

43 Robert Munro, Ancient Scottish Lake-Dwellings
or Crannogs, with a Supplementary Chapter on
Remains of Lake-Dwellings in England.
Edinburgh: David Douglas, 1882; The Lake-
Dwellings of Europe. London, Paris, and
Melbourne: Cassell and Co., 1890

44 Ibid., 545–546

45 Ibid., 551; In criticising Keller, Munro ignored
the 1878 edition of Keller's book, The Lake
Dwellings of Switzerland and Other Parts of
Europe, 2nd edition, vol. 1, 410, 425, where
Keller adopted Franks' definition of Celtic art
to describe Iron-Age sites

46 Franks, 'Notes on a Sword Found in
Catterdale, Yorkshire, Exhibited by Lord
Wharncliffe, and Other Examples of the Same
Kind', Archaeologia 45 (1877), 264

47 Munro, The Lake-Dwellings of Europe, 552

48 Ibid., 490

49 Pitt Rivers, Excavations in Bokerly and
Wansdyke, Dorset and Wilts. 1888-1891.

Privately printed, 1892

50 Munro, 'Introductory Chapter' to Arthur
Bulleid and Harold St George Gray, The
Glastonbury Lake Village: A Full Description of
the Excavations and the Relics Discovered, 1892-
1907, vol. 1. The Glastonbury Antiquarian
Society, 1911, 9

51 Arthur Bulleid, 'The Lake Village Near
Glastonbury', Proceedings of the Somersetshire
Archaeological and Natural History Society 40
(1894), 150; 'The Lake Village at Glastonbury.
– Report of the Committee', BAAS Report
1894, 431-434

52 Munro, 'Introductory Chapter', 15

53 'The Lake Village at Glastonbury. – Report of
the Committee', BAAS Report 1895, 519

54 Munro, 'Introductory Chapter', 34

55 Dawkins, 'The Place of the Iberic Race in
British Ethnology', in Arthur Bulleid and
Harold St. George Gray, The Glastonbury Lake
Village: A Full Description of the Excavations and
the Relics Discovered, 1892-1907, vol. 2. The
Glastonbury Antiquarian Society, 1917, 689–
700

56 Evans, 'On a Late-Celtic Urn-Field at
Aylesford, Kent, and on the Gaulish, Illyro-
Italic, and Classical Connexions of the Forms
of Pottery and Bronze-Work There
Discovered', Archaeologia 52 (1890), 317

57 Ibid., 324-325

58 Ibid., 323

59 Ibid., 338

60 Ibid., 386-387

61 Ibid., 388

62 Ibid., 339, 388

63 Allen, Celtic Art, xvi

64 Ibid., 72

65 Noted in Barry Cunliffe, Iron Age Communities
in Britain: An Account of England, Scotland and
Wales from the Seventh Century BC until the
Roman Conquest, 3rd edition. London and
New York: Routledge, 1991, 2

66 Arnold, The Study of Celtic Literature; Charles
de Gaulle, 'The Celts of the Nineteenth
Century: An Appeal to the Living
Representatives of the Celtic Race'. trans. and
ed. J. Davenport Mason, The Cambrian Journal
7. March, 1864, 1-55

67 Arnold, The Study of Celtic Literature, 25, 83

68 Ibid., 57

69 Ibid., xxix, 148

70 Donald Masson, Vestiga Celtica: Celtic Footprints

in Philology, Ethics, and Religion. Edinburgh: Maclachlan and Stewart, 1882

71 John Rhys, 'The Early Ethnology of the British Isles', *The Scottish Review* 15(April, 1890), 234

72 *Ibid.*, 250; 'Traces of a Non-Aryan Element in the Celtic Family: Being the Second "Rhind Lecture"', *The Scottish Review* 16 (July, 1890), 30-47; 'The Mythographical Treatment of Celtic Ethnology: Being the Third "Rhind Lecture"', *The Scottish Review* 16 (October, 1890), 240-256

73 Rhys, 'The Spread of Gaelic in Scotland: Being the Fifth "Rhind Lecture"', *The Scottish Review* 17 (April, 1891), 349; 'Certain National Names of the Aborigines of the British Isles: Being the Sixth Rhind Lecture', *The Scottish Review* 18 (July, 1891), 143

74 Rhys, *Early Britain: Celtic Britain*, 3rd edition. London: Society for the Promotion of Christian Knowledge, 1904, 277

75 Lubbock, *Mr. Gladstone and the Nationalities of the United Kingdom: A Series of Letters to the 'Times'*. London: Bernard Quaritch, 1887

76 Beddoe, 'On the Ancient and Modern Ethnography of Scotland', 257

77 Beddoe, 'The Anthropological History of Europe: Being the First Rhind Lecture', *The Scottish Review* 19. April, 1892, 406

78 Beddoe, 'The Anthropological History of Europe: The Second Rhind Lecture', *The Scottish Review* 20. July, 1892, 156

79 Beddoe, 'The Anthropological History of Europe: Sixth Lecture', *The Scottish Review* 22. July, 1893, 102

80 *Ibid.*, 92

81 Beddoe, *The Races of Britain: A Contribution to the Anthropology of Western Europe*. Bristol: J.W. Arrowsmith and London: Trübner and Co., 1885, 18

82 *Ibid.*, 206-207

83 *Ibid.*, 299

84 Lubbock, *Mr. Gladstone and the Nationalities of the United Kingdom*

85 'Ethnographical Survey of the United Kingdom. – First Report of the Committee', BAAS *Report* 1893, 621

86 James Urry, 'Englishmen, Celts, and Iberians: The Ethnographic Survey of the United Kingdom, 1892-1899', *Functionalism Historicized: Essays on British Social Anthropology*, ed. George W. Stocking Jr. Madison: University of Wisconsin Press, 1984, 96-101

87 William Z. Ripley, *The Races of Europe: A Sociological Study*. New York: D. Appleton and Co., 1899, 121

88 Henri Hubert, *The Rise of the Celts*, vol. 1. London: Kegan Paul, Trench, Trubner, and Co., 1934, 15

Epilogue

1 James, *The Atlantic Celts*, 136

2 *Ibid.*, 145

3 e.g., Barry Cunliffe, *The Ancient Celts*. Oxford: Oxford University Press, 1997, 268

4 James, *The Atlantic Celts*, 136-137

5 Nick Merriman, 'Value and Motivation in Pre-history: The Evidence for "Celtic Spirit"', ed. Ian Hodder, *The Archaeology of Contextual Meanings*. Cambridge: Cambridge University Press, 1987, 111-116

6 Michael Dietler, '"Our Ancestors the Gauls": Archaeology, Ethnic Nationalism, and the Manipulation of Celtic Identity in Modern Europe', *American Anthropologist* 96 (1994), 599

7 James, 'Celts, Politics and Motivation in Archaeology', 206, 208

8 Collis, *The Celts*, 225-226

INDEX

If you are interested in purchasing other books published by Tempus,
or in case you have difficulty finding any Tempus books in your local bookshop,
you can also place orders directly through our website

www.tempus-publishing.com